Overcoming Depression: Using Cognitive Behavioural Therapy and Evidence-Based Approaches

jayden james

Published by Talking Therapies UK, 2025.

OVERCOMING DEPRESSION: USING COGNITIVE BEHAVIOURAL THERAPY AND EVIDENCE-BASED APPROACHES

First edition. November 19, 2025.

ISBN: 979-8232270841

Written by jayden james.

For Russell, Paul and Isabella James

OVERCOMING DEPRESSION

A Comprehensive Guide to Recovery

Using Cognitive Behavioural Therapy and Evidence-Based Approaches

Written by Jayden Josh James

Talking Therapies UK

www.talkingtherapies.co.uk

Disclaimer

This book is designed to provide helpful information on the subjects discussed. It is not meant to be used, nor should it be used, to diagnose or treat any medical condition. For diagnosis or treatment of any medical problem, consult your own clinician. The publisher and author are not responsible for any specific health needs that may require medical supervision and are not liable for any damages or negative consequences from any treatment, action, application, or preparation to any person reading or following the information in this book.

Whilst every effort has been made to ensure the accuracy of information contained within this book, the author and publisher accept no responsibility for errors or omissions.

Published by Talking Therapies UK

www.talkingtherapies.co.uk

Foreword

Depression is one of the most common mental health difficulties affecting millions of people worldwide. It is not a sign of weakness, nor is it something you can simply snap out of. Depression is a genuine health condition that affects how you think, feel, and function in daily life. The good news is that depression is treatable, and recovery is possible.

This book has been written to provide you with a comprehensive, evidence-based guide to understanding and overcoming depression. Drawing primarily on Cognitive Behavioural Therapy (CBT), one of the most thoroughly researched and effective treatments for depression, this guide will take you step by step through the recovery process. Whether you are experiencing depression for the first time or have been struggling for years, the strategies and techniques presented here can help you reclaim your life.

Throughout this book, you will learn about the nature of depression, how it develops and is maintained, and most importantly, what you can do about it. You will discover practical strategies to challenge negative thinking patterns, increase positive activities, improve your sleep and routine, manage difficult emotions, and build resilience against future episodes. We will also explore how depression affects relationships and provide guidance on navigating these challenges.

This guide is designed to be used as a self-help resource that you can work through at your own pace. However, it is important to remember that this book is not a substitute for professional help. If you are experiencing severe depression, particularly if you are having thoughts of self-harm or suicide, please seek immediate support from your GP, a mental health professional, or emergency services.

Recovery from depression is a journey, and like any journey, it requires patience, effort, and commitment. There will be good days and difficult days. Progress is rarely linear. But with the right tools, support, and determination, you can overcome depression and build a more fulfilling life.

We at Talking Therapies UK have supported countless individuals on their journey to recovery from depression. We have witnessed firsthand the transformative power of evidence-based psychological therapy. Our hope is that this book will serve as a valuable companion on your own journey towards better mental health and wellbeing.

Remember, seeking help is a sign of strength, not weakness. By picking up this book, you have already taken an important first step. We wish you every success on your journey to recovery.

Chapter 1: Understanding Depression

What Is Depression?

Depression, also known as major depressive disorder or clinical depression, is far more than simply feeling sad or having a bad day. It is a serious mental health condition characterised by persistent feelings of sadness, hopelessness, and a loss of interest or pleasure in activities that were once enjoyed. Depression affects how you feel, think, and behave, and can lead to a variety of emotional and physical problems.

Unlike the temporary feelings of sadness that everyone experiences from time to time in response to life's challenges, clinical depression persists for weeks, months, or even years if left untreated. It interferes significantly with your ability to function in daily life, affecting your work, relationships, and overall quality of life.

Risk Factors and Demographics

Educational attainment also correlates with depression rates, with lower levels of education associated with higher depression prevalence. This relationship likely reflects multiple factors, including the correlation between education and socioeconomic status, the potential protective effect of cognitive skills and resources gained through education, and the link between early life adversity, educational disruption, and mental health difficulties.

Socioeconomic factors significantly influence depression risk and outcomes. People living in poverty are at substantially higher risk of experiencing depression, with some studies suggesting rates two to three times higher than in more affluent populations. This relationship is bidirectional: poverty increases the risk of depression through increased stress, reduced access to resources, and greater exposure to adverse circumstances, whilst depression can lead to or exacerbate poverty through reduced earning capacity, increased healthcare costs, and impaired ability to manage financial affairs. Unemployment, financial strain, poor housing conditions, and food insecurity all independently contribute to depression risk.

Age also plays a significant role in depression prevalence and presentation. Whilst depression can occur at any age, the average age of onset is in the mid-twenties, with half of all cases beginning by age fourteen and three-quarters by age twenty-four. However, depression in children, adolescents, and older adults may present differently than in adults, sometimes making it more difficult to recognise. Adolescent depression, for instance, may manifest more as irritability and behavioural problems rather than sadness. In older adults, depression often coexists with physical health problems and may be mistaken for cognitive decline or other age-related conditions.

The prevalence of depression varies across different demographic groups and life stages. Women are approximately twice as likely as men to experience depression (Kuehner, 2017) during their lifetime, though this gender difference is complex and influenced by biological, psychological, and social factors. The reasons for this disparity are multifaceted and include hormonal differences, different rates of exposure to certain types of trauma and stress, differences in help-seeking behaviour, and potentially differences in how depression manifests and is diagnosed across genders.

In the United Kingdom specifically, mental health problems, including depression, account for approximately 23 per cent of the total burden of disease, making them the largest single cause of disability. The Mental Health Foundation reports that each year, one in six people in England reports experiencing a common mental health problem such as anxiety or depression. Furthermore, mental health problems are responsible for the largest proportion of days lost from work in Britain, with depression being a leading contributor to this statistic.

Depression represents one of the most significant public health challenges of our time. The World Health Organisation's comprehensive Global Burden of Disease (James et al., 2018) Study consistently ranks depression among the top causes of disability-adjusted life years worldwide. This means that when we consider both years lost to premature death and years lived with disability, depression emerges as one of the most impactful health conditions affecting humanity. The economic burden is staggering, with estimates suggesting that depression costs the global economy over one trillion US dollars annually in lost productivity alone. This figure does not include the substantial costs of healthcare provision, social support services, or the immeasurable personal costs to individuals and families.

Depression is remarkably common. According to the World Health Organisation (WHO, 2020), more than 264 million people of all ages suffer from depression globally. It is a leading cause of disability worldwide and a major contributor to the overall burden of disease. In the United Kingdom, approximately one in four people will experience a mental health problem each year, with depression and anxiety being the most prevalent conditions.

It is crucial to understand that depression is not a character flaw or a sign of personal weakness. It is a legitimate medical condition with biological, psychological, and social components. Just as someone with diabetes needs treatment to manage their blood sugar levels, someone with depression needs appropriate support and treatment to recover.

Signs and Symptoms of Depression

Depression manifests differently in different people, but there are common signs and symptoms that clinicians look for when making a diagnosis. These symptoms can be broadly categorised into emotional, cognitive (thinking), physical, and behavioural changes.

Emotional Symptoms

Hopelessness is perhaps the most dangerous symptom of depression because it erodes motivation to seek help or engage in recovery efforts. When you feel hopeless, you believe that nothing will improve, that you will always feel this way, and that no intervention or effort will make a difference. This belief, whilst a symptom of depression rather than an accurate reflection of reality, feels absolutely true and convincing when you are in its grip. Hopelessness manifests as thoughts such as 'I will never feel better,' 'Nothing helps,' 'This is how I am now,' or 'There is no point in trying.' It creates a self-fulfilling prophecy where the belief that nothing will help prevents you from engaging in activities or treatments that might actually help, thus confirming the original belief.

The emptiness characteristic of depression is particularly difficult for those who have not experienced it to understand. It is not simply an absence of happiness but rather a profound sense of internal void. Many people describe feeling hollow, as though something essential has been removed from inside them. This emptiness can be deeply disturbing. You might look at things that used to move you emotionally—a beautiful sunset, a child laughing, a piece of music you once loved—and feel nothing. It is as though your emotional responses have been switched off. This emotional numbness extends to positive and negative emotions alike. You do not feel happier, but nor do you experience emotions with their usual intensity. Some people describe this as feeling like a robot going through the motions of life without any internal experience.

To truly understand the emotional experience of depression, we must go beyond simple descriptions and explore the lived reality of these symptoms. The persistent low mood of depression is qualitatively different from ordinary sadness. When you experience normal sadness in response to a specific event, such as loss or disappointment, the sadness typically varies in intensity, responds to positive events or distractions, and gradually diminishes over time. The sadness of depression, in contrast, is pervasive, persistent, and largely non-responsive to circumstances. It permeates every aspect of your experience, colouring your perception of everything around you. One person described it as living under a dark cloud that follows you everywhere, casting a shadow over even the brightest moments. Another likened it to viewing the world through grey-tinted glasses where all the colour has been drained from life.

The emotional symptoms of depression are often the most recognisable. You may experience a persistent low mood that doesn't lift, even when something positive happens. This is often described as feeling empty, hopeless, or numb. Many people with depression describe feeling as though they are trapped in a dark pit with no way out.

Loss of interest or pleasure in activities you once enjoyed, known as anhedonia, is another hallmark of depression. Things that used to bring you joy, whether that's spending time with friends, pursuing hobbies, or engaging in sexual activity, no longer feel rewarding. This can be particularly distressing as it may feel as though you've lost touch with who you are.

Feelings of worthlessness, excessive guilt, and self-criticism are also common. You may blame yourself for things that aren't your fault or focus excessively on past failures. These feelings can be so overwhelming that they dominate your thinking and colour your perception of yourself and the world around you.

Irritability and frustration, even over small matters, can increase when you're depressed. You may find yourself snapping at loved ones or feeling unreasonably angry about minor inconveniences. This can strain relationships and add to feelings of guilt and shame.

Cognitive Symptoms

Depression significantly affects how you think. One of the most common cognitive symptoms is difficulty concentrating, remembering details, or making decisions. You may find yourself reading the same page of a book multiple times without taking in the information, or struggling to follow conversations. This can affect your performance at work or in education and may lead to additional stress and worry.

These concentration difficulties are not simply a matter of not trying hard enough. Depression affects the prefrontal cortex and other brain regions involved in attention, working memory, and executive function. Research using neuroimaging techniques has demonstrated that people experiencing depression show reduced activation in brain regions associated with sustained attention and cognitive control. This means that the difficulty you experience in concentrating is rooted in actual changes in brain function, not a lack of willpower or motivation. (Rock et al., 2014)

Memory problems in depression typically affect what we call 'episodic memory' – the memory for specific events and experiences. You might struggle to remember what you did yesterday, what someone told you this morning, or where you put your keys. These memory difficulties are closely linked to attention problems. When depression impairs your ability to focus your attention, it becomes difficult to encode new memories effectively. Additionally, depression is associated with rumination – repetitive, circular thinking about problems and negative experiences – which can consume mental resources that would otherwise be available for encoding and retrieving memories.

Decision-making becomes particularly challenging during depression, even for relatively simple choices. You might stand in front of your wardrobe unable to decide what to wear, spend an inordinate amount of time choosing what to have for lunch, or find yourself paralysed when facing more significant decisions about work, relationships, or treatment options. This indecisiveness stems from several factors. Depression reduces your confidence in your own judgement, makes it difficult to imagine positive outcomes from any choice, and impairs the cognitive processes involved in weighing options and predicting consequences. Moreover, the general slowing of thought processes in depression means that what would normally be an automatic or quick decision becomes laboured and effortful.

Perhaps the most characteristic cognitive feature of depression is the presence of negative automatic thoughts. These are involuntary, often lightning-quick thoughts that pop into your mind unbidden and typically carry a negative interpretation of yourself, your experiences, or your future. Aaron Beck, the founder of cognitive therapy, identified what he called the 'cognitive triad' of depression: negative thoughts about the self ('I am worthless,' 'I am a failure,' 'I am unlovable'), negative thoughts about the world and experiences ('Nothing ever goes right,' 'Everyone is against me,' 'Life is unbearable'), and negative thoughts about the future ('Things will never get better,' 'I will always feel this way,' 'There is no hope').

These negative thoughts in depression are not based on a balanced or realistic assessment of the situation. Instead, they reflect systematic errors in thinking, which Beck called 'cognitive distortions'. These include all-or-nothing thinking, where you see things in black-and-white categories with no middle ground; overgeneralisation, where you view a single negative event as a never-ending pattern of defeat; mental filter, where you pick out a single negative detail and dwell on it exclusively; disqualifying the positive, where you reject positive experiences by insisting they 'don't count'; jumping to conclusions through mind reading (assuming you know what others are thinking) or fortune telling (predicting that things will turn out badly); magnification or minimisation, where you exaggerate the importance of negative things or inappropriately shrink the importance of positive things; emotional reasoning, where you assume that your negative emotions necessarily reflect the way things really are; should statements, where you try to motivate yourself with 'shoulds' and 'shouldn'ts' which create guilt and frustration; labelling, where you attach a negative label to yourself rather than describing the specific behaviour; and personalisation, where you see yourself as the cause of negative events for which you are not primarily responsible.

The negative thinking patterns in depression create and maintain a vicious cycle. Negative thoughts trigger negative emotions, which in turn generate more negative thoughts, creating a downward spiral that can be difficult to escape. These thoughts feel entirely true and accurate when you are depressed, even though objective evidence might contradict them. This is because depression affects not just what you think about, but how you process information. There is evidence that depression is associated with a 'negative cognitive bias' – a tendency to pay more attention to negative information, to remember negative experiences more readily than positive ones, and to interpret ambiguous information in a negative way.

Figure 1: The Vicious Cycle of Depression

The Vicious Cycle of Depression

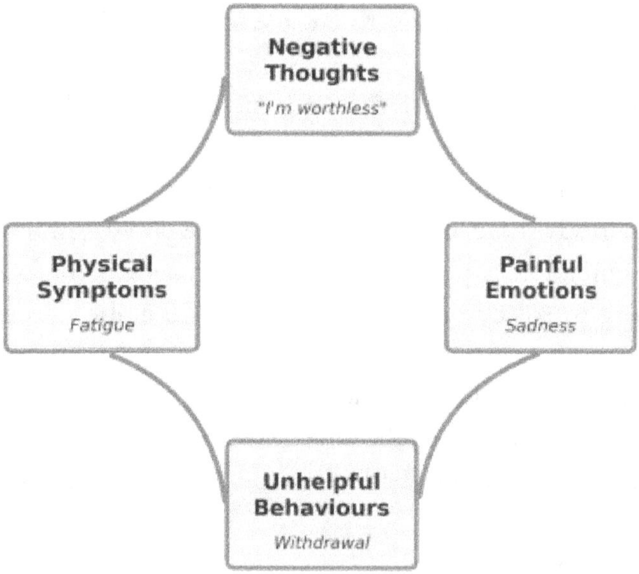

Each component reinforces the others

This negative cognitive bias operates largely automatically and outside of conscious awareness, influencing how you perceive and interpret the world around you. For example, if someone passes you in the corridor without saying hello, your depression-influenced thinking might immediately jump to the conclusion that they dislike you or are deliberately ignoring you, whereas in reality they might simply have been preoccupied with their own thoughts. These interpretive biases accumulate over time, reinforcing the negative view of yourself and your world that is characteristic of depression.

Rumination, the tendency to engage in repetitive, passive thinking about one's symptoms, problems, and negative experiences, is another key cognitive feature of depression. Unlike productive problem-solving, rumination involves dwelling on problems without moving towards solutions. You might find yourself lying awake at night replaying conversations, analysing what you said or did wrong, worrying about what others think of you, or brooding over past mistakes and failures. This ruminative thinking style has been shown to prolong and intensify depressed mood, impair problem-solving abilities, and reduce motivation to engage in potentially mood-enhancing activities.

Research by Susan Nolen-Hoeksema and colleagues (Nolen-Hoeksema et al., 2008) has demonstrated that people who ruminate in response to depressed mood are at increased risk of developing major depression, and those who already have depression experience longer and more severe episodes. Rumination is particularly pernicious because it feels as though you are trying to solve your problems by thinking about them, when in fact you are simply rehearsing negative material and reinforcing negative patterns of thinking. The difference between rumination and productive reflection is that productive reflection leads to insights and action plans, whereas rumination simply circles around the same negative thoughts without resolution.

Physical Symptoms

Depression is not solely a disorder of the mind; it profoundly affects the body as well. The physical symptoms of depression are often what initially bring people to seek medical help, as they can be alarming and significantly impact quality of life. Understanding that these physical symptoms are a legitimate part of depression, not separate medical problems, is important for both accurate diagnosis and effective treatment.

Fatigue and low energy are among the most common and debilitating physical symptoms of depression. This is not ordinary tiredness that improves with rest; it is a profound exhaustion that persists regardless of how much sleep you get. You might feel physically heavy, as though you are moving through thick treacle. Simple tasks that you previously took for granted – having a shower, preparing a meal, getting dressed – can feel overwhelmingly effortful. This fatigue affects not just physical energy but mental energy as well. You may feel mentally exhausted even after minimal cognitive effort, finding that activities requiring concentration or decision-making leave you feeling drained.

The mechanisms underlying depression-related fatigue are complex and multifactorial. Depression is associated with changes in the hypothalamic-pituitary-adrenal (Stetler & Miller, 2011) axis, which regulates the body's stress response and energy metabolism. Research has shown alterations in cortisol patterns in people with depression, which can affect energy levels and physical functioning. Additionally, inflammation, which has been increasingly recognised as playing a role in depression, can contribute to feelings of fatigue and malaise. The neurotransmitter changes in depression, particularly alterations in serotonin, noradrenaline, and dopamine systems, also affect arousal, motivation, and physical energy. (Dunlop & Nemeroff, 2007)

Sleep disturbance is another hallmark physical symptom of depression, though it manifests differently in different people. Some people experience insomnia, finding it difficult to fall asleep, waking frequently during the night, or waking far earlier than desired in the morning and being unable to return to sleep. This early morning waking, sometimes called 'terminal insomnia', is particularly characteristic of depression. You might find yourself awake at three or four in the morning, your mind racing with worries and negative thoughts, unable to switch off and return to sleep.

Conversely, some people with depression experience hypersomnia – sleeping excessively, yet still not feeling rested. You might sleep for ten, twelve, or even more hours per day, yet wake feeling as tired as when you went to bed. You may struggle to get out of bed in the morning, hit the snooze button repeatedly, or find yourself napping during the day. This excessive sleep can be understood partly as an escape from the pain of depression, but it also reflects genuine changes in sleep architecture and regulation in depression.

Research using polysomnography has demonstrated that depression is associated with characteristic changes in sleep structure. These include reduced slow-wave sleep (deep sleep), increased rapid eye movement sleep, shortened time to the first REM period, and increased sleep fragmentation. These changes mean that even when you are sleeping, the quality of that sleep is compromised, which contributes to continued fatigue and impaired daytime functioning. (Steiger & Kimura, 2010)

Changes in appetite and weight are common in depression, though like sleep disturbance, these can go in either direction. Some people experience a significant loss of appetite and unintentional weight loss. Food loses its appeal, eating feels like a chore, and you may need to force yourself to eat even small amounts. You might not feel hungry at all, or find that everything tastes bland and unappealing. This can lead to substantial weight loss, which in severe cases can become medically concerning.

Other people experience increased appetite and weight gain, particularly craving carbohydrates and comfort foods. This is sometimes referred to as 'atypical depression' when it occurs alongside other specific symptoms such as hypersomnia and a feeling of being physically heavy. The increased appetite may be partly explained by the body's attempt to boost serotonin levels through carbohydrate consumption, as carbohydrates temporarily increase tryptophan levels, which is a precursor to serotonin. However, this provides only brief relief and can lead to a cycle of emotional eating and weight gain, which may then contribute to further low self-esteem and depression.

Physical aches and pains are frequently reported in depression, even in the absence of any identifiable physical cause. You might experience unexplained headaches, back pain, joint pain, or general bodily discomfort. These pains are not imaginary; they represent real physical sensations. Depression appears to lower pain thresholds and increase pain sensitivity, making you more aware of and reactive to physical discomfort. Additionally, the same neurotransmitter systems (particularly serotonin and noradrenaline) that are implicated in depression also play important roles in pain modulation, which explains the overlap between depression and pain conditions.

Digestive problems are another common physical manifestation of depression. The gut and brain are closely connected through what is known as the gut-brain axis (Cryan & Dinan, 2012), and disturbances in mood can significantly affect digestive function. You might experience nausea, constipation, diarrhoea, abdominal pain, or changes in bowel habits. Some research suggests that depression is associated with changes in the gut microbiome (the community of bacteria and other microorganisms that live in the digestive tract), though the exact nature and direction of this relationship is still being investigated.

Psychomotor changes refer to alterations in movement and motor activity. In depression, these changes can manifest as either psychomotor retardation (slowing down) or psychomotor agitation (restlessness). Psychomotor retardation is more common and involves slowed movements, reduced facial expressions, slower speech with increased pauses, and an overall sense of being slowed down. An observer might notice that you move more slowly, take longer to respond to questions, or speak in a monotone with less inflection than usual.

Psychomotor agitation, though less common, can also occur in depression. This involves restlessness, an inability to sit still, pacing, hand-wringing, or fidgeting. You might feel an inner sense of agitation or tension that manifests in these physical movements. Sometimes, both retardation and agitation can be present in the same person at different times or even simultaneously, with an internal sense of agitation despite outward slowing of movement.

Changes in libido and sexual function are frequently associated with depression. Many people experience a significant reduction in sexual desire and interest. Sexual activity that was previously enjoyable may no longer feel appealing, or you may be unable to become aroused or reach orgasm. These changes can strain intimate relationships and add to feelings of guilt, inadequacy, or difference from one's former self. It is important to note that certain antidepressant medications can also affect sexual function, so distinguishing between depression-related and medication-related sexual difficulties is important, though both require sensitive discussion with healthcare providers.

Behavioural Symptoms

Depression profoundly affects behaviour, often in ways that perpetuate and worsen the depression itself. Understanding these behavioural changes is crucial because they represent targets for intervention in cognitive behavioural therapy and other evidence-based treatments. Behaviour change is often more achievable than immediate mood change, and positive behavioural changes can create an upward spiral that gradually improves mood and thinking patterns.

Social withdrawal is one of the most characteristic behavioural changes in depression. You may find yourself declining invitations, avoiding social situations, or spending more and more time alone. This withdrawal can be driven by multiple factors. You might feel that you have nothing to contribute to conversations, worry that others will judge you negatively, lack the energy for social interaction, or simply find that activities that used to be enjoyable no longer provide pleasure. However, social withdrawal creates a vicious cycle. The less you engage socially, the more isolated you feel, and isolation itself worsens depression. Furthermore, withdrawing from others means missing out on potentially supportive interactions and positive experiences that could help improve mood.

The social withdrawal in depression can be understood through the lens of behavioural activation theory, which proposes that depression is maintained by a reduction in behaviour that could potentially bring rewards or positive experiences. When you withdraw socially, you reduce your exposure to positive reinforcement from social interactions, which maintains the depression. Moreover, other people in your life may initially increase their support when you first become depressed, but over time, as you continue to withdraw and reject overtures of help or companionship, they may themselves pull back, further reducing your social support network precisely when you need it most.

Reduced activity and motivation are central to depression's behavioural impact. You may find it increasingly difficult to initiate activities, even those that are necessary or that you previously enjoyed. Projects are started but not finished, household chores pile up, personal hygiene may slip, and you might spend increasing amounts of time in passive activities such as lying in bed or sitting on the sofa. This inactivity is not laziness or a conscious choice; it reflects the genuine motivational deficits associated with depression.

The relationship between activity and mood in depression is complex and bidirectional. Depression causes reduced activity through its effects on energy, motivation, and the ability to anticipate or experience pleasure. However, this reduced activity then maintains and worsens the depression. When you do less, you have fewer opportunities for positive experiences, achievement, or pleasure. You may also lose the sense of structure and purpose that activities provide, which can contribute to feelings of worthlessness and meaninglessness. Furthermore, physical inactivity contributes to reduced fitness, which can increase fatigue and reduce energy levels, creating another vicious cycle.

Procrastination and avoidance behaviours often increase markedly during depression. Tasks that require attention, decision-making, or effort feel overwhelming, leading to repeated postponement. You might find yourself putting off important tasks, ignoring bills or correspondence, or avoiding dealing with problems. This avoidance provides short-term relief from the anxiety or difficulty associated with the task, which reinforces the avoidance behaviour. However, in the longer term, avoidance typically makes problems worse. Tasks that could have been manageable become more difficult as deadlines pass, bills accumulate, or situations deteriorate, creating additional stress and confirming negative beliefs about the inability to cope.

Changes in work or academic performance are common behavioural manifestations of depression. The concentration difficulties, reduced energy, slowed thinking, and decreased motivation associated with depression all impact your ability to function effectively in work or educational settings. You might miss deadlines, make more mistakes, struggle to keep up with the workload, or find it difficult to contribute in meetings or classes. These difficulties can lead to concerns about job security or academic performance, which add to stress and worsen depression. In some cases, people may take time off work or withdraw from education due to their depression, which, whilst sometimes necessary for recovery, can also lead to isolation, loss of structure, and financial concerns.

Self-neglect is another important behavioural sign of depression. This might include neglecting personal hygiene, not eating properly, failing to take prescribed medications for other health conditions, or ignoring warning signs of physical health problems. In severe depression, even basic self-care tasks such as washing, brushing teeth, or changing clothes can feel overwhelming. This self-neglect can have consequences for physical health and can contribute to feelings of shame or worthlessness, particularly when others comment on changes in appearance or when you become aware that you are not looking after yourself as you once did.

Increased use of alcohol or other substances is a concerning behavioural change that some people experience during depression. You might drink more alcohol or use substances in an attempt to relieve emotional pain, improve sleep, or simply to feel different from how you feel when depressed. This represents a form of self-medication, but it is invariably counterproductive. Alcohol is a central nervous system depressant that worsens depression, disrupts sleep quality, can interact dangerously with antidepressant medications, and creates the risk of developing a substance use disorder in addition to depression. Substance use as a coping strategy needs to be addressed as part of depression treatment.

Reassurance-seeking is a behavioural pattern that can develop in depression. You might repeatedly ask loved ones for reassurance that things will be okay, that you are loved, that you are not a burden, or that you will recover. Whilst seeking occasional reassurance is normal and can be helpful, excessive reassurance-seeking can become problematic. The relief provided by reassurance is typically short-lived, leading to a need for repeated reassurance. This can strain relationships, as others may become frustrated with constant requests for reassurance, particularly when the reassurance they provide does not seem to help for long. Moreover, over-reliance on external reassurance prevents you from developing your own internal resources for managing anxiety and uncertainty.

Risk-taking or reckless behaviour can occur in some people with depression, though this is less common than withdrawal and inactivity. This might include financial recklessness, unsafe sexual behaviour, reckless driving, or other behaviours that show a disregard for consequences. This can be understood as an attempt to feel something different from the numbness of depression, to distract from emotional pain, or may reflect a sense of hopelessness about the future that reduces normal concern about consequences. Any such behaviours require immediate attention as they pose risks to safety and wellbeing.

The Diagnosis of Depression

Depression is diagnosed based on the presence of specific symptoms over a defined time period. Mental health professionals in the United Kingdom typically use either the International Classification of Diseases (currently

ICD-11, published by the World Health Organisation) or the Diagnostic and Statistical Manual of Mental Disorders (currently DSM-5, published by the American Psychiatric Association) as diagnostic frameworks. Whilst there are minor differences between these systems, both recognise that depression involves a persistent and pervasive disturbance in mood, accompanied by other characteristic symptoms, that significantly impairs functioning.

According to the ICD-11, a diagnosis of depressive episode requires the presence of depressed mood or loss of interest or pleasure in activities (anhedonia) for most of the day, nearly every day, for at least two weeks. In addition to this core symptom, several of the following must be present: reduced concentration and attention, reduced self-esteem and self-confidence, ideas of guilt and unworthiness, pessimistic views of the future, ideas or acts of self-harm or suicide, disturbed sleep, and diminished appetite. The symptoms must represent a change from previous functioning and cause significant distress or impairment in personal, family, social, educational, occupational, or other important areas of functioning.

The DSM-5 criteria are broadly similar, requiring five or more specific symptoms to be present during the same two-week period and to represent a change from previous functioning. At least one of the symptoms must be either depressed mood or loss of interest or pleasure. The additional symptoms that count towards diagnosis include significant weight loss or gain or change in appetite, insomnia or hypersomnia nearly every day, psychomotor agitation or retardation observable by others, fatigue or loss of energy, feelings of worthlessness or excessive guilt, diminished ability to think or concentrate or indecisiveness, and recurrent thoughts of death or suicidal ideation.

It is important to note that depression exists on a spectrum of severity. Both diagnostic systems recognise mild, moderate, and severe depressive episodes based on the number of symptoms present, their intensity, and the degree of functional impairment. In mild depression, whilst the symptoms are distressing, you are usually able to continue with most activities, though they may require more effort than usual. Moderate depression involves greater symptom intensity and more marked difficulties in continuing with ordinary activities. Severe depression is characterised by marked and distressing symptoms, with considerable or complete loss of ability to function in social or occupational roles.

Severe depression may occur with or without psychotic features. Psychotic features include delusions (fixed false beliefs) or hallucinations (perceptual experiences without external stimuli, most commonly auditory hallucinations or hearing voices). The content of psychotic symptoms in depression is typically mood-congruent, meaning they align with depressive themes. Common depressive delusions include beliefs about being worthless, being punished for imagined wrongdoings, having a serious illness, or having caused harm to others. Psychotic depression requires urgent psychiatric assessment and treatment, often including both medication and psychological therapy, and sometimes requiring inpatient care for safety.

Making a diagnosis of depression requires ruling out other potential explanations for the symptoms. Many medical conditions can produce symptoms similar to depression, including thyroid disorders (particularly hypothyroidism), vitamin deficiencies (especially vitamin B12 and folate deficiency), anaemia, diabetes, neurological conditions, chronic pain conditions, and sleep disorders. Certain medications can also cause or contribute to depressive symptoms, including some blood pressure medications, steroids, and hormonal treatments. For this reason, if you present to your GP with symptoms of depression, they will typically conduct or arrange blood tests and a physical examination to rule out medical causes before finalising a diagnosis of depression.

It is also important to distinguish depression from normal sadness or grief. Bereavement and loss naturally cause sadness and many symptoms that resemble depression, including disturbed sleep, reduced appetite, difficulty concentrating, and social withdrawal. However, in normal grief, these symptoms typically fluctuate over time, improve gradually, and are predominantly focused on the loss rather than involving the pervasive negative view of self, world, and future characteristic of depression. Moreover, in grief, there can be moments of pleasure or humour connected to memories of the deceased, whereas in depression, the loss of ability to experience pleasure is more complete and pervasive.

That said, grief and depression can coexist, and prolonged or complicated grief can develop into depression. The distinction between normal grief and depression following loss is not always clear-cut, and in cases where symptoms are severe, persistent (extending well beyond what would be culturally expected for grief), or include features particularly suggestive of depression (such as pervasive worthlessness or suicidal ideation), treatment for depression may be appropriate even in the context of bereavement.

Depression must also be distinguished from other mental health conditions that can involve depressed mood. Bipolar disorder involves episodes of depression alternating with episodes of mania or hypomania (elevated mood, increased energy, reduced need for sleep, racing thoughts, and sometimes reckless behaviour). If someone has experienced even a single manic or hypomanic episode, their diagnosis would be bipolar disorder rather than depression, and treatment approaches differ significantly. This is why a thorough psychiatric history, including questions about past episodes of elevated mood, is important in diagnosis.

Adjustment disorders involve emotional or behavioural symptoms in response to an identifiable stressor, occurring within three months of the stressor and resolving within six months after the stressor or its consequences have ended. If the response to stress is more severe or persistent than would be expected and meets full criteria for depression, then major depressive disorder rather than adjustment disorder would be diagnosed. This distinction has implications for treatment planning and prognosis.

Persistent depressive disorder (previously called dysthymia) is a form of chronic depression characterised by depressed mood for most of the day, for more days than not, for at least two years. The symptoms are typically less severe than in major depression but their chronic nature means they can be equally debilitating, affecting identity, relationships, and quality of life. It is possible to experience major depressive episodes superimposed on persistent depressive disorder, sometimes referred to as 'double depression'.

Premenstrual dysphoric disorder involves mood symptoms that occur regularly in the week before menstruation and remit within a few days after the onset of menses. Perinatal depression encompasses depression that occurs during pregnancy or in the year after giving birth. Seasonal affective disorder (SAD) involves recurrent depression with a seasonal pattern, most commonly with episodes beginning in autumn or winter and remitting in spring. These are considered specifiers or subtypes of depression rather than entirely separate conditions, but recognising them can inform treatment planning.

The diagnostic process typically involves a comprehensive assessment by a healthcare professional. This will include a detailed history of your symptoms, including when they started, how they have progressed, what makes them better or worse, and how they affect your daily functioning. The clinician will ask about your past psychiatric history, including any previous episodes of depression or other mental health difficulties, and what treatments you have received. Family history of mental health problems is relevant, as is your personal and social history, including major life events, current stressors, relationship status, living situation, employment or educational status, and use of alcohol or other substances.

Standardised questionnaires are often used to support diagnosis and assess severity. Common tools include the Patient Health Questionnaire-9 (PHQ-9), which asks about the frequency of nine depressive symptoms over the past two weeks, and the Hospital Anxiety and Depression Scale (HADS), which assesses both anxiety and depression. These questionnaires can provide a quantitative measure of symptom severity and can be repeated over time to track progress during treatment. However, they are screening and monitoring tools rather than diagnostic instruments in themselves; diagnosis requires a comprehensive clinical assessment.

Types and Subtypes of Depression

Whilst the term 'depression' is often used as a single diagnosis, in reality depression can present in various forms, each with particular characteristics that may influence treatment approaches. Understanding these different presentations can help you recognise your own experience and understand why certain treatments might be recommended.

Major Depressive Disorder

Major depressive disorder, often simply called major depression or clinical depression, is what most people mean when they talk about depression. It involves discrete episodes of depression lasting at least two weeks (though episodes typically last much longer if untreated) in which you experience the symptoms described earlier in this chapter. Between episodes, you may return to your normal level of functioning, though some people experience residual symptoms even between major episodes. Major depression can be a single episode, meaning it occurs once in a person's lifetime, but more commonly it is recurrent, with multiple episodes occurring over the course of a lifetime.

The likelihood of recurrence increases with each episode. After a first episode of major depression, there is approximately a 50 per cent chance of having another episode. After two episodes, the risk of a third rises to around 70 per cent, and after three episodes, the risk of further episodes approaches 90 per cent. This pattern of recurrence is one reason why ongoing vigilance for early warning signs and sometimes longer-term treatment or maintenance strategies are important, even after recovery from an episode.

Major depression can occur with various specifiers that describe particular features of the episode. Depression with anxious distress involves prominent anxiety symptoms alongside the depressive symptoms, such as feeling tense or wound up, feeling restless, worrying excessively, or fearing that something awful might happen. This combination of depression and anxiety is extremely common, with research suggesting that more than half of people with major depression also meet criteria for an anxiety disorder.

Depression with mixed features includes some symptoms that are characteristic of mania or hypomania, such as elevated mood, increased energy, racing thoughts, or increased activity, occurring alongside predominantly depressive symptoms. This is distinct from bipolar disorder but may indicate increased risk for later development of bipolar disorder and may require different treatment approaches than depression without mixed features.

Melancholic depression represents a particularly severe form of major depression characterised by profound anhedonia (complete inability to experience pleasure), lack of mood reactivity (mood does not improve even temporarily in response to positive events), early morning waking, marked psychomotor changes, significant appetite or weight loss, and excessive guilt. People with melancholic features often describe a quality to their mood that feels distinctly different from normal sadness. Melancholic depression has been particularly associated with biological factors and may be more responsive to medication than to psychological therapy alone, though combined treatment is often most effective.

Persistent Depressive Disorder

Persistent depressive disorder, formerly known as dysthymia, involves chronic low-grade depression lasting for at least two years in adults (one year in children and adolescents). The symptoms are generally less severe than in major depression, but their persistence over years can be profoundly debilitating. You might be able to continue functioning in most areas of life, but everything feels harder, requires more effort, and brings less satisfaction. Many people with persistent depressive disorder describe depression as being so much a part of their life that they can barely remember what it feels like not to be depressed.

The chronic nature of persistent depressive disorder means it significantly shapes your identity, worldview, and relationships. You may have developed ways of coping with or compensating for the depression that have become so ingrained they feel like part of your personality. Some people describe themselves as 'just a pessimistic person' or 'not a naturally happy person', not recognising that their characteristic way of experiencing the world reflects an ongoing mood disorder rather than an immutable personality trait.

It is possible to experience episodes of major depression superimposed on persistent depressive disorder. When this occurs, it is sometimes called 'double depression'. You might live for years with the chronic low-level symptoms of persistent depressive disorder, then periodically experience more severe episodes meeting criteria for major depression, before returning to your chronic baseline once the major episode resolves. This pattern requires treatment that addresses both the acute major depressive episodes and the underlying persistent depression.

Because persistent depressive disorder is chronic and often begins early in life (many people develop it in adolescence or young adulthood), it can be particularly resistant to treatment. However, treatment is both possible and important. Both psychological therapies, particularly cognitive behavioural therapy, and antidepressant medications have been shown to be effective for persistent depressive disorder, with combination treatment often showing the best outcomes. The chronic nature of the condition means treatment may need to be longer-term than for episodic major depression.

Atypical Depression

Despite its name, atypical depression is actually quite common, occurring in perhaps 15 to 30 per cent of people with depression. The term 'atypical' is used because the features differ from what was historically considered the typical presentation of melancholic depression. The key feature of atypical depression is mood reactivity—your mood brightens, at least temporarily, in response to positive events. If something good happens, your mood improves for a while, even though you remain generally depressed.

Other characteristic features of atypical depression include increased appetite and weight gain (rather than the decreased appetite typical of melancholic depression), hypersomnia (sleeping too much rather than too little), a feeling of heaviness in the arms and legs described as 'leaden paralysis', and heightened sensitivity to interpersonal rejection. This rejection sensitivity means that you may be particularly vulnerable to feeling hurt or upset by perceived criticism or rejection, which can significantly impact relationships and social functioning.

The pattern of atypical depression is often characterised by particular difficulty in the mornings, with mood and energy sometimes improving somewhat as the day progresses—the opposite pattern to melancholic depression, where mornings are often the worst time. People with atypical depression may describe feeling weighted down, as though they are carrying heavy burdens, and may sleep excessively but still feel unrefreshed. The increased appetite often specifically involves craving carbohydrates or sweet foods.

Atypical depression often begins earlier in life than melancholic depression and tends to follow a more chronic course. It is more common in women than men and may be associated with other conditions such as anxiety disorders and seasonal pattern depression. Some research suggests that people with atypical depression may respond particularly well to a specific class of antidepressants called monoamine oxidase inhibitors (MAOIs), though these are now less commonly used due to dietary restrictions and potential interactions. However, other antidepressants and psychological therapies are also effective for atypical depression.

Seasonal Affective Disorder

Seasonal affective disorder (SAD) involves recurrent episodes of depression that follow a seasonal pattern, most commonly beginning in autumn or winter and remitting in spring or summer. This pattern must occur for at least two consecutive years to be diagnosed as SAD. The winter pattern is far more common than summer pattern SAD. People with winter pattern SAD typically experience the atypical features of depression: increased sleep, increased appetite with weight gain, craving for carbohydrates, and a feeling of heaviness or fatigue.

The mechanism underlying seasonal affective disorder is thought to involve the effects of reduced daylight exposure on circadian rhythms (the body's internal clock), melatonin regulation, and possibly serotonin levels. During winter months, reduced daylight can lead to disruption of normal circadian patterns, with consequences for mood, sleep, and energy regulation. Some people appear to be particularly vulnerable to these effects, developing full depressive episodes in response to seasonal changes in light exposure.

The geographical prevalence of SAD follows an interesting pattern, with higher rates at higher latitudes where winter day length is shorter. In the United Kingdom, it is estimated that around 2 to 3 per cent of the population experiences full SAD, with a much larger proportion (perhaps 10 to 20 per cent) experiencing milder winter blues or subsyndromal SAD. Women are diagnosed with SAD more frequently than men, with a ratio of approximately 4:1.

Because SAD has a clear temporal pattern and a hypothesised mechanism involving light exposure, it can be treated with light therapy (also called bright light therapy or phototherapy) in addition to standard treatments for depression. Light therapy involves daily exposure to a bright light box (typically 10,000 lux) for 30 minutes to an hour each morning. Research has demonstrated that light therapy can be as effective as antidepressant medication for seasonal depression, with benefits often apparent within one to two weeks. However, standard depression treatments, including antidepressant medications and psychological therapies, are also effective for SAD and may be preferred by some people or used in combination with light therapy.

Perinatal Depression

Perinatal depression refers to depression that occurs during pregnancy (antenatal or prenatal depression) or following childbirth (postnatal depression). The perinatal period, encompassing pregnancy and the first year after delivery, represents a time of particular vulnerability to depression. Approximately ten to fifteen per cent of women experience depression during pregnancy, and a similar proportion develop postnatal depression, making perinatal depression one of the most common complications of childbearing. However, these figures likely underestimate the true prevalence as perinatal depression is often underrecognised and undertreated.

During pregnancy, significant hormonal changes occur, including dramatic increases in oestrogen and progesterone. Following delivery, these hormones drop precipitously, which is thought to contribute to mood disturbance in vulnerable individuals. However, hormonal changes alone do not fully explain perinatal depression. Psychological factors including anxiety about the health of the baby, concerns about parenting ability, changes in identity and relationships, loss of independence, and the physical demands of pregnancy and early parenthood all contribute. Social factors such as lack of support, relationship difficulties, financial stress, and previous trauma or mental health problems also increase risk.

Antenatal depression presents particular challenges because symptoms such as fatigue, changes in appetite, and sleep disturbance are common in pregnancy even in the absence of depression, making diagnosis more difficult. Women experiencing antenatal depression may struggle to enjoy their pregnancy, may have intrusive anxious thoughts about the baby's health, and may feel guilty about not experiencing the joy they expected or believe they should feel. There are concerns about the impact of untreated depression on the developing baby, as maternal stress and depression can affect foetal development, though the risks of untreated depression generally outweigh the small risks associated with most treatments.

Postnatal depression typically develops within the first three months after delivery, though it can occur any time in the first year. It is important to distinguish postnatal depression from the 'baby blues', which affect up to eighty per cent of women in the first week after delivery. Baby blues involve mood swings, tearfulness, anxiety, and irritability but are short-lived, typically resolving within two weeks without treatment. Postnatal depression is more severe, persistent, and functionally impairing. Women with postnatal depression may experience profound sadness, anxiety about the baby's wellbeing, feelings of inadequacy as a mother, difficulty bonding with the baby, intrusive thoughts about harm coming to the baby, or even thoughts of harming the baby themselves.

The impact of postnatal depression extends beyond the mother to affect the infant and the whole family. Maternal depression can interfere with mother-infant bonding, affect the mother's ability to respond sensitively to infant cues, and potentially impact infant development. Partners of women with postnatal depression are themselves at increased risk of depression. Untreated postnatal depression can persist for months or years, significantly affecting family functioning and child development. However, with appropriate treatment, most women recover well.

Risk factors for perinatal depression include previous history of depression or anxiety, previous perinatal depression, lack of social support, relationship difficulties, stressful life events during pregnancy or postpartum, complications during pregnancy or delivery, unplanned or unwanted pregnancy, young maternal age, and adverse childhood experiences. Women with a history of perinatal depression have up to a fifty per cent risk of recurrence in subsequent pregnancies, making monitoring and early intervention particularly important.

Treatment of perinatal depression requires careful consideration of the potential risks and benefits of different interventions during pregnancy and whilst breastfeeding. Psychological therapies, particularly cognitive behavioural therapy and interpersonal therapy, are effective and do not carry the concerns about medication that some women have. For moderate to severe depression, antidepressant medication may be recommended. Most modern antidepressants, particularly selective serotonin reuptake inhibitors, have been extensively studied in pregnancy and breastfeeding and the evidence suggests that the risks to the baby are small, whilst the risks of untreated depression are significant. The decision about medication should be made collaboratively between the woman and her healthcare providers, weighing the individual circumstances and preferences.

Perinatal mental health services have been developed in many areas to provide specialist support for women experiencing mental health difficulties during pregnancy and postpartum. These services offer assessment, treatment, and support tailored to the unique needs of this period. Health visitors and midwives play important roles in identifying women who may be struggling and facilitating access to support. Peer support from other mothers who have experienced perinatal depression can also be valuable.

Perinatal depression encompasses both depression during pregnancy (antenatal or prenatal depression) and depression in the year following childbirth (postnatal or postpartum depression). This is not a separate type of depression in terms of symptoms—the symptoms are the same as in major depression occurring at other times. However, the perinatal period is recognised as a time of particular vulnerability to depression, and perinatal depression has specific implications for both the mother and child that warrant particular attention.

Postnatal depression is relatively common, affecting approximately 10 to 15 per cent of women in the year after giving birth, though many cases go unrecognised and untreated. It is important to distinguish postnatal depression from the 'baby blues', which affects up to 80 per cent of new mothers in the first week or two after birth and involves mood swings, tearfulness, and anxiety that resolve spontaneously without treatment. Postnatal depression is more severe, persistent, and interferes significantly with functioning, requiring professional intervention.

Symptoms of postnatal depression include all the typical symptoms of depression but may also involve particular difficulties bonding with the baby, excessive anxiety about the baby's health or wellbeing, intrusive thoughts about harm coming to the baby, or thoughts about self-harm. These symptoms can be particularly distressing and may be accompanied by intense guilt and shame, feelings of being a bad mother, or fears about disclosing symptoms to health professionals in case the baby is taken away. Such fears, whilst understandable, often prevent women from seeking the help they need.

Multiple factors contribute to perinatal depression. Hormonal changes during pregnancy and after childbirth are significant, with dramatic shifts in oestrogen, progesterone, and other hormones that can affect mood regulation. Sleep deprivation in the postnatal period is a powerful trigger for depression. The major life changes and adjustments required by becoming a parent can be overwhelming. Previous history of depression, lack of social support, relationship difficulties, and stressful life events all increase risk. Depression during pregnancy also increases the risk of postnatal depression.

Perinatal depression has implications beyond the mother's wellbeing. Untreated antenatal depression has been associated with poorer pregnancy outcomes, and postnatal depression can affect mother-infant bonding and interaction, with potential consequences for the child's emotional and cognitive development. However, with appropriate treatment, these risks can be substantially reduced. Treatment for perinatal depression may include psychological therapy (particularly CBT or interpersonal therapy), antidepressant medication (with careful consideration of potential effects on the baby during pregnancy or breastfeeding), social support interventions, and practical help. Many women recover fully with treatment, and good outcomes for both mother and child are the norm when depression is recognised and treated appropriately.

It is worth noting that whilst postnatal depression is more commonly discussed in relation to mothers, fathers and non-gestational partners can also experience depression in the perinatal period. Estimates suggest that 5 to 10 per cent of new fathers experience postnatal depression, with higher rates when the mother is also depressed. The transition to parenthood, sleep deprivation, changes in relationship dynamics, financial pressures, and feeling excluded from the mother-baby bond can all contribute to depression in partners. Partners' mental health is important both in its own right and because it affects their ability to support the mother and baby.

Psychotic Depression

Psychotic depression, also known as major depressive disorder with psychotic features, represents a severe form of depression characterised by the presence of delusions, hallucinations, or both, in addition to the typical symptoms of major depression. Psychotic depression affects approximately fifteen to twenty per cent of people hospitalised with depression and about one in four people experiencing severe depression. It is a serious condition that requires prompt and intensive treatment, as it is associated with higher suicide risk and greater functional impairment than non-psychotic depression.

The psychotic features in psychotic depression are typically mood-congruent, meaning they align with depressive themes. Delusions commonly involve themes of guilt, sin, punishment, personal inadequacy, poverty, or somatic illness. For example, a person might hold the fixed false belief that they have committed some terrible, unforgivable sin, that they are being punished for past wrongdoing, that they have caused harm to others, or that they have a serious illness despite medical evidence to the contrary. These delusions differ from the negative thoughts in non-psychotic depression in their fixed, unshakeable quality and their disconnection from reality.

Nihilistic delusions are particularly characteristic of psychotic depression. These involve beliefs that parts of one's body have ceased to exist or function, that one is dead, or that the world is ending or has ended. Cotard's syndrome, though rare, is an extreme form of nihilistic delusion in which the person believes they are dead or do not exist. Poverty delusions involve fixed beliefs about financial ruin despite evidence to the contrary. Persecutory delusions, whilst more common in other psychotic disorders, can occur in psychotic depression, often with depressive themes such as believing one is being punished or targeted because one deserves it.

Hallucinations in psychotic depression are less common than delusions but do occur, most often as auditory hallucinations. These typically involve hearing voices that are critical, accusatory, or command self-harm. The voices might tell the person they are worthless, that they deserve to die, or instruct them to harm themselves. Visual hallucinations are less common but can occur, sometimes involving disturbing or frightening images. Unlike the hallucinations in schizophrenia, which may have elaborate or bizarre content, hallucinations in psychotic depression typically have depressive themes and are experienced as extremely distressing.

The presentation of psychotic depression can be confused with other psychotic disorders, particularly schizophrenia or schizoaffective disorder. The key distinction is that in psychotic depression, psychotic symptoms occur only during episodes of severe depression and resolve when the depression improves. In schizophrenia, psychotic symptoms typically persist even when the mood is normal. The timing, content, and course of psychotic symptoms help differentiate these conditions, though careful assessment is required.

Psychotic depression often develops gradually, with psychotic symptoms emerging as depression becomes more severe. Early in the course, the boundary between severe negative thoughts and delusions may be unclear. As depression worsens, thoughts become more fixed, more removed from reality, and less responsive to evidence or reassurance, crossing the threshold into true delusions. Some people experience psychotic symptoms only during the most severe periods of depression, whilst others develop psychotic features more readily with each episode.

The impact of psychotic depression on functioning is typically profound. The combination of severe depression and psychotic symptoms makes it extremely difficult or impossible to maintain normal activities. People with psychotic depression may be unable to work, care for themselves, or maintain relationships. Hospitalisation is often necessary, both to provide intensive treatment and to ensure safety, as suicide risk is elevated. The presence of command hallucinations instructing self-harm or delusions about deserving death or punishment creates a particular risk.

Treatment of psychotic depression differs from treatment of non-psychotic depression and typically requires a combination of antidepressant and antipsychotic medication. Antidepressants alone are usually insufficient when psychotic features are present. The combination of an antidepressant with an antipsychotic medication is more effective than either medication alone. Electroconvulsive therapy (ECT) is particularly effective for psychotic depression and may be considered first-line treatment, especially when rapid response is needed due to safety concerns or severe functional impairment. ECT often produces faster and more complete responses in psychotic depression than medication alone.

Following recovery from an episode of psychotic depression, maintenance treatment with medication is typically recommended for an extended period to prevent relapse. People who have experienced psychotic depression are at higher risk of recurrence, and future episodes are likely to include psychotic features again. Long-term management may involve continuing both antidepressant and antipsychotic medication, though some individuals may be able to discontinue the antipsychotic once depression has fully remitted, whilst continuing the antidepressant. Psychological therapy can be beneficial once acute psychotic symptoms have resolved, helping to address underlying vulnerabilities and develop relapse prevention strategies.

Psychotic depression, also known as major depressive disorder with psychotic features, occurs when severe depression is accompanied by some form of psychosis. Psychosis involves a loss of contact with reality, manifesting as delusions (fixed false beliefs) or hallucinations (perceiving things that are not present). Approximately 15 to 20 per cent of people hospitalised for depression have psychotic features, though the condition can also occur in community settings where it may go unrecognised.

The delusions in psychotic depression typically have themes that are mood-congruent, meaning they align with the depressed mood. Common delusional themes include beliefs about having committed unforgivable sins, having a terminal illness despite medical evidence to the contrary, having lost all money or possessions, or having caused harm to others. For instance, someone might be convinced they have caused their family irreparable damage or that they are being punished for past wrongdoings. These beliefs are held with absolute certainty despite clear evidence to the contrary.

Hallucinations in psychotic depression, when they occur, are usually auditory rather than visual. The voices heard typically convey critical, accusatory, or derogatory messages consistent with the person's depressed state. Someone might hear voices telling them they are worthless, that they deserve to die, or accusing them of terrible things. Unlike hallucinations in schizophrenia, which may have neutral or command content, hallucinations in psychotic depression almost always reinforce negative self-perception and hopelessness.

Psychotic depression represents a psychiatric emergency requiring urgent treatment. The presence of psychotic symptoms significantly increases the risk of suicide, as delusions may include themes of death being the only escape or of suicide being a deserved punishment. People with psychotic depression are also at risk of neglecting self-care to dangerous degrees, as delusions might include beliefs that they do not deserve food or that their body is already dead.

Treatment for psychotic depression typically requires a combination of antidepressant medication and antipsychotic medication, as antidepressants alone are rarely sufficient. In severe cases, or when medication is ineffective, electroconvulsive therapy (ECT) may be recommended. ECT has a particularly high success rate for psychotic depression, with response rates of 80 to 90 per cent. Hospitalisation is often necessary to ensure safety and allow for intensive treatment. Psychological therapy can be helpful once psychotic symptoms have resolved sufficiently.

The presence of psychotic features does not necessarily mean a worse long-term prognosis, but it does require more intensive acute treatment. With appropriate treatment, most people with psychotic depression recover fully, though they remain at higher risk for future episodes, which may or may not include psychotic features. Close monitoring and maintenance treatment are typically recommended to reduce recurrence risk.

Bipolar Depression

Whilst this book focuses primarily on unipolar depression (major depressive disorder), it is important to understand bipolar depression because it can initially present identically to unipolar depression. Bipolar disorder involves episodes of depression alternating with episodes of mania (bipolar I disorder) or hypomania (bipolar II disorder). The depressive episodes in bipolar disorder look the same as those in major depression—they involve the same symptoms of low mood, loss of interest, sleep and appetite changes, and so forth. The key difference is that people with bipolar disorder also experience periods of abnormally elevated, expansive, or irritable mood.

During manic episodes (in bipolar I disorder), mood is abnormally and persistently elevated or irritable for at least one week. People experiencing mania may feel euphoric, invincible, or extraordinarily capable. They typically need little sleep yet have abundant energy. Thoughts race, speech becomes rapid and difficult to interrupt, and attention jumps from topic to topic. Self-esteem becomes inflated, sometimes reaching grandiose proportions—someone might believe they have special powers, connections to famous people, or solutions to complex problems. Behaviour becomes impulsive and risky, with poor judgement about consequences. People might spend money recklessly, engage in sexual indiscretions, make foolish business investments, or drive dangerously. True mania is severe enough to cause marked impairment in functioning, often requiring hospitalisation.

Hypomanic episodes (in bipolar II disorder) involve similar symptoms but are less severe and do not cause marked impairment or require hospitalisation. During hypomania, someone might feel unusually productive, creative, and energetic. They might sleep less, talk more, and take on multiple projects simultaneously. Whilst the mood and behaviour are noticeably different from usual, the person can still function and may even function better than usual in some respects. However, the mood change is observable to others and represents a clear departure from normal functioning.

Why is distinguishing bipolar depression from unipolar depression important? The treatment differs significantly. Antidepressant medications, whilst effective for unipolar depression, can trigger manic or hypomanic episodes in people with bipolar disorder and may worsen the long-term course of the illness. The primary treatment for bipolar disorder involves mood stabilising medications (such as lithium, valproate, or certain antipsychotic medications) which prevent both manic and depressive episodes. Psychological therapy is also important, with a focus on recognising early warning signs of mood episodes, maintaining regular routines, and ensuring medication adherence.

Diagnosing bipolar disorder can be challenging because people typically seek help during depressive episodes rather than during manic or hypomanic episodes (which may feel good or go unrecognised as abnormal). Many people with bipolar disorder are initially misdiagnosed with unipolar depression. Careful assessment of mood history is therefore crucial. If you have experienced periods of unusually elevated, expansive, or irritable mood lasting several days or more, it is essential to discuss this with a mental health professional, as it significantly affects treatment planning.

The depressive episodes in bipolar disorder can be particularly challenging to treat and may have some distinctive features compared to unipolar depression, including more sleep (hypersomnia), increased appetite, leaden paralysis (limbs feeling heavy), and particularly severe loss of energy. However, these features are not universal, and many people with bipolar depression have symptoms indistinguishable from unipolar depression. Careful longitudinal assessment of mood patterns, rather than cross-sectional symptom assessment alone, is necessary for accurate diagnosis.

Treatment-resistant depression (TRD) refers to depression that has not responded adequately to at least two different antidepressant medications given at adequate doses for a sufficient duration. Approximately one-third of people with major depressive disorder do not achieve remission with their first antidepressant medication, and about ten to fifteen per cent meet criteria for treatment-resistant depression after multiple treatment trials. Treatment-resistant depression represents a significant clinical challenge, causing prolonged suffering, substantial functional impairment, and increased risk of suicide and medical comorbidity.

The definition of treatment-resistant depression varies across studies and clinical practice, but most definitions require failure to respond to at least two antidepressants from different classes, each taken at therapeutic doses for at least four to six weeks. Some definitions require failure of three or more medications, whilst others include failure to respond to psychological therapy as well as medication. The concept of treatment-resistant depression acknowledges that whilst most people with depression improve with standard first-line treatments, a substantial minority requires more intensive or specialised intervention.

Before concluding that depression is treatment-resistant, it is essential to ensure that previous treatments have been truly adequate. Many cases of apparent treatment resistance actually reflect inadequate treatment trials. Common problems include insufficient medication dose, insufficient duration of treatment (stopping before therapeutic effects have had time to develop), poor adherence to medication due to side effects or other factors, presence of comorbid conditions that complicate treatment, and psychosocial factors that maintain depression despite biological treatment.

A thorough review of previous treatments, including verification of doses, duration, and adherence, should be conducted before labelling depression as treatment-resistant.

Pseudo-resistance can also occur when the diagnosis is incorrect. What appears to be treatment-resistant depression may actually be bipolar disorder (where antidepressants alone are insufficient and may worsen the condition), a primary anxiety disorder with secondary depressive symptoms, or depression secondary to another medical condition or substance use that has not been addressed. Careful reassessment of the diagnosis is an important step when depression does not respond to standard treatments.

Several factors increase the risk of treatment-resistant depression. Chronic or recurrent depression, earlier age of onset, greater severity of depression, presence of psychotic features, high levels of anxiety, comorbid personality disorder, history of trauma (particularly childhood trauma), concurrent medical conditions, and lack of social support all predict poorer response to standard treatments. Genetic factors also play a role, with treatment response showing some heritability. Understanding these risk factors can help identify individuals who may need more intensive treatment from the outset. (Sullivan et al., 2000)

The approach to treatment-resistant depression typically follows a sequential strategy. After ensuring that previous treatments have been adequate and that the diagnosis is correct, options include optimisation (increasing the dose of the current antidepressant to the maximum tolerated dose), switching (changing to a different antidepressant, ideally from a different class), augmentation (adding another medication to enhance the effects of the antidepressant), or combination (using two antidepressants together). Each strategy has evidence supporting its use, and the choice depends on individual factors including previous treatments tried, side effect profile, and patient preference.

Augmentation strategies involve adding medications that are not themselves antidepressants but that can enhance antidepressant effects. Lithium augmentation has the strongest evidence base and involves adding lithium to an existing antidepressant. The mechanism is not fully understood, but lithium appears to potentiate antidepressant effects and can produce improvement in people who have not responded to antidepressants alone. Thyroid hormone augmentation, typically with liothyronine (T3), is another evidence-based strategy. Atypical antipsychotics, particularly aripiprazole, quetiapine, and olanzapine, are increasingly used as augmentation agents and have regulatory approval for this indication in some countries.

Electroconvulsive therapy (ECT) is one of the most effective treatments for treatment-resistant depression, with response rates of fifty to seventy per cent even in people who have not responded to multiple medications. ECT involves inducing a brief seizure under general anaesthesia using electrical stimulation. Modern ECT is safe and well-tolerated, though it does carry some risk of temporary cognitive side effects, particularly memory difficulties that usually resolve after treatment ends. ECT is particularly indicated when depression is severe, when psychotic features are present, when suicide risk is high, or when rapid response is needed.

Repetitive transcranial magnetic stimulation (rTMS) is a newer non-invasive brain stimulation technique approved for treatment-resistant depression in many countries. rTMS involves applying magnetic pulses to specific areas of the brain, typically the dorsolateral prefrontal cortex, which is involved in mood regulation. Treatment involves daily sessions over several weeks. Whilst generally less effective than ECT, rTMS has fewer side effects and does not require anaesthesia, making it more acceptable to some patients. Response rates in treatment-resistant depression range from thirty to forty per cent.

Other neurostimulation approaches being investigated for treatment-resistant depression include vagus nerve stimulation, which involves surgical implantation of a device that stimulates the vagus nerve; deep brain stimulation, involving surgical implantation of electrodes in specific brain regions; and magnetic seizure therapy, which induces seizures using magnetic fields rather than electrical current. These approaches are currently reserved for the most severe, refractory cases due to their invasive nature and limited availability, but ongoing research may expand their role.

Ketamine and esketamine represent a novel pharmacological approach to treatment-resistant depression. These medications, historically used as anaesthetics, work through different mechanisms than traditional antidepressants, acting on the glutamate system rather than the serotonin, noradrenaline, or dopamine systems. They can produce rapid improvements in depression, sometimes within hours or days rather than weeks. Esketamine nasal spray has been approved for treatment-resistant depression in several countries. Treatment involves administration under medical supervision, typically twice weekly initially. The rapid onset of action makes ketamine particularly valuable for people with acute suicidality, though the duration of effect can be limited and repeated treatments may be needed.

Psychological therapies remain important in treatment-resistant depression, even though most definitions focus on medication resistance. Cognitive behavioural therapy, particularly when delivered intensively, can benefit people who have not responded to medication. The Cognitive Behavioural analysis System of Psychotherapy (CBASP) was specifically developed for chronic and treatment-resistant depression and combines elements of cognitive, behavioural, interpersonal, and psychodynamic approaches. Interpersonal therapy and psychodynamic therapy may also help, particularly when interpersonal problems or long-standing personality factors contribute to depression maintenance.

Addressing lifestyle factors and psychosocial contributors to depression is particularly important in treatment-resistant cases. Regular exercise, sleep hygiene, stress management, social connection, and addressing ongoing life stressors or difficulties all contribute to recovery. For some people, chronic life stress, relationship problems, occupational difficulties, or other ongoing adversities maintain depression regardless of biological treatments. Comprehensive treatment addressing both biological and psychosocial factors typically produces the best outcomes in treatment-resistant depression.

Treatment-Resistant Depression

Depression in the Context of Other Medical Conditions

Depression can occur as a direct consequence of medical conditions or as a psychological reaction to living with chronic illness. The distinction is sometimes challenging, as physical illness affects mood both through biological mechanisms and through the psychological burden of symptoms, disability, and lifestyle changes. However, regardless of the pathway, depression in the context of medical illness deserves recognition and treatment.

Certain medical conditions have particularly strong associations with depression. Neurological conditions such as stroke, multiple sclerosis, Parkinson's disease, and epilepsy frequently co-occur with depression. Stroke depression affects approximately one-third of stroke survivors and can significantly impair rehabilitation and recovery. In Parkinson's disease, depression affects 40 to 50 per cent of patients and may precede the motor symptoms. Multiple sclerosis is associated with depression rates two to three times higher than in the general population.

Endocrine disorders commonly affect mood. Hypothyroidism (underactive thyroid) can cause symptoms that closely mimic depression, including fatigue, low mood, concentration difficulties, and weight gain. Hyperthyroidism (overactive thyroid) can cause anxiety and mood instability. Cushing's syndrome, involving excessive cortisol production, is strongly associated with depression. Diabetes, particularly Type 2 diabetes, has depression rates approximately double that of the general population, with complex bidirectional relationships—depression increases diabetes risk, and diabetes increases depression risk.

Cardiovascular disease and depression have a well-established association. Depression affects 15 to 30 per cent of people after myocardial infarction (heart attack) and is associated with worse cardiac outcomes, increased mortality, and reduced quality of life. The relationship is bidirectional—depression is also a risk factor for developing cardiovascular disease. Similarly, chronic pain conditions, including fibromyalgia, chronic back pain, and arthritis, co-occur with depression at high rates, with each condition exacerbating the other.

Cancer is another condition with high depression rates, affecting 15 to 25 per cent of cancer patients, though rates vary depending on cancer type, stage, and treatment phase. Depression in cancer patients can be difficult to recognise because symptoms like fatigue, appetite loss, and sleep disturbance may be attributed to the cancer or its treatment. However, the psychological symptoms—persistent sadness, hopelessness, loss of pleasure—are key indicators of depression rather than cancer alone.

Chronic infectious diseases, including HIV/AIDS and hepatitis C, are associated with elevated depression rates. HIV-associated depression affects 20 to 30 per cent of people living with HIV, with multiple contributing factors including neurobiological effects of the virus, medication side effects, stigma, and psychological adjustment to chronic illness. Treatment of depression in HIV-positive individuals improves both mental health and adherence to antiretroviral therapy, which is crucial for physical health outcomes.

When depression occurs in the context of medical illness, both conditions require treatment. Treating depression does not mean ignoring the medical condition, and addressing the medical condition alone may not resolve depression. Integrated treatment approaches that address both physical and mental health tend to produce the best outcomes. The psychological therapies described in this book, particularly cognitive behavioural therapy, have been adapted for various medical conditions and have demonstrated effectiveness in reducing depression in medically ill populations.

It is important to note that certain medications used to treat medical conditions can contribute to depression as a side effect. These include corticosteroids (used for inflammation and autoimmune conditions), some cardiovascular medications, hormonal treatments, and certain cancer chemotherapy agents. If you develop depression after starting a new medication, this should be discussed with your doctor, though you should never stop prescribed medication without medical guidance.

Substance-Induced Depressive Disorder

Depression can be triggered or exacerbated by substance use, including both illicit drugs and alcohol. Substance-induced depressive disorder occurs when depressive symptoms arise during or soon after substance intoxication or withdrawal. The relationship between substance use and depression is complex and bidirectional—substance use can cause depression, and depression can lead to increased substance use as people attempt to self-medicate distressing symptoms.

Alcohol is one of the most common substances associated with depression. Whilst alcohol may provide temporary relief from low mood or anxiety, it is a central nervous system depressant that ultimately worsens depression. Chronic alcohol use alters brain chemistry in ways that increase vulnerability to depression. Additionally, the lifestyle consequences of problematic alcohol use—relationship difficulties, employment problems, health complications—contribute to depressed mood. Studies show that reducing or stopping alcohol consumption often leads to significant improvement in depressive symptoms, sometimes resolving depression entirely.

Cannabis use, particularly heavy or chronic use, has been associated with increased rates of depression, though the causal direction remains debated. Some research suggests cannabis use increases depression risk, particularly when use begins in adolescence. Others argue that people with emerging depression may be more likely to use cannabis. What is clear is that for some individuals, cannabis use maintains or worsens depression. The amotivational syndrome sometimes seen with chronic cannabis use—characterised by reduced drive, apathy, and diminished interest in previously enjoyed activities—overlaps considerably with depressive symptoms.

Stimulant drugs, including cocaine, amphetamines, and methamphetamine, typically produce euphoria during intoxication but often trigger significant depression during withdrawal. The neurochemical rebound following stimulant use can produce profound dysphoria, fatigue, increased sleep, and increased appetite—sometimes called a "crash." With repeated use, the depressive symptoms can become more persistent and severe. Similarly, MDMA (ecstasy) use is commonly followed by several days of low mood, sometimes termed "midweek blues," reflecting temporary depletion of serotonin in the brain.

Opioid use disorder is highly comorbid with depression, with rates of major depression in people with opioid dependence ranging from 30 to 50 per cent. The relationship is complex—depression may predate opioid use, may develop as a consequence of opioid use and its lifestyle impact, or may emerge during withdrawal. Opioid withdrawal itself produces significant dysphoria and depression-like symptoms. Treatment of opioid use disorder, whether through abstinence-based approaches or medication-assisted treatment (such as methadone or buprenorphine), often improves depressive symptoms, though co-occurring depression may require specific treatment.

Determining whether depression is substance-induced or independent can be challenging and has important treatment implications. Generally, if depressive symptoms preceded substance use, persist during extended periods of abstinence, or are more severe than would be expected from substance use alone, independent depression is likely present and requires specific treatment. However, in many cases, the wisest approach is to address substance use first and reassess depressive symptoms after a period of sustained abstinence. Often, depressive symptoms improve considerably or resolve once substance use ceases, though this may take weeks or months as the brain's chemistry rebalances.

Treatment for substance-induced depression involves both addressing substance use and treating depressive symptoms. Cognitive behavioural therapy is effective for both substance use disorders and depression and can address how these conditions interact. Antidepressant medication may be considered, though effectiveness can be compromised by ongoing substance use. Integrated treatment programmes that address both conditions simultaneously tend to produce better outcomes than treating either condition in isolation. Support groups, such as Alcoholics Anonymous or Narcotics Anonymous, can provide valuable peer support for maintaining abstinence.

The Experience of Depression

To truly understand depression, we must go beyond clinical descriptions and diagnostic criteria to consider the lived experience of those who suffer from this condition. Depression is not simply sadness amplified; it is a qualitatively different state that profoundly alters how one experiences oneself, others, and the world. People with depression often describe feeling trapped, as though they are viewing life from behind glass, able to see normality but unable to access it. The world appears grey, muted, devoid of colour and vibrancy. Experiences that should evoke emotion, whether positive or negative, provoke only numbness or indifference.

The subjective experience of time changes in depression. Time feels distorted, with minutes feeling like hours when you are experiencing acute distress, yet days and weeks blur together indistinguishably. The past feels like it happened to someone else, a distant time when you were a different person capable of feeling and functioning. The present feels endless, an unbroken stretch of greyness with no relief. The future appears non-existent or threatening, a blank void or a continuation of present suffering. This distortion of temporal experience contributes to the sense of hopelessness that characterises severe depression: if you cannot imagine a different future, hope becomes impossible.

Depression affects the sense of self in fundamental ways. You may feel that depression has consumed your personality, that you can no longer remember who you were before depression or imagine who you might be without it. The things that once defined you – your interests, values, roles, relationships – feel distant and irrelevant. You might describe feeling like a shell, going through the motions of life whilst feeling fundamentally empty inside. This loss of self is one of the most distressing aspects of depression and one that is difficult for others to understand. It is not simply that you are sad; it is that you, as you knew yourself, seem to have disappeared.

Physical sensations in depression are often described in metaphorical terms that capture their oppressive quality. People speak of heavy weights on their chest or shoulders, of moving through treacle or quicksand, of being submerged underwater where everything is slow and muffled. The fatigue of depression is not simple tiredness but profound exhaustion that sleep does not relieve, a bone-deep weariness that makes even small movements feel like immense efforts. Some describe feeling as though their body is made of lead, as though gravity has increased its pull specifically on them. These are not mere figures of speech but attempts to communicate a genuinely altered physical experience.

The experience of depression is often marked by a profound sense of isolation and disconnection. Even when surrounded by people who care about you, you feel utterly alone, convinced that no one could possibly understand what you are experiencing. This isolation is compounded by difficulty expressing your experience. Words feel inadequate to convey the depth of your distress. When you try to explain how you feel, it comes out flat or incomplete, failing to communicate the intensity of your suffering. This communication difficulty can lead to frustration on both sides: you feel misunderstood and alone, whilst others feel helpless, not knowing how to help or whether their efforts make any difference.

Guilt is a pervasive feature of the depression experience. You feel guilty for being depressed, for being unable to function normally, for burdening others with your problems, for not being able to simply 'snap out of it'. You feel guilty about not enjoying things you know you should enjoy, about letting people down, about not being the person you think you should be. This guilt is typically disproportionate and irrational, but it feels utterly justified in the moment. You might recognise intellectually that depression is an illness not a choice, yet still feel profound shame about having it, as though it represents some fundamental moral or personal failure.

The sense of hopelessness in depression is particularly dangerous because it undermines motivation to seek help or persist with treatment. When you feel hopeless, you believe that nothing will ever improve, that you will feel this way forever, that treatment will not work for you even if it works for others. This hopelessness can be so convincing that the objective evidence for depression's treatability feels irrelevant to your specific case. You might acknowledge that others recover but remain certain that you will not. This is why hopelessness is so closely associated with suicidality: when you truly believe that your suffering is permanent and unchangeable, death can seem like the only escape.

For many people, depression involves constant internal struggle. Part of you knows intellectually that your negative thoughts may not be true, that things may not be as hopeless as they seem, that you should reach out for help. But another part of you, the part currently in control, insists that everything is hopeless, that you are fundamentally worthless, that nothing can help. This internal battle is exhausting. You might spend hours trying to convince yourself to do something simple, like getting out of bed or making a phone call, with competing voices arguing about whether there is any point, whether you have the energy, whether it will make any difference. This constant internal conflict consumes enormous mental energy, leaving even less available for actually managing life.

Despite the overwhelming nature of depression, many people manage to maintain a façade of functioning, at least for periods. You might hold down a job, maintain relationships, and appear outwardly relatively normal whilst internally experiencing profound distress. This 'high-functioning depression' or 'smiling depression' is exhausting, requiring enormous energy to present a normal face to the world whilst privately struggling. The discrepancy between your internal experience and external presentation can be confusing for others and can make your suffering feel even more isolating. When you do reveal your struggles, others may be surprised, having seen no signs of difficulty, which can feel invalidating of your experience.

Understanding the subjective experience of depression is important not only for those experiencing it but also for their loved ones and healthcare providers. This understanding fosters compassion, both self-compassion and compassion from others. It helps explain behaviours that might otherwise be interpreted as laziness, selfishness, or not caring. It validates the reality and severity of depression as a profoundly debilitating condition. Most importantly, understanding that these experiences, however convincing they feel, are symptoms of depression rather than accurate reflections of reality creates the possibility of questioning and challenging them. The hopelessness, worthlessness, and conviction that nothing will help are products of depression, not truth. Recovery is possible, even when depression makes it impossible to believe.

Understanding depression from a clinical perspective—its symptoms, types, and prevalence—provides necessary context, but it tells only part of the story. To truly comprehend depression, we must also understand what it feels like to live with this condition day by day. The lived experience of depression encompasses not just the presence of symptoms but the profound way those symptoms alter your relationship with yourself, others, and the world around you.

Depression is often described as feeling like you are living under a thick, heavy blanket that muffles everything. Colours seem less vibrant. Food loses its taste. Music that once moved you now sounds flat and distant. Conversations that would normally engage you feel like they are happening far away, as though you are separated from life by an invisible barrier. This sense of disconnection extends to your own emotions—even when you want to feel something, anything, there is often just a dull emptiness where feelings used to be.

Many people with depression describe a profound sense of heaviness, as though gravity has somehow increased. Getting out of bed requires enormous effort. Taking a shower feels like climbing a mountain. Tasks that once were automatic—brushing teeth, getting dressed, preparing food—become challenges that demand what feels like superhuman willpower. This physical heaviness is not laziness or lack of motivation; it is a genuine symptom that makes even the simplest actions feel impossibly difficult.

The cognitive experience of depression extends beyond the difficulty concentrating mentioned earlier. Thoughts become slower and stickier, as though wading through thick mud. Decision-making, even about trivial matters, becomes overwhelming. Should I have tea or coffee? What should I wear? These tiny choices can precipitate internal debates that last for frustrating lengths of time. This cognitive sluggishness is called psychomotor retardation and can be noticeable to others—your speech may slow, your movements may become more deliberate, and you may pause longer before responding to questions.

Depression fundamentally alters your relationship with time. The past becomes a catalogue of regrets and failures. Positive memories either become inaccessible or are reinterpreted through a negative filter—that job promotion was just luck, that relationship was bound to fail anyway. The present feels unbearable, each moment something to endure rather than experience. And the future seems impossibly bleak. When you are depressed, you literally cannot imagine feeling better. This is not simply pessimism; it is a cognitive change where your brain loses the ability to project positive outcomes. The future appears as an unrelenting continuation of current misery, stretching endlessly ahead.

This inability to imagine recovery creates one of depression's cruellest paradoxes: you desperately want to feel better, yet you cannot believe you ever will. This makes seeking help feel pointless. Why bother going to therapy when you "know" it will not work? Why try treatment when you are "certain" nothing can help? This hopelessness itself is a symptom, not a fact, but when you are in its grip, it feels absolutely true. Understanding that hopelessness is a symptom rather than reality is crucial—it means that what feels like clear-sighted realism is actually a distortion caused by the depression itself.

The social impact of depression is profound and often creates a vicious cycle that maintains the condition. Depression makes you want to withdraw from others, yet isolation worsens depression. Social interactions feel exhausting. Keeping up conversation requires energy you do not have. Smiling and appearing normal feels like an exhausting performance. Yet when you are alone, the negative thoughts intensify and the sense of disconnection deepens. Friends may stop inviting you to events after repeated cancellations, which confirms your belief that no one cares about you, even though it is your depression-driven withdrawal that created the situation.

Depression also affects how you perceive others' responses to you. When depressed, you are more likely to interpret neutral or ambiguous social cues negatively. A friend's brief text message becomes evidence they are annoyed with you. A colleague's distracted greeting confirms your belief that people find you boring. This negative interpretation bias operates automatically and feels accurate, even though it is a cognitive distortion. These misinterpretations then influence your behaviour—you might avoid the friend or colleague, which can actually create the rejection you feared.

For many people, depression brings intense guilt and self-criticism. You may berate yourself for being depressed, viewing it as weakness or failure. "I should be stronger," "I have nothing to be depressed about," "Other people have it worse than me"—these thoughts are common but deeply unhelpful. They add a layer of suffering on top of the depression itself. You are not just depressed; you are depressed about being depressed and angry at yourself for not being able to just "snap out of it." This self-criticism often reflects harsh internal standards and perfectionism that predate the depression but become amplified by it.

Depression also affects your sense of identity. When symptoms persist for weeks or months, you may begin to lose touch with who you were before. Your interests, personality, sense of humour, and capabilities all seem to have disappeared, replaced by this flattened, joyless version of yourself. You may think, "This is just who I am now," believing the depression has fundamentally changed you. This loss of identity can be frightening and demoralising. It is crucial to understand that depression is not your identity—it is a condition that obscures your true self, like clouds blocking the sun. Your personality, interests, and capabilities remain; they are simply inaccessible whilst the depression is active.

The physical symptoms of depression—fatigue, sleep disturbance, appetite changes, physical pain—add another layer of difficulty. Chronic tiredness makes everything harder. Sleep problems mean you never feel rested. Changes in appetite and weight can affect self-image and physical health. Many people with depression experience physical pain—headaches, backaches, muscle tension, or unexplained aches throughout the body. These physical symptoms are not "all in your head"; they are real manifestations of depression that occur because the brain systems that regulate mood are connected to systems that regulate pain, sleep, appetite, and energy.

Perhaps one of the most challenging aspects of depression is how it affects motivation and then punishes you for the lack of motivation. Depression depletes the very resources—energy, concentration, hope—that you need to fight it. You know you should exercise, maintain social connections, keep up with responsibilities, but depression makes these things feel impossible. Then you criticise yourself for not doing them, which worsens the depression. This creates a downward spiral where depression symptoms reduce functioning, reduced functioning increases depression symptoms, and self-criticism amplifies both.

Depression also disrupts your relationship with pleasure and accomplishment. Activities that used to bring joy—seeing friends, pursuing hobbies, watching favourite films—no longer do so. This loss of pleasure, called anhedonia, is one of depression's core symptoms. Initially, you might try to engage in previously enjoyed activities, but when they feel flat and unrewarding, you stop trying. This makes sense in the moment but eliminates potential sources of positive experience that might gradually help lift mood. Similarly, accomplishments feel meaningless. You might complete a significant task at work, but instead of satisfaction, you feel nothing or immediately discount the achievement as insignificant.

Understanding the lived experience of depression helps explain why it is so difficult to simply "think positive" or "look on the bright side" as well-meaning others might suggest. Depression is not simply negative thinking that can be overcome with willpower. It is a pervasive change in brain function that affects thinking, feeling, physical sensation, motivation, and perception. The cognitive behavioural approach you will learn in this book does not ask you to think positive thoughts while ignoring reality. Instead, it teaches you to recognise the specific ways depression distorts thinking and to develop more balanced, accurate thoughts that take into account both difficulties and resources, both problems and possibilities.

What Causes Depression?

The question "what causes depression?" does not have a simple answer. Depression is not caused by a single factor but rather arises from the complex interaction of multiple biological, psychological, and social influences. Understanding this multicausal nature is important because it helps explain why depression affects some people and not others, why it occurs at particular times, and why comprehensive treatment often requires addressing multiple contributing factors.

For many years, scientific understanding of depression was dominated by competing theories—was it biological or psychological, genetic or environmental, a brain disease or a reaction to life circumstances? We now understand that these are not competing explanations but different levels of analysis of the same phenomenon. Biological changes in the brain do occur in depression, and these changes have psychological manifestations. Psychological experiences and environmental stressors can trigger biological changes. The mind and brain are not separate entities but different ways of describing the same underlying processes.

Biological Factors

The biological factors contributing to depression are complex, involving multiple interacting systems including neurotransmitter systems, neuroendocrine function, inflammatory processes, circadian rhythm regulation, and structural and functional brain changes. Understanding these biological mechanisms is important for several reasons: it validates depression as a legitimate medical condition rather than personal weakness, it explains why medication can be helpful in treatment, it highlights the importance of addressing physical health in depression recovery, and it provides insight into the complex interplay between biological and psychosocial factors in depression causation and maintenance.

Neurotransmitter systems have long been central to biological theories of depression. The monoamine hypothesis, developed in the 1960s, proposed that depression results from deficiencies in monoamine neurotransmitters, particularly serotonin, noradrenaline (norepinephrine), and dopamine. This hypothesis arose from observations that drugs affecting these neurotransmitter systems could improve depression, and that drugs depleting these neurotransmitters could induce depression in vulnerable individuals. Whilst the simple version of this hypothesis (that depression is caused by a chemical imbalance) has proven inadequate to explain the complexity of depression, neurotransmitter systems clearly play important roles.

Serotonin is involved in mood regulation, sleep, appetite, and numerous other functions. People with depression show various abnormalities in serotonin function including reduced serotonin synthesis, altered receptor sensitivity, and abnormalities in serotonin transporter function. Selective serotonin reuptake inhibitors (SSRIs), which increase serotonin availability in the synapse, are effective antidepressants, though their therapeutic effects take weeks to develop, suggesting the mechanism is more complex than simply increasing serotonin levels. Recent research indicates that serotonin may influence neuroplasticity and the brain's capacity to adapt and change, which may be how SSRIs ultimately produce their effects. (Cipriani et al., 2018)

Noradrenaline is involved in alertness, energy, and attention, and is part of the body's stress response system. Depression is associated with abnormalities in noradrenaline function. Some antidepressants, such as serotonin-noradrenaline reuptake inhibitors (SNRIs), work by affecting both serotonin and noradrenaline. The noradrenaline system interacts closely with the hypothalamic-pituitary-adrenal (HPA) axis, which regulates the stress response. Dysregulation of both noradrenaline and the HPA axis is common in depression, particularly in depression associated with stress or trauma.

Dopamine is crucial for motivation, reward processing, and the experience of pleasure. The anhedonia characteristic of depression, the inability to experience pleasure, is thought to relate particularly to dopamine dysfunction. People with depression show reduced activation in dopamine-rich brain regions in response to rewards. This may explain why activities that should be pleasurable feel flat and why motivation is so impaired in depression. Some antidepressants, particularly those used in treatment-resistant depression, affect dopamine function. The role of dopamine in depression is increasingly recognised as important, though historically it received less attention than serotonin and noradrenaline.

The hypothalamic-pituitary-adrenal (HPA) axis regulates the body's stress response through the production of cortisol and other stress hormones. In depression, the HPA axis is often hyperactive, with elevated cortisol levels and failure of the normal feedback mechanisms that shut down cortisol production when stress passes. Chronic elevation of cortisol has numerous negative effects including suppression of neurogenesis, reduction in brain-derived neurotrophic factor, damage to neurons particularly in the hippocampus, disruption of sleep, effects on immune function, and metabolic changes. The HPA axis abnormalities in depression may be both a consequence of chronic stress and a perpetuating factor maintaining depression.

Brain-derived neurotrophic factor (BDNF) is a protein that supports the growth, survival, and differentiation of neurons. It plays a crucial role in neuroplasticity, the brain's ability to adapt and change. People with depression have reduced levels of BDNF, particularly in the hippocampus and prefrontal cortex, brain regions involved in mood regulation and showing structural changes in depression. Antidepressants increase BDNF levels, and this effect may be central to their therapeutic action. Stress reduces BDNF, whilst exercise and positive experiences increase it. The BDNF hypothesis of depression proposes that reduced neuroplasticity, reflected in low BDNF, is a core feature of depression.

Neurogenesis, the birth of new neurons, continues in certain brain regions throughout life, particularly the hippocampus. Depression is associated with reduced neurogenesis, whilst antidepressants promote neurogenesis. The time course of increased neurogenesis following antidepressant treatment matches the time course of clinical improvement, suggesting neurogenesis may be important for recovery. Stress inhibits neurogenesis, providing another mechanism through which chronic stress contributes to depression. Factors that promote neurogenesis, including exercise, learning, and environmental enrichment, may have antidepressant effects partly through this mechanism.

Structural brain changes are consistently found in depression using neuroimaging techniques. The hippocampus, involved in memory and stress regulation, shows reduced volume in depression, with greater reduction associated with longer duration and more episodes of depression. The prefrontal cortex, involved in emotional regulation, decision-making, and executive function, also shows reduced volume and altered activity in depression. The amygdala, involved in processing emotions particularly fear and threat, often shows increased activity in depression. These structural changes are thought to both result from depression and to maintain it, creating vulnerability to future episodes.

Functional brain changes in depression involve altered activity and connectivity in brain networks involved in mood regulation, cognitive control, and response to rewards. The default mode network, active during rest and involved in self-referential thinking, shows increased activity and connectivity in depression, which may relate to rumination. The cognitive control network, involved in directing attention and regulating thoughts and emotions, shows reduced activity. The reward network shows reduced responsiveness to positive stimuli. These functional changes help explain many symptoms of depression including rumination, difficulty with attention and concentration, and anhedonia.

Inflammation is increasingly recognised as playing a role in depression. Many people with depression have elevated levels of inflammatory markers such as C-reactive protein, interleukin-6, and tumour necrosis factor alpha. Inflammatory cytokines can affect mood, energy, sleep, and appetite, producing symptoms resembling depression. Inflammation may contribute to depression through effects on neurotransmitter metabolism, HPA axis function, neuroplasticity, and neurogenesis. Medical conditions associated with inflammation, such as cardiovascular disease and diabetes, show high rates of comorbid depression. Anti-inflammatory interventions show some promise as augmentation strategies in treatment-resistant depression.

Circadian rhythm dysregulation is common in depression. The circadian system regulates the sleep-wake cycle, hormone production, body temperature, and numerous other physiological processes over the twenty-four-hour cycle. Depression is associated with abnormalities in circadian rhythms including delayed or disrupted sleep-wake cycles, altered timing of cortisol and melatonin production, and reduced amplitude of circadian rhythms. Light therapy, which helps re-entrain circadian rhythms, is effective for seasonal affective disorder and shows some benefit in non-seasonal depression. Interventions that strengthen circadian rhythms, including regular sleep-wake times and morning light exposure, can support depression recovery.

Genetic factors contribute to depression risk, with heritability estimated at thirty to forty per cent based on twin and family studies. However, depression is polygenic, meaning many genes each contribute small effects rather than a single gene causing depression. Genes involved in neurotransmitter function, stress response, neuroplasticity, and circadian rhythms have been associated with depression risk, though findings are often inconsistent across studies. Gene-environment interactions are important: genetic vulnerability may only lead to depression in the presence of environmental stressors. Epigenetic changes, modifications to gene expression rather than to the genetic code itself, may be one mechanism through which environmental experiences interact with genetic vulnerability to influence depression risk.

Physical health and depression are bidirectionally related. Chronic medical conditions including cardiovascular disease, diabetes, cancer, chronic pain conditions, neurological conditions, and thyroid disorders are associated with elevated rates of depression. Depression in turn increases risk for various physical health problems and worsens outcomes in existing conditions. The mechanisms linking physical and mental health are multiple, including shared biological pathways (such as inflammation), behavioural factors (depression reduces self-care and adherence to medical treatments), and psychological factors (chronic illness is stressful and can lead to loss and disability). Addressing physical health is an important component of comprehensive depression treatment.

Neurotransmitters are chemicals that facilitate communication between nerve cells in the brain. Three neurotransmitters—serotonin, noradrenaline (also called norepinephrine), and dopamine—have been particularly implicated in depression. Serotonin is involved in regulating mood, sleep, appetite, and pain perception. Noradrenaline affects energy, attention, and arousal. Dopamine is crucial for motivation, pleasure, and reward. Depression is associated with disruptions in the functioning of these neurotransmitter systems, though the relationship is more nuanced than simply having "too little" of these chemicals.

The neurotransmitter hypothesis gained support from observations about antidepressant medications. Drugs that increase serotonin and noradrenaline availability in the brain often relieve depression. However, the full picture is more complex. Antidepressants increase neurotransmitter levels within hours, but mood improvement typically takes weeks. This suggests that the therapeutic effect involves longer-term changes in brain cell function and connectivity rather than simple chemical correction. Current understanding suggests that depression involves disruptions in the brain's capacity to regulate mood, with neurotransmitters being part of a more complex system of cellular communication and adaptation.

Brain structure and function also differ in depression. Neuroimaging studies have identified several brain regions that show altered activity or structure in depressed individuals. The prefrontal cortex, involved in planning, decision-making, and regulating emotion, often shows reduced activity in depression. The hippocampus, important for memory and stress regulation, may show reduced volume in people with chronic or recurrent depression. The amygdala, which processes emotions, particularly negative emotions, often shows increased activity in depression. These changes help explain many depression symptoms—diminished prefrontal cortex function contributes to difficulties with concentration and decision-making; hippocampal changes affect memory and stress response; amygdala hyperactivity increases sensitivity to negative information.

The stress response system plays a crucial role in depression. When you encounter stress, your body releases cortisol and other stress hormones that mobilise resources to deal with threats. This is adaptive in the short term, but chronic stress leads to prolonged elevation of cortisol, which can damage brain cells, particularly in the hippocampus. Many people with depression show dysregulation of the stress response system, with elevated cortisol levels and an inability to shut off the stress response after stressors have passed. This creates a vicious cycle where stress triggers depression, and depression increases vulnerability to stress.

Inflammation is increasingly recognised as playing a role in depression. People with depression often have elevated levels of inflammatory markers in their blood. Inflammation affects the brain in multiple ways, including influencing neurotransmitter metabolism and reducing the production of new neurons. The immune system and nervous system are intricately connected, and chronic activation of inflammatory processes may contribute to depression in some individuals. This helps explain why medical conditions involving inflammation, such as rheumatoid arthritis or cardiovascular disease, have high rates of co-occurring depression.

Genetics clearly influence depression risk. If you have a first-degree relative (parent, sibling, or child) with depression, your risk is two to three times higher than someone without such family history. Twin studies suggest that genetic factors account for approximately 40 to 50 per cent of depression risk. However, no single "depression gene" has been identified. Instead, many genes, each with small effects, contribute to vulnerability. These genes affect neurotransmitter systems, stress response, brain development, and other processes relevant to mood regulation. Importantly, genetic risk is not deterministic—having genetic vulnerability does not mean you will definitely develop depression, and lacking family history does not make you immune.

Psychological Factors

How you think about yourself, your experiences, and your future significantly influences depression risk. Cognitive theories of depression, which form the foundation of cognitive behavioural therapy, propose that negative thinking patterns both contribute to and maintain depression. These patterns include negative automatic thoughts (immediate, involuntary negative interpretations of situations), negative core beliefs about the self (such as "I am inadequate" or "I am unlovable"), and negative thinking styles that lead you to interpret ambiguous situations negatively, focus selectively on negative information, and discount positive experiences.

Attribution style—how you explain the causes of events—influences depression vulnerability. People who habitually explain negative events with internal ("it's my fault"), stable ("things are always like this"), and global ("this affects everything in my life") attributions are more prone to depression than those who use external, unstable, and specific attributions. For instance, after failing an exam, one person might think "I'm stupid (internal), I'll never succeed (stable), I'm a failure at everything (global)" whilst another might think "The test was unusually difficult (external), I didn't study enough this time (unstable), I need to prepare differently for this subject (specific)." These habitual explanation patterns develop early in life and influence how you respond to difficulties.

Rumination—repetitively focusing on the causes, meanings, and consequences of negative feelings—is strongly associated with depression. When you ruminate, you think repeatedly about your problems, why you feel bad, what your symptoms mean, but without making progress toward solutions. Rumination feels like problem-solving but is actually a form of mental wheel-spinning that intensifies and prolongs negative mood. Women ruminate more than men on average, which may partly explain higher depression rates in women. Rumination can be distinguished from productive reflection—rumination is abstract ("Why am I such a failure?"), repetitive, and focused on problems, whilst productive reflection is concrete, moves toward solutions, and includes broader perspectives.

Personality characteristics influence depression risk. Neuroticism—the tendency to experience negative emotions intensely and frequently—is the personality trait most strongly associated with depression. High neuroticism does not cause depression directly but creates vulnerability by influencing how strongly and how long you feel distressed in response to negative events. Perfectionism, particularly the aspects involving harsh self-criticism and fear of negative evaluation by others, is also associated with depression. Perfectionism sets unrealistic standards, leading to frequent experiences of failure and self-criticism. Low self-esteem is both a risk factor for depression and a symptom of it, creating another self-perpetuating cycle.

Early adverse experiences shape psychological vulnerability to depression. Childhood trauma—including abuse, neglect, loss of a parent, and household dysfunction—significantly increases lifelong depression risk. These experiences affect psychological development in multiple ways: they shape beliefs about the self ("I am worthless"), others ("People cannot be trusted"), and the world ("The world is dangerous"). They affect the development of emotion regulation skills, making it harder to manage negative feelings. They influence attachment patterns, affecting adult relationships. And they have biological effects, altering stress response systems and even affecting gene expression through epigenetic mechanisms.

Social and Environmental Factors

Stressful life events frequently precede depression onset. Major life stressors—bereavement, relationship breakdown, job loss, serious illness, financial crisis—can trigger depression in vulnerable individuals. Not all stressful events carry equal risk. Events that involve loss, humiliation, or entrapment are particularly depressogenic. Loss events include bereavement, divorce, or job loss. Humiliation events involve public embarrassment or revelation of damaging information. Entrapment situations involve feeling stuck in intolerable circumstances with no escape, such as an abusive relationship or overwhelming debt. Chronic stressors, such as ongoing financial difficulties or caregiving responsibilities, also increase depression risk through accumulated strain.

Social support plays a crucial protective role. Having close, confiding relationships buffers against depression following stress. Social support provides practical assistance, emotional validation, and perspective that helps you cope with difficulties. Conversely, social isolation and loneliness significantly increase depression risk. This is not simply about the number of social contacts but about the quality of relationships. A few close, supportive relationships are more protective than many superficial acquaintances. Problematic relationships—marked by criticism, conflict, or controlling behaviour—can increase rather than decrease depression risk.

Socioeconomic factors influence depression risk through multiple pathways. Lower income and education levels are associated with higher depression rates. Poverty creates chronic stress through financial insecurity, poor housing, unsafe neighbourhoods, and limited access to resources. It also limits opportunities for positive experiences and reduces sense of control over one's life. Employment status matters—unemployment increases depression risk not only through financial stress but also through loss of structure, purpose, and social contacts that work provides. Job insecurity and work stress, including high demands with low control, also elevate depression risk.

Cultural factors influence both the experience and expression of depression. Different cultures have different concepts of mental health and emotional experience, affecting how people understand and describe their distress. In some cultures, psychological distress is primarily expressed through physical symptoms—a pattern called somatisation. In others, expressing emotional pain openly is culturally unacceptable, leading to minimisation or denial of symptoms. Cultural factors also affect help-seeking—in cultures where mental health problems carry strong stigma, people may delay seeking help until symptoms are severe. Understanding cultural context is important for recognising depression across diverse populations and providing culturally sensitive treatment.

Life stage and developmental factors affect depression risk and presentation. Adolescence and early adulthood are periods of elevated risk, partly due to biological brain development continuing into the mid-20s and partly due to the life transitions and identity formation challenges of this period. Older adulthood brings different risks—retirement can trigger depression through loss of purpose and social contacts; bereavement becomes more common; health problems accumulate; and cognitive changes can affect mood regulation. Women face particular vulnerability during periods of hormonal change—puberty, menstruation, pregnancy and postpartum, and menopause—though the mechanisms are complex and involve biological, psychological, and social factors.

The Biopsychosocial Model and the Stress-Vulnerability Framework

The biopsychosocial model integrates biological, psychological, and social factors into a comprehensive understanding of depression. Rather than asking whether depression is biological or psychological, this model recognises that it is both. Biological factors create vulnerabilities or resiliences at the neural level. Psychological factors involve how you think about and respond to experiences. Social factors include your relationships, environment, and life circumstances. These factors constantly interact—biological vulnerabilities make you more sensitive to stress; stressful experiences trigger biological changes; psychological patterns influence which situations feel stressful; social support affects how you cope with difficulties.

The stress-vulnerability model, also called the diathesis-stress model, provides a useful framework for understanding why some people develop depression whilst others, facing similar circumstances, do not. The model proposes that depression results from the interaction between vulnerability factors (predispositions that increase risk) and stress factors (triggers that precipitate the disorder). Vulnerabilities include genetic factors, early adverse experiences, personality characteristics, and negative thinking patterns. These create a lower threshold for depression. Stressful life events then act as triggers that push vulnerable individuals past the threshold into depression.

This model helps explain several phenomena. First, it accounts for the fact that depression often, but not always, follows stress—those with high vulnerability may develop depression with relatively minor stress, whilst those with low vulnerability may remain resilient even facing severe stress. Second, it explains why depression sometimes seems to come "out of nowhere"—if vulnerability is high, even minor stressors may trigger an episode. Third, it helps explain recurrence—each episode of depression may increase vulnerability for future episodes, lowering the threshold for subsequent depression. This sensitisation effect means that first episodes often follow major stress, whilst later episodes may occur with less obvious triggers.

Importantly, the stress-vulnerability model suggests multiple intervention points. You cannot change your genes or undo early adverse experiences, but you can modify other vulnerability factors. Cognitive behavioural therapy targets negative thinking patterns, reducing psychological vulnerability. Lifestyle changes, including exercise, sleep, and stress management, can reduce biological vulnerability. Building social support and developing coping skills reduces the impact of stressors.

Reducing rumination and developing mindfulness skills changes how you respond to negative thoughts and feelings. Understanding depression as arising from multiple interacting factors, rather than a single cause, opens up multiple pathways for treatment and prevention.

Coping styles represent another psychological factor. Active, problem-focused coping strategies, where people identify problems and take steps to address them, are generally associated with better outcomes. In contrast, avoidance-based coping, where people withdraw from difficulties, deny problems, or engage in distraction without addressing underlying issues, tends to be associated with worse outcomes and increased depression risk. Emotion-focused coping strategies, such as seeking social support, reappraising situations more positively, or using relaxation techniques, can be helpful in situations where problems cannot be directly solved, but some emotion-focused strategies, such as rumination or self-blame, are unhelpful. Depression itself tends to impair effective coping, creating a vicious cycle where poor coping maintains depression, and depression further undermines coping capacity.

Social and Environmental Factors

Social and environmental factors play a crucial role in depression, both in triggering initial episodes and in maintaining symptoms. The relationship between life stress and depression is well-established. Stressful life events, particularly those involving loss, humiliation, or entrapment, are strongly associated with depression onset. Significant losses might include bereavement, relationship breakdown, job loss, financial setbacks, or loss of health or role. Events involving humiliation or degradation, such as public failure, rejection, or betrayal, are particularly depressogenic. Situations of entrapment, where people feel stuck in intolerable circumstances with no escape route, such as abusive relationships, overwhelming caregiving responsibilities, or impossible work situations, are also powerful triggers for depression.

The impact of stressful events depends not only on the objective severity of the event but also on its meaning to the individual, the context in which it occurs, and the resources available for coping. An event that feels overwhelming to one person might be manageable for another, depending on factors such as social support, prior experience, coping skills, and other concurrent stressors. Chronic stress, ongoing difficulties that persist over time rather than discrete events, can be particularly problematic. Examples include long-term relationship conflict, chronic work stress, ongoing financial hardship, persistent caregiving demands, or chronic physical health problems. Chronic stress is exhausting, depletes coping resources, and provides no relief or recovery period.

Social support, defined as the availability of people who provide emotional support, practical help, guidance, and companionship, is one of the most important protective factors against depression. Strong social support can buffer the impact of stress, making stressful events less likely to trigger depression. Conversely, lack of social support, social isolation, and loneliness are major risk factors for depression. This is not simply about the number of social contacts but about the quality of relationships. One or two close, confiding relationships where people feel understood and valued can be more protective than numerous superficial acquaintances. However, depression itself interferes with social relationships, as people withdraw from social contact, feel unworthy of others' care, struggle to communicate, or become irritable and difficult to be around. This withdrawal then increases isolation, creating another vicious cycle that maintains depression.

Family environment and relationship dynamics influence depression risk. Growing up in a family characterised by criticism, overcontrol, lack of emotional warmth, or inconsistent parenting is associated with increased depression risk. Insecure attachment patterns developed in childhood, particularly anxious or avoidant attachment, can increase vulnerability to depression in adulthood by affecting how people relate to others, regulate emotions, and cope with stress. Current family or relationship difficulties, including conflict, domestic violence, lack of emotional intimacy, or relationship breakdown, are both triggers for depression and barriers to recovery.

Childhood adversity has enduring effects on depression risk. Adverse childhood experiences such as physical, sexual, or emotional abuse, neglect, witnessing domestic violence, parental mental illness, parental substance abuse, parental separation or divorce, or having an incarcerated household member, are associated with substantially increased risk of depression throughout life. The more types of adversity experienced, the greater the risk. These effects appear to operate through multiple pathways, including effects on brain development, stress response systems, attachment patterns, development of negative core beliefs about self and others, and reduced access to protective factors such as education and stable relationships. Importantly, whilst childhood adversity increases risk, it does not make depression inevitable, and many people who experience significant adversity do not develop depression, highlighting the importance of resilience factors.

Socioeconomic factors are relevant to depression. Lower socioeconomic status, measured by income, education, or occupational status, is associated with higher rates of depression. This association likely reflects multiple factors, including greater exposure to stress, fewer resources for coping with stress, reduced access to healthcare and psychological treatment, and potentially greater exposure to other risk factors such as poor housing, neighbourhood disadvantage, or violence. Unemployment is particularly strongly associated with depression, likely through loss of income, loss of structure and purpose, loss of social contacts and identity associated with work, and the stress and uncertainty of job seeking.

Cultural factors influence how depression is experienced, expressed, and understood. Some cultures emphasise somatic symptoms (physical manifestations) of depression more than emotional symptoms. Stigma around mental health varies across cultures and can affect whether people seek help. Cultural values regarding emotional expression, individualism versus collectivism, and attitudes towards professional help all influence depression presentation and treatment seeking. An understanding that incorporates cultural context is important for recognising and treating depression effectively.

The interaction between biological, psychological, and social factors is crucial to understand. These factors do not operate independently but influence each other in complex ways. For example, genetic vulnerability might only lead to depression in the presence of significant life stress (gene-environment interaction). Early adverse experiences can affect brain development and stress response systems (social factors affecting biology). Chronic stress can alter neurotransmitter function (environment affecting biology). Negative thinking patterns can lead to social withdrawal and relationship problems (psychological factors affecting social factors). Depression changes brain function and neurotransmitter systems (psychology affecting biology). This biopsychosocial model of depression recognises that understanding and treating depression requires attention to multiple levels of influence.

Recognising Depression: Signs and Symptoms

Recognising depression is the crucial first step towards recovery. Depression affects every aspect of functioning, with symptoms spanning emotional, cognitive, physical, and behavioural domains. Understanding the full range of symptoms helps people identify when they might be experiencing depression, validate their experiences, and understand why depression has such a pervasive impact on their lives.

Core Emotional Symptoms

The hallmark emotional symptom of depression is persistent low mood or sadness. This is not ordinary sadness that everyone experiences from time to time in response to disappointments or losses. Rather, it is a pervasive, unremitting feeling of sadness, emptiness, or numbness that persists most of the day, nearly every day, for at least two weeks. The low mood is often present from the moment of waking and pervades all activities throughout the day. Some people describe feeling 'flat' or 'dead inside' rather than actively sad. Others experience their mood as a heavy, oppressive weight that makes everything feel difficult and pointless.

Equally characteristic is anhedonia, the loss of interest or pleasure in previously enjoyable activities. Hobbies and pastimes that once brought satisfaction become boring or feel like too much effort. Social activities that were once pleasurable become obligations to be avoided. Even fundamental pleasures such as food, sex, or time with loved ones lose their appeal. This loss of pleasure is not a choice or lack of trying, but reflects a fundamental change in the ability to experience positive emotions. People often describe feeling 'nothing' when engaging in activities, as if their emotional responses have been switched off.

Feelings of worthlessness or excessive guilt are prominent emotional features of depression. People may believe they are fundamentally flawed, bad, or inadequate. They ruminate on past mistakes, blowing them out of proportion and condemning themselves harshly. Normal human failings become evidence of their unworthiness. They may feel they are a burden to others and that people would be better off without them. Guilt can extend to inappropriate areas, with people blaming themselves for things outside their control or taking responsibility for others' unhappiness. These feelings are maintained by the negative thinking patterns characteristic of depression and feel absolutely real and justified, even when observers can see they are distorted.

Anxiety frequently accompanies depression. Many people with depression experience significant worry, restlessness, irritability, and physical symptoms of anxiety such as tension, rapid heartbeat, or stomach discomfort. The co-occurrence of depression and anxiety is the rule rather than the exception, with estimates suggesting 50 to 60 per cent of people with depression also meet criteria for an anxiety disorder. Anxiety in depression might focus on worries about the future, concerns about health, fears about being unable to cope, or generalised tension without a specific focus. This combination of depression and anxiety is sometimes termed 'anxious depression' and can be particularly distressing and impairing.

Irritability, whilst less traditionally emphasised as a depression symptom, is common, particularly in men and adolescents. People may feel constantly annoyed, snap at others over minor issues, have a short fuse, or experience anger that feels out of proportion to the situation. This irritability can damage relationships and increase social isolation, creating additional problems whilst reflecting the underlying depressive process.

Cognitive Symptoms

Depression profoundly affects thinking processes. Concentration difficulties are nearly universal in depression. People struggle to focus on conversations, reading, television programmes, or work tasks. Their minds wander, they lose track of what they were doing, and they need to read the same passage multiple times without retaining information. Complex tasks become overwhelming. Decision-making, even about simple matters such as what to eat or what to wear, feels impossibly difficult. People become paralysed by indecision, unable to weigh options or commit to choices.

Memory problems are also common, with people forgetting appointments, conversations, or where they put things.

These cognitive difficulties have important practical consequences, affecting work performance, academic achievement, and ability to manage daily responsibilities. They also contribute to the negative self-evaluation characteristic of depression, as people interpret their cognitive difficulties as further evidence of their inadequacy or incompetence, not recognising that these problems are symptoms of depression that will improve with treatment.

Negative thinking, as discussed earlier in relation to psychological causes, is a defining cognitive feature of depression. Thoughts become systematically negatively biased, focusing on failures whilst discounting successes, interpreting ambiguous situations in the worst possible light, predicting negative outcomes, and generating harsh self-criticism. These negative thoughts feel absolutely true and arise automatically without conscious effort. They are experienced as facts about reality rather than interpretations that might be questioned. This sense of certainty makes negative thoughts particularly powerful in maintaining depression.

Suicidal thoughts are a particularly serious cognitive symptom of depression. These range from passive thoughts that life is not worth living or that it would be better not to wake up, through to active thoughts about ending one's life and specific plans for suicide. Suicidal thinking in depression typically stems from the combination of unbearable emotional pain, hopelessness about the future (believing things will never improve), and the belief that one is a burden to others. It is crucial to recognise that suicidal thoughts are symptoms of depression, not rational assessments of one's situation. They reflect the depressed brain's distorted processing of information and typically resolve with effective treatment. However, they require immediate clinical attention and should always be taken seriously.

Physical Symptoms

Depression is accompanied by numerous physical symptoms, which can sometimes be the most prominent or distressing features. Sleep disturbance is extremely common, affecting over 80 per cent of people with depression. The pattern varies between individuals. Many people experience insomnia, including difficulty falling asleep (lying awake for hours), frequent waking during the night, or early morning waking (waking hours before intended and being unable to return to sleep). In contrast, some people experience hypersomnia, sleeping excessively, having difficulty waking, and feeling unrefreshed despite extended sleep. Sleep problems are particularly troublesome because poor sleep worsens all other symptoms of depression, creating another vicious cycle.

Appetite and weight changes are also very common. Many people with depression experience reduced appetite, with food seeming unappealing and eating feeling like a chore. This can lead to significant weight loss. Conversely, some people, particularly those with atypical depression, experience increased appetite, especially for carbohydrates and sweets, leading to weight gain. These changes in eating patterns can be distressing in themselves and can contribute to negative feelings about oneself.

Fatigue and loss of energy are hallmark physical symptoms. People feel exhausted even after a full night's sleep. Simple tasks require enormous effort. Getting out of bed, showering, or preparing a meal can feel as difficult as running a marathon would normally feel. This profound fatigue is not simply tiredness that can be overcome with willpower or rest, but reflects the physiological changes in depression. It makes behavioural activation particularly challenging, as people must push themselves to engage in activities when feeling profoundly exhausted.

Psychomotor changes refer to alterations in movement and speech. Some people experience psychomotor retardation, with movements becoming slow, speech becoming quiet and slow, and thinking feeling slowed down. They may sit motionless for long periods, struggle to initiate actions, and appear sluggish. Others experience psychomotor agitation, with inability to sit still, constant restlessness, pacing, hand-wringing, or fidgeting. Psychomotor changes are observable by others and can be particularly pronounced in severe depression.

Pain and physical discomfort are frequently reported. Headaches, back pain, muscle aches, stomach problems, chest tightness, and other physical symptoms can occur without clear medical cause. These symptoms are real, not imagined, and reflect the complex connections between brain, mind, and body. They often lead people to seek medical attention for physical complaints without recognising depression as the underlying issue, resulting in extensive medical investigations that find no physical cause. Recognition that physical symptoms can be manifestations of depression is important for appropriate diagnosis and treatment.

Behavioural Symptoms

Depression affects behaviour in multiple ways. Social withdrawal is extremely common. People stop seeing friends, avoid social invitations, withdraw from family members, and isolate themselves. This withdrawal stems from multiple factors: lack of energy and motivation, belief that one is not good company, difficulty experiencing pleasure from social interaction, anxiety about being with others, and feelings of worthlessness, making people believe others would prefer not to be around them. Unfortunately, social withdrawal reduces access to social support and positive experiences, maintaining the depression.

Reduced activity and productivity are characteristic behavioural features. People stop engaging in hobbies, exercise less or stop entirely, neglect household tasks, struggle to meet work responsibilities, and reduce self-care activities. The reduction in activity results from fatigue, lack of motivation, inability to experience pleasure, and the overwhelming effort required for even simple tasks. However, inactivity then maintains depression by removing sources of achievement, pleasure, and structure from life, creating another vicious cycle where depression leads to inactivity, and inactivity maintains depression.

Avoidant behaviours become more prevalent. People avoid situations, tasks, or decisions that feel overwhelming or anxiety-provoking. They procrastinate, put things off, or make excuses to avoid confronting difficulties. Whilst avoidance provides short-term relief from anxiety or overwhelm, it maintains depression by preventing people from engaging with life, solving problems, or experiencing mastery and accomplishment.

Changes in personal care and hygiene often occur. People may stop showering regularly, wear the same clothes repeatedly, neglect grooming, or stop caring for their living environment. These changes reflect the profound lack of energy and motivation in depression, as well as feelings of worthlessness, making self-care seem pointless. Neglect of personal care can then increase feelings of shame and unworthiness, further maintaining the depression.

The pervasive nature of depression symptoms across emotional, cognitive, physical, and behavioural domains explains why depression is so disabling. Every aspect of functioning is affected, creating a perfect storm where symptoms reinforce each other in multiple vicious cycles. Understanding this helps explain why depression cannot be overcome through willpower alone and validates the need for systematic intervention to break these cycles and restore functioning.

Chapter 2: The Cognitive Model of Depression

The cognitive model of depression, developed by Aaron T. Beck in the 1960s and refined through decades of research, provides a comprehensive framework for understanding how thoughts, emotions, and behaviours interact to create and maintain depression. This model forms the foundation of cognitive behavioural therapy (CBT), one of the most extensively researched and effective psychological treatments for depression. Understanding the cognitive model helps make sense of the depression experience and provides a roadmap for recovery. (Hofmann et al., 2012)

Figure 2: The Cognitive Model of Depression

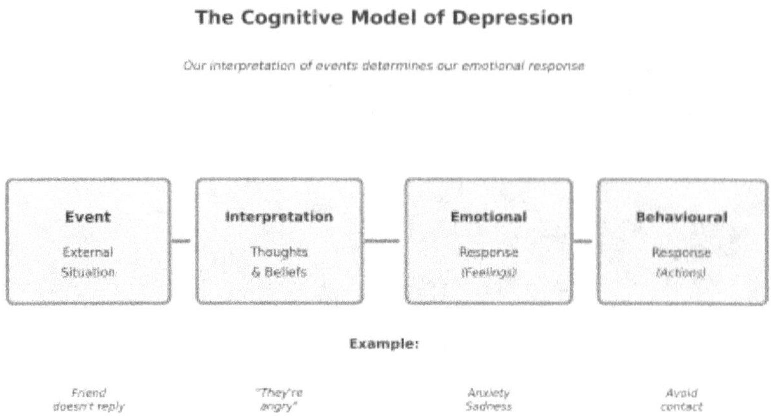

Core Principles of the Cognitive Model

The cognitive model of depression, developed by Aaron Beck in the 1960s and refined over subsequent decades, revolutionised our understanding and treatment of depression. Prior to Beck's work, depression was primarily understood through psychoanalytic frameworks emphasising unconscious conflicts and loss, or through biological models focusing solely on neurochemical imbalances. The cognitive model offered a new perspective, proposing that depression results from systematic biases in how people process information and interpret their experiences. This model has generated an enormous body of research and led to the development of cognitive behavioural therapy, one of the most effective treatments for depression. (Hofmann et al., 2012)

At the heart of the cognitive model is the idea that our thoughts mediate the relationship between events and our emotional responses. In other words, it is not events themselves that cause depression, but rather how we interpret and think about those events. Two people experiencing the same adverse event may respond very differently depending on how they understand and make sense of what happened. This insight is empowering because, whilst we cannot always control external events, we can learn to identify and modify unhelpful thinking patterns, thereby changing our emotional responses.

Beck proposed that depression is characterised by a negative cognitive triad: negative views of the self, negative views of the world and current experiences, and negative views of the future. People with depression tend to view themselves as defective, inadequate, or worthless. They interpret their experiences in systematically negative ways, focusing on negative aspects whilst discounting or failing to notice positive aspects. They view the future as hopeless, believing that their negative circumstances are permanent and unchangeable. This cognitive triad forms the basis of the pervasive negativity that characterises depressive thinking.

The negative cognitive triad is maintained and reinforced by cognitive distortions, which are systematic errors in thinking that bias information processing towards negative interpretations. Beck identified numerous cognitive distortions, including all-or-nothing thinking, overgeneralisation, mental filtering, discounting the positive, jumping to conclusions, magnification and minimisation, emotional reasoning, should statements, labelling, and personalisation. These thinking errors operate largely automatically, influencing how we perceive situations before we have consciously reflected on them. Learning to recognise and challenge these cognitive distortions is a central component of cognitive therapy for depression.

Underlying the negative thoughts and cognitive distortions are core beliefs or schemas, which are fundamental assumptions about oneself, others, and the world that develop through early experiences and continue to shape information processing throughout life. Core beliefs in depression typically involve themes of worthlessness, unlovability, helplessness, or defectiveness. For example, someone might hold the core belief 'I am fundamentally unlovable' or 'I am a failure'. These core beliefs are often rigid, overgeneralised, and resistant to change because they have been repeatedly confirmed by selective attention to information that supports them, whilst information contradicting them is discounted or dismissed.

Core beliefs give rise to intermediate beliefs, which include attitudes, rules, and assumptions that guide behaviour and interpretation of experiences. For instance, the core belief 'I am worthless' might generate the intermediate belief 'I must achieve perfectly to have any value' or 'if people really knew me, they would reject me'. These intermediate beliefs create vulnerability to depression by setting up rigid, conditional standards for self-worth that are difficult or impossible to consistently meet. When these standards are not met, the underlying core beliefs are activated, triggering the negative automatic thoughts and emotional responses characteristic of depression.

The cognitive model also emphasises the role of information processing biases in maintaining depression. People with depression show attentional biases towards negative information, more readily noticing negative aspects of situations and negative facial expressions, whilst overlooking positive information. Memory biases lead to better recall of negative memories and difficulty retrieving positive memories. Interpretation biases cause ambiguous situations to be interpreted in negative ways. These processing biases create a self-perpetuating cycle in which depressive thinking patterns repeatedly find confirmation in experience, even when alternative, more balanced interpretations are equally or more valid.

Research has extensively validated the cognitive model of depression. Numerous studies have demonstrated that negative thinking patterns predict the development and maintenance of depression, that changes in negative thinking during therapy correlate with symptomatic improvement, and that interventions targeting cognitive processes produce significant reductions in depression. Neuroimaging studies have identified neural correlates of cognitive biases in depression, demonstrating altered activity in brain regions involved in emotional processing, attention, and cognitive control. The cognitive model has proven both scientifically sound and clinically useful.

Importantly, the cognitive model does not deny the role of biological factors in depression. Rather, it proposes that biological, psychological, and social factors interact in complex ways to produce and maintain depression. Genetic vulnerability, neurochemical imbalances, and stressful life events all contribute to depression, but these factors exert their influence partly through their effects on cognitive processes. For example, stress affects the hypothalamic-pituitary-adrenal axis, which in turn influences information processing in brain regions involved in attention and memory. The cognitive model provides a framework for understanding how these multiple levels of causation interact.

The central premise of the cognitive model is that our thoughts, feelings, and behaviours are intimately interconnected, with each influencing the others. How we think about a situation affects how we feel emotionally and what we do behaviourally. In turn, our emotional state influences what thoughts come to mind and how we interpret situations. Our behaviours can confirm or disconfirm our thoughts and beliefs, and can influence our mood directly. This interconnection means that changing any one component – thoughts, feelings, or behaviours – can produce changes in the others.

A crucial insight of the cognitive model is that it is not situations themselves that directly cause our emotional responses, but rather our interpretation of situations. Two people can experience the same objective situation but have completely different emotional reactions because of differences in how they interpret the situation. For example, if a friend walks past without saying hello, one person might think 'They're ignoring me, they must not like me anymore' and feel hurt and rejected, whilst another person might think 'They must have been preoccupied and didn't notice me' and feel neutral or mildly concerned about their friend. The situation is identical, but the interpretation differs, leading to different emotional consequences.

This principle has profound implications. It means that we are not passive victims of our circumstances, helplessly at the mercy of external events. Rather, we actively construct our emotional experience through how we interpret and think about events. This opens the possibility of changing our emotional experience by changing our thinking. This does not mean that external events do not matter or that we can simply 'think positively' to overcome depression. Negative events genuinely are stressful and distressing. However, the cognitive model suggests that our interpretation of events, the meanings we assign to them, and the conclusions we draw about ourselves, others, and the future, all significantly influence whether we become depressed and how severe the depression becomes.

Levels of Cognition

The cognitive model distinguishes between different levels of cognition that operate in depression. At the most accessible level are automatic thoughts, also called negative automatic thoughts or NATs. These are the thoughts that pop into our minds automatically throughout the day, often so quickly and habitually that we barely notice them. They arise spontaneously in response to situations and represent our immediate interpretations or reactions. In depression, automatic thoughts are predominantly negative and reflect the depressed way of viewing oneself, the world, and the future.

Automatic thoughts have several important characteristics. They are automatic, arising without deliberate effort. They are plausible, seeming reasonable and believable in the moment. They are often brief and abbreviated, sometimes consisting of just a few words or even images rather than complete sentences. They are specific to situations, triggered by particular circumstances or events. Despite being spontaneous and brief, automatic thoughts have powerful effects on mood and behaviour. A fleeting thought such as 'I'm useless' can trigger a cascade of depressed feelings.

Common themes in automatic thoughts in depression include self-criticism ('I'm a failure,' 'I'm worthless,' 'I can't do anything right'), negative predictions ('Things will never improve,' 'I'll never be happy,' 'Everything will go wrong'), negative interpretations ('They think I'm boring,' 'I've let everyone down,' 'Nothing I do matters'), and self-defeating conclusions ('Why bother trying,' 'There's no point,' 'I might as well give up'). Identifying automatic thoughts is a key skill in CBT, as it makes the previously invisible thought processes visible and available for examination and modification.

Beneath automatic thoughts lie intermediate beliefs, which are attitudes, rules, and assumptions that shape how we interpret situations and generate automatic thoughts. These intermediate beliefs are more stable and general than automatic thoughts but less deeply ingrained than core beliefs. They often take the form of conditional rules or assumptions, such as 'If I make a mistake, it means I'm incompetent,' 'I must be perfect or I'm a failure,' 'If people really knew me, they wouldn't like me,' or 'I need others' approval to be worthwhile.' These rules and assumptions are not constantly conscious but become activated in relevant situations, generating the stream of automatic thoughts.

At the deepest level are core beliefs, which are fundamental, absolute beliefs about oneself, others, and the world. Core beliefs typically develop in childhood and adolescence through experiences with caregivers, peers, and significant events. They become the lens through which all subsequent experiences are interpreted. In depression, core beliefs are typically negative and fall into several common categories. Beliefs about oneself as helpless or inadequate include thoughts such as 'I am weak,' 'I am incompetent,' 'I am powerless,' 'I am vulnerable.' Beliefs about oneself as unlovable or worthless include 'I am unlovable,' 'I am unacceptable,' 'I am worthless,' 'I am defective.' These core beliefs are typically not in conscious awareness most of the time but exert a powerful influence on thinking, feeling, and behaving.

The three levels of cognition operate together. When a situation occurs, core beliefs influence how the situation is processed. This processing generates intermediate beliefs or rules about how to interpret the situation, which in turn produce automatic thoughts. These automatic thoughts then affect mood and behaviour. For example, someone with a core belief 'I am inadequate' might hold the intermediate belief 'If I don't succeed at everything, it proves I'm inadequate.' When faced with a difficult task, this generates automatic thoughts such as 'I can't do this,' 'I'm going to fail,' which trigger anxiety and demotivation, potentially leading to avoidance or half-hearted effort, which then confirms the original beliefs.

Cognitive Distortions

The cognitive model identifies specific patterns of distorted thinking that are common in depression and that maintain negative mood. These cognitive distortions, also called thinking errors or cognitive biases, represent systematic ways in which thinking deviates from logical, balanced processing of information. Recognising these patterns in one's own thinking is an important skill because it allows people to question thoughts that feel absolutely true but are actually distorted interpretations.

All-or-nothing thinking, also called black-and-white thinking or dichotomous thinking, involves viewing situations, people, or experiences in extreme categories with no middle ground. Things are either perfect or terrible, people are either all good or all bad, and experiences are either complete successes or total failures. This distortion is problematic because life rarely fits into such extreme categories, and this thinking style makes any imperfection feel like complete failure. For example, 'If I'm not perfect at this, I'm a complete failure' represents all-or-nothing thinking.

Overgeneralisation involves reaching broad conclusions based on single events or limited evidence. If one negative event occurs, it is seen as part of a never-ending pattern. Words such as 'always,' 'never,' 'everyone,' 'no one,' 'everything,' 'nothing' are markers of overgeneralisation. For example, after one social interaction goes poorly, thinking 'I always mess up social situations' or 'No one likes me' represents overgeneralisation.

Mental filtering involves focusing exclusively on negative aspects of a situation whilst ignoring or filtering out positive aspects. Even when a situation contains both positive and negative elements, attention becomes completely focused on the negatives. It is as if positive information cannot pass through the filter and register consciously. For example, after giving a presentation that included one small mistake, focusing entirely on that mistake whilst dismissing all the positive feedback and successful elements demonstrates mental filtering.

Disqualifying the positive involves acknowledging positive experiences but immediately dismissing them as not counting for some reason. Positive events are explained away, minimised, or reframed as negative. For example, when someone gives a compliment, responding with 'They're just being polite' or 'They haven't seen my flaws yet' disqualifies the positive. When something goes well, explaining it as 'Just luck' or 'Anyone could have done that' dismisses the achievement.

Jumping to conclusions involves making negative interpretations without adequate evidence. This distortion takes two main forms. Mind reading involves assuming we know what others are thinking, usually assuming they are thinking negatively about us. For example, 'They think I'm boring' or 'She doesn't like me' without any actual evidence. Fortune telling involves predicting negative outcomes with certainty. For example, 'I'm going to fail this exam' or 'This won't work out' or 'Things will never get better.' These predictions feel like facts but are actually guesses dressed up as certainties.

Magnification and minimisation involve exaggerating the importance of negative events or personal flaws whilst minimising the importance of positive events or personal strengths. Negative events are blown out of proportion ('This is a catastrophe'), whilst achievements are shrunk ('It wasn't important'). This distortion is sometimes called the 'binocular effect,' as if viewing negatives through a magnifying end of binoculars and positives through the diminishing end. For example, magnifying a small mistake at work into proof of complete incompetence whilst minimising years of good performance.

Emotional reasoning involves assuming that negative feelings reflect objective reality. 'I feel inadequate, therefore I am inadequate.' 'I feel like a failure, therefore I am a failure.' 'I feel overwhelmed; therefore, the situation is impossible.' This distortion treats feelings as evidence of truth, ignoring that depression feelings are influenced by depressed thinking and do not necessarily reflect reality accurately. Feelings are real and valid, but they are not always accurate guides to external reality.

Should statements involve using rigid rules about how things 'should' or 'must' be, creating unrealistic expectations and harsh self-criticism when these expectations are not met. 'I should be able to cope with this,' 'I must succeed at everything,' 'I shouldn't feel this way,' 'They should appreciate me.' These inflexible demands create frustration, guilt, and anger. When directed at oneself, should statements generate guilt and inadequacy. When directed at others, they generate anger and resentment. When directed at the world, they generate frustration and disappointment.

Labelling involves attaching global negative labels to oneself based on specific behaviours or situations. Rather than saying 'I made a mistake,' labelling says 'I am a failure.' Rather than 'That didn't go well,' labelling says 'I am useless.' This distortion involves taking a specific event or characteristic and using it to define one's entire identity. Labels are over-simplifications that ignore the complexity of human beings and create rigid, negative self-concepts that are difficult to change.

Personalisation involves assuming responsibility for negative events that are not actually within one's control or blaming oneself for outcomes that have multiple causes. If something goes wrong, it must be one's fault. If someone is upset, one must have caused it. If a team project fails, it is all down to one's own inadequacy. This distortion ignores the multiple factors that influence outcomes and leads to excessive guilt and self-blame.

Recognising these cognitive distortions in one's own thinking does not immediately change the depression, but it is an important first step. It introduces the possibility that thoughts are interpretations rather than facts, and that alternative, more balanced interpretations might exist. This creates space for examining and modifying thinking patterns, which is central to cognitive therapy.

Maintaining Cycles in Depression

The cognitive model emphasises that depression is maintained through multiple vicious cycles where symptoms perpetuate each other. Understanding these cycles is crucial because they explain why depression persists and point towards intervention strategies. Breaking any link in these cycles can begin to reverse the depression.

The thought-feeling cycle is perhaps the most fundamental maintaining cycle. Negative thoughts trigger depressed feelings, and depressed feelings in turn, make negative thoughts more likely and more accessible. When the mood is low, the mind becomes biased towards negative information. Negative memories are more easily recalled, negative interpretations of events come to mind more readily, and positive information is harder to process and remember. This mood-congruent processing means that depression creates the very thinking patterns that maintain depression. The cycle continues: negative thoughts depress mood, depressed mood generates more negative thoughts, further depressing mood.

The behaviour-mood cycle involves the relationship between activity and mood. Depression causes reduced activity through fatigue, lack of motivation, and anhedonia. However, reduced activity then maintains depression by removing sources of pleasure, achievement, and structure from life. Days become empty and purposeless. There are no accomplishments to feel good about, no pleasures to enjoy, and no sense of progress or purpose. This emptiness deepens depression, which further reduces activity. Additionally, reduced activity often includes reduced exercise and social contact, both of which are independently beneficial for mood, so their reduction further maintains depression.

The avoidance-anxiety cycle is particularly relevant when depression and anxiety co-occur. Anxiety about situations, tasks, or social interactions leads to avoidance. Avoidance provides short-term relief from anxiety but has several negative consequences that maintain problems. Avoidance prevents people from discovering that their fears are exaggerated or that they can cope with difficult situations. It removes opportunities for success and achievement. It can create practical problems as important tasks remain undone. It often generates guilt and self-criticism. All of these consequences contribute to depression and anxiety. The anxiety remains because it was never faced, and depression worsens because avoidance removes opportunities for positive experiences.

The social withdrawal cycle is particularly powerful. Depression leads to social withdrawal through fatigue, lack of enjoyment in social interaction, beliefs about being a burden, and anxiety about social situations. However, social withdrawal then increases loneliness, removes access to social support, reduces opportunities for positive experiences and meaningful connections, and often generates worry that relationships are being damaged. These consequences worsen depression, leading to further withdrawal.

The rumination cycle involves repeatedly thinking about one's problems, symptoms, and possible causes without reaching any resolution or taking any action. Rumination is tempting because it feels like problem-solving and because distraction from depressive thoughts is difficult. However, rumination maintains depression by keeping attention focused on negative aspects of one's situation, interfering with effective problem-solving (because rumination is repetitive and passive rather than active and goal-directed), preventing engagement in mood-improving activities, and often occurring late at night, interfering with sleep. The more one ruminates, the more depressed one feels, generating more material for rumination.

The sleep-mood cycle operates because depression disrupts sleep, but poor sleep then worsens all symptoms of depression. Fatigue increases, concentration deteriorates, emotional regulation becomes more difficult, irritability increases, and motivation decreases. This worsens the depression, which further disrupts sleep. Breaking this cycle by improving sleep can have substantial benefits for overall mood and functioning.

Understanding these maintenance cycles helps explain why depression can feel like being stuck in quicksand – the harder one struggles, the deeper one sinks. It also provides hope, because whilst there are multiple maintaining cycles, breaking any one of them can begin to create positive momentum. Treatment strategies target these cycles systematically, interrupting the maintaining processes and gradually reversing the downward spiral into a recovery trajectory.

Chapter 3: Beginning Your Recovery: First Steps

Recovery from depression is possible. This statement, which might feel difficult to believe when in the midst of depression, is supported by robust evidence. The majority of people who experience depression, even severe depression, recover with appropriate treatment. Recovery might take time and persistence, and the path might not be smooth, but recovery is the expected outcome. This chapter outlines the crucial first steps in your recovery journey.

Acknowledging and Accepting That You Are Experiencing Depression

The first step in recovery is recognising and accepting that you are experiencing depression. This might seem obvious, but many people struggle for extended periods before reaching this acknowledgement. Depression carries stigma, with unhelpful cultural messages suggesting that depression reflects personal weakness, lack of willpower, or moral failing. People often feel ashamed of their depression, believing they should be able to cope better or that they have no right to feel depressed. These beliefs can prevent people from acknowledging the reality of their situation and seeking help.

Acknowledging depression is not giving in or accepting defeat. Rather, it is recognising reality so that you can respond effectively. If you twisted your ankle, acknowledging the injury would be the first step towards treating it appropriately. Denying the injury and trying to walk normally would delay healing and potentially worsen the damage. The same principle applies to depression. Acknowledgement allows you to take appropriate action rather than continuing ineffective strategies that maintain the problem.

Acceptance of depression does not mean resignation or believing that nothing can be done. Acceptance means acknowledging the current reality without judgment or self-criticism, recognising that depression is a genuine health condition rather than a character flaw, and understanding that recovery will take time and effort. Acceptance involves self-compassion, treating yourself with the same kindness and understanding you would offer a friend facing similar difficulties. Self-criticism and shame worsen depression, whilst self-compassion supports recovery.

Many people experience initial relief when they recognise their difficulties as depression. Symptoms that seemed inexplicable suddenly make sense. The experience feels validated. There is a framework for understanding what is happening and a clear direction for treatment. Whilst the diagnosis of depression is not welcome, the clarity it provides can be helpful. You are not weak, lazy, or inadequate; you are experiencing a treatable condition with well-established interventions.

Seeking Professional Help

Seeking professional help for depression is one of the most important steps you can take towards recovery. Whilst self-help strategies can be beneficial, and this book provides many evidence-based techniques you can use independently, professional support significantly improves outcomes, particularly for moderate to severe depression. Professional help provides expert assessment to ensure accurate diagnosis, access to evidence-based treatments, monitoring of progress and safety, support and encouragement during difficult periods, and adjustment of treatment approaches if initial strategies are not effective. Research consistently demonstrates that people who receive professional treatment for depression recover more quickly and completely than those who rely solely on self-help.

Many people delay seeking professional help for depression due to stigma, shame, beliefs that they should be able to manage alone, concerns about cost or accessibility, fears about what treatment might involve, or simply not recognising that what they are experiencing is depression rather than personal weakness or character flaw. These barriers are understandable but ultimately counter-productive. Depression is a medical condition deserving of proper assessment and treatment. Seeking help demonstrates strength and wisdom, not weakness. Early intervention typically leads to better outcomes and shorter duration of illness than delayed treatment.

The first point of contact for professional help in the United Kingdom is typically your General Practitioner (GP). GPs are trained to recognise and assess depression, can prescribe antidepressant medication if appropriate, and can refer to specialist mental health services or psychological therapy services. When consulting your GP about depression, it can be helpful to prepare in advance. Consider keeping a diary of your symptoms for a week or two before the appointment, noting mood, sleep, energy levels, and functioning. Write down key points you want to convey, as anxiety or depression itself can make it difficult to think clearly during the appointment. Be as honest and specific as possible about your symptoms and their impact on your life.

During the assessment, your GP will ask about your symptoms, how long they have been present, their severity and impact on functioning, any previous episodes of depression or other mental health difficulties, your physical health and any medications you are taking, use of alcohol or other substances, recent life events and stressors, family history of mental health problems, and whether you have thoughts of self-harm or suicide. These questions, whilst sometimes uncomfortable to answer, are necessary to ensure accurate assessment and appropriate treatment recommendations. Your GP may also use standardised questionnaires to assess symptom severity and monitor progress over time.

Following the assessment, your GP may recommend various treatment approaches depending on the severity and nature of your depression. For mild depression, your GP might initially suggest watchful waiting, self-help resources, exercise, or brief psychological interventions. For moderate depression, psychological therapy (typically cognitive behavioural therapy or counselling) is usually recommended as first-line treatment, sometimes in combination with antidepressant medication. For severe depression, medication is typically recommended, often alongside psychological therapy. If your depression is particularly severe, is not responding to treatment, or involves psychotic features or significant suicide risk, referral to specialist mental health services may be necessary.

Accessing psychological therapy in the NHS is facilitated by the Improving Access to Psychological Therapies (NHS Talking Therapies) programme, which provides evidence-based psychological treatments for depression and anxiety. Most NHS Talking Therapies accept self-referrals, meaning you can refer yourself directly without going through your GP, though GP referral is also common. NHS Talking Therapies offer telephone assessments to determine the most appropriate level and type of support.

Treatment typically involves cognitive behavioural therapy or counselling delivered in individual or group format. NHS Talking Therapies aim to see people within eighteen weeks of referral, though waiting times vary by area.

In addition to NHS services, private psychological therapy is available, though costs vary considerably. Chartered Clinical Psychologists, Counselling Psychologists, and accredited Cognitive Behavioural Therapists can be found through professional bodies such as the British Psychological Society and the British Association for Behavioural and Cognitive Psychotherapies. Some charities offer free or low-cost counselling. Employee Assistance Programmes provided by many employers often include access to counselling. University counselling services provide support for students. Various routes to accessing professional support exist, and persistence in finding appropriate help is worthwhile.

If you are experiencing thoughts of suicide or self-harm, or if you are in crisis and feel unable to keep yourself safe, immediate help is available. You can contact the Samaritans any time on 116 123, attend your local Accident and Emergency department, call NHS 111 for urgent health advice, or call 999 if you are in immediate danger. Many areas have Crisis Resolution and Home Treatment Teams that provide intensive home-based support to prevent hospital admission. These services are there to help you through crisis periods and connect you with ongoing support.

The therapeutic relationship with your healthcare provider is an important factor in treatment success. Research demonstrates that the quality of the therapeutic relationship predicts treatment outcomes across different types of therapy and for different conditions. A good therapeutic relationship is characterised by trust, collaboration, understanding, and genuine care. If you do not feel comfortable with a particular healthcare provider, it is entirely appropriate to request seeing someone else. Finding the right fit can make a significant difference to your engagement with treatment and your recovery.

Seeking professional help is strongly recommended for depression. Whilst self-help can play an important role, and this book aims to provide comprehensive guidance, professional support significantly improves outcomes. Professional help provides expert assessment to confirm the diagnosis, rule out other conditions, and identify any complicating factors.

It provides access to evidence-based treatments, including psychological therapy and medication. It offers monitoring of symptoms and risk, ensuring safety and tracking progress. It provides expertise in adjusting treatment if initial approaches are insufficient. For all these reasons, professional help is valuable even for people working through self-help resources.

The usual first point of contact is your general practitioner (GP). GPs are trained in recognising and managing depression and can provide initial assessment, prescribe medication if appropriate, refer to specialist mental health services if needed, and offer ongoing monitoring and support. When seeing your GP, it helps to be open about the full range of your symptoms, including emotional, cognitive, physical, and behavioural symptoms. Mention the duration and severity of symptoms, the impact on your functioning, and any factors that might be relevant such as recent stresses, family history, or previous episodes. If you are experiencing suicidal thoughts, it is crucial to mention this, as it affects the urgency and type of help offered.

If your GP refers you for psychological therapy, waiting times can vary considerably depending on location and service capacity. In England, the Improving Access to Psychological Therapies (NHS Talking Therapies) programme provides evidence-based psychological treatments for depression and anxiety. Self-referral is often possible without needing a GP referral. Private psychological therapy is also available and might have shorter waiting times, though it involves cost. When selecting a private therapist, ensure they have appropriate qualifications and are registered with a professional body such as the British Association for Behavioural and Cognitive Psychotherapies (BABCP) for CBT, the British Psychological Society (BPS), or the UK Council for Psychotherapy (UKCP).

For severe depression, crises, or significant risk, more immediate or intensive help might be needed. Crisis services, which vary by area but might include crisis resolution teams or psychiatric liaison services accessible through your GP or Accident and Emergency departments, provide urgent assessment and support. The Samaritans offer 24-hour emotional support by phone (116 123) and are available to talk to anyone experiencing distress. Mental health charity helplines such as Mind (0300 123 3393) provide information and support. In emergencies where there is an immediate risk of harm, attending Accident and Emergency or calling emergency services is appropriate.

The Role of Medication

Antidepressant medication is an effective treatment for moderate to severe depression, with robust evidence from many hundreds of clinical trials demonstrating that antidepressants significantly reduce depressive symptoms. Antidepressants work by influencing neurotransmitter systems in the brain, particularly serotonin, noradrenaline, and dopamine. Different classes of antidepressants work through different mechanisms, though all aim to normalise the neurotransmitter imbalances associated with depression.

Selective serotonin reuptake inhibitors (SSRIs) are the most commonly prescribed antidepressants, considered first-line treatment due to their effectiveness and generally more tolerable side effect profile compared to older antidepressants. SSRIs work by blocking the reuptake of serotonin in the brain, increasing its availability. Common SSRIs include fluoxetine, sertraline, citalopram, escitalopram, and paroxetine.

Serotonin-noradrenaline reuptake inhibitors (SNRIs) work by blocking the reuptake of both serotonin and noradrenaline. Common SNRIs include venlafaxine and duloxetine. SNRIs might be used when SSRIs have been ineffective or when particular symptoms, such as physical pain, are prominent.

Other antidepressants work through various mechanisms. Mirtazapine enhances both serotonin and noradrenaline transmission through a different mechanism than SNRIs and can be particularly helpful for sleep and appetite problems. Bupropion primarily affects dopamine and noradrenaline and might be useful when low energy and motivation are prominent. Tricyclic antidepressants (TCAs) such as amitriptyline are older medications that are effective but generally have more side effects than newer antidepressants, so they are typically used when other options have not worked. Monoamine oxidase inhibitors (MAOIs) are rarely used now due to dietary restrictions and drug interactions but can be effective for atypical depression and treatment-resistant depression.

Important points about antidepressants include the following. Antidepressants typically take two to four weeks to begin working, with full effects often taking six to eight weeks. Improvement is usually gradual rather than dramatic. It is important to continue taking medication even when starting to feel better, as stopping too soon often leads to relapse. Treatment is typically continued for at least six months after symptoms have resolved, and often longer for recurrent depression. Stopping antidepressants should be done gradually under medical supervision, as sudden discontinuation can cause unpleasant withdrawal symptoms.

Side effects of antidepressants vary by medication but can include nausea, headaches, increased anxiety initially, sexual difficulties, weight changes, sleep problems, or drowsiness. Side effects are usually most prominent in the first couple of weeks and often improve with time. If side effects are troublesome, discussing them with your doctor is important, as dose adjustment or changing to a different medication might help. The benefits of treatment typically outweigh side effects for moderate to severe depression, but individual experiences vary.

The decision whether to take antidepressants is personal and should be made in discussion with your doctor, considering severity of depression, previous treatment responses, personal preferences, and potential risks and benefits. For mild depression, psychological therapy alone might be sufficient. For moderate to severe depression, combination treatment with both medication and psychological therapy is often most effective. Some people have strong preferences for or against medication, and these preferences should be respected where possible whilst ensuring effective treatment.

Antidepressants are not addictive in the sense of creating cravings or requiring escalating doses. However, they should not be stopped abruptly due to potential withdrawal effects. Antidepressants do not change your personality or prevent you from experiencing normal emotions. They do not make problems disappear but can reduce symptom severity sufficiently to allow you to engage more effectively with addressing underlying problems. They are not a substitute for making life changes or developing coping skills, but they can create the platform from which such changes become possible.

Building Your Support Network

Social support is one of the most important factors in recovery from depression. Research consistently shows that strong social support predicts better outcomes, whilst isolation predicts worse outcomes. Building and maintaining your support network should be a priority, even though depression makes this feel difficult.

Support can come from various sources. Family members and close friends who understand your situation and provide emotional support, practical help, and companionship are invaluable. However, it is important to recognise that while loved ones want to help, they might not always know how. Communicating clearly about what kind of support is helpful allows them to support you effectively. You might need someone to listen without trying to fix things, or you might need practical help with tasks, or you might need encouragement to engage in activities. Different people in your network might provide different types of support.

Support groups, whether face-to-face or online, connect you with others who have experienced depression. This can reduce feelings of isolation and provide understanding from people who truly comprehend what depression feels like. Shared experiences, coping strategies, and hope from others who have recovered can be powerfully helpful. Mind, the mental health charity, offers peer support programmes and can provide information about local groups. Online forums and communities also exist, though quality and safety vary, so some caution is needed.

Workplace support might be relevant if you are employed. Many employers have employee assistance programmes offering confidential counselling and support. Occupational health services can advise on workplace adjustments that might help you manage whilst recovering. Being open with your employer about your depression is a personal decision depending on workplace culture and your relationship with your manager, but awareness can allow reasonable adjustments under disability discrimination legislation.

Professional support through your treatment team – your GP, therapist, psychiatrist, or other mental health professionals – is a crucial part of your support network. Building a good working relationship with your treatment providers, being honest about symptoms and difficulties, and actively engaging with treatment recommendations all support recovery.

It is also important to recognise that not all relationships are supportive. Some relationships might be actively harmful, involving criticism, invalidation, or abuse. Other relationships might be well-intentioned but unhelpful, with friends or family inadvertently saying things that worsen depression, such as 'just think positive,' 'snap out of it,' or 'others have it worse.' Protecting yourself from unhelpful responses might involve limiting contact with certain people, being selective about what you share, or educating people about how they can help. This book's later chapters address relationships and depression in more detail.

Chapter 4: Behavioural Activation: Taking Action to Improve Mood (Martell et al., 2001)

Behavioural activation is one of the most powerful and well-evidenced techniques for overcoming depression. The fundamental principle is deceptively simple: increase engagement in valued, meaningful activities, and mood will improve. This principle might seem too simple to be effective, particularly when depression makes even basic activities feel impossibly difficult. However, decades of research demonstrate that behavioural activation is highly effective, with some studies suggesting it is as effective as cognitive therapy or antidepressant medication for treating depression.

Understanding the Rationale

Behavioural activation is founded on a fundamental principle: our actions influence our emotions. When we engage in activities, particularly those that provide a sense of accomplishment, pleasure, or connection, positive emotions follow. Conversely, when we withdraw from activities and become passive, negative emotions intensify. This relationship between behaviour and mood creates a vicious cycle in depression. Depression reduces motivation and energy, leading to reduced activity. Reduced activity means fewer opportunities for positive experiences, which lowers mood further, which then makes activity even more difficult. Behavioural activation breaks this cycle by deliberately increasing activity even when motivation is low.

Figure 3: Breaking the Motivation Trap

The theoretical foundation of behavioural activation lies in learning theory, particularly the concept of reinforcement. Positive reinforcement occurs when a behaviour leads to a pleasant consequence, making that behaviour more likely to occur in the future. Depression involves reduced positive reinforcement: the activities that normally provide pleasure or satisfaction no longer do so, or we stop engaging in them, cutting ourselves off from sources of positive reinforcement. Behavioural activation systematically reintroduces positive reinforcement by scheduling and engaging in potentially rewarding activities, even when we do not feel motivated. Over time, this exposure to positive reinforcement helps shift the balance from the predominance of negative experiences to a more balanced mix of positive and negative experiences.

Charles Ferster, a behaviourist, was among the first to apply operant conditioning principles to understanding depression in the 1970s. He proposed that depression results from insufficient response-contingent positive reinforcement and excessive punishment or loss of reinforcement. Peter Lewinsohn developed these ideas into a comprehensive behavioural model and treatment approach, proposing that depression occurs when the frequency of response-contingent positive reinforcement falls below a critical level. This can happen due to lack of reinforcing events in the environment, lack of skills to obtain reinforcement, or inability to enjoy reinforcement due to high anxiety or other interfering emotions. Behavioural activation directly addresses these factors by identifying and scheduling rewarding activities, building relevant skills, and providing structured exposure that allows positive emotions to develop.

Christopher Martell, Sona Dimidjian, and Ruth Herman-Dunn refined and modernised behavioural activation for contemporary practice, developing detailed treatment protocols that have been subjected to rigorous research evaluation. Their approach emphasises identifying valued life directions, examining how current patterns of avoidance and withdrawal maintain depression, and systematically increasing engagement in valued activities whilst reducing avoidance. This modern behavioural activation has proven as effective as cognitive therapy for depression in multiple randomised controlled trials, and it may be particularly effective for severe depression. Its straightforward nature makes it accessible to many people and suitable for delivery in various settings.

The mechanisms through which behavioural activation produces its effects are multiple. Firstly, increased activity provides greater opportunity for positive reinforcement through pleasurable experiences, sense of accomplishment, and social connection. Secondly, activity disrupts rumination by occupying attention with engagement in the present moment rather than dwelling on negative thoughts about past or future. Thirdly, activity provides evidence against negative thoughts, demonstrating that you are capable of doing things even when depressed. Fourthly, activity produces physiological changes including increased endorphin release and improved sleep-wake regulation. Fifthly, returning to normal routines and responsibilities rebuilds self-efficacy and sense of control. Finally, social activities specifically provide connection, belonging, and validation from others.

Behavioural activation is particularly valuable in depression because it does not require you to change your thinking or to feel motivated before taking action. Unlike cognitive approaches that focus on changing thoughts, behavioural activation focuses on changing behaviour first, with the understanding that mood and thinking will follow. This is important because in depression, trying to think differently or to generate motivation before acting is extremely difficult. Negative thoughts feel completely true, and motivation is absent. Waiting for thoughts to change or motivation to return before becoming active can mean waiting indefinitely. Behavioural activation sidesteps this problem by asking you to change behaviour first, creating experiences that then shift thinking and mood.

The principle of 'action before motivation' is counterintuitive but crucial. In normal circumstances, we feel motivated first, then act. Motivation precedes action. In depression, this normal sequence is reversed. We must act first, and motivation follows. The activation itself generates energy and motivation, even though it does not feel this way before you start. This is why the first step, getting started with an activity, is typically the hardest. Once you have started and engaged in the activity, it becomes easier, and completing the activity provides a sense of satisfaction and demonstrates that action is possible even when motivation is absent.

Behavioural activation also addresses a key maintaining factor in depression: avoidance. Depression leads people to avoid situations that trigger distress, such as social situations, challenging tasks, or situations that remind them of losses or failures. Whilst avoidance provides short-term relief from discomfort, it maintains depression by preventing disconfirmation of negative beliefs, reducing positive reinforcement, and often creating additional problems as responsibilities and relationships are neglected. Behavioural activation involves approaching, rather than avoiding, important life activities and situations. This approach is graded and supported, allowing you to gradually confront avoided situations whilst developing confidence and demonstrating to yourself that you can cope.

Behavioural activation addresses one of the key maintaining cycles in depression: the inactivity-depression cycle. When people become depressed, they naturally withdraw from activities. This withdrawal happens for understandable reasons. Fatigue makes activity feel exhausting. Anhedonia means activities no longer bring pleasure. Low motivation and hopelessness make effort seem pointless. Concentration difficulties make complex activities overwhelming. Social anxiety or feelings of worthlessness lead to social withdrawal. In the short term, reducing activity might feel like the only manageable response to overwhelming fatigue and low mood.

However, whilst reducing activity provides short-term relief from demands, it has devastating longer-term consequences. When activity decreases, sources of pleasure disappear from life. There are no enjoyable experiences to lift mood. Sources of achievement and mastery disappear. There is no sense of accomplishment or competence. Structure and routine collapse. Days become empty and directionless. Social contact reduces. Loneliness increases and support becomes less available. Physical fitness declines. Energy levels drop further. Practical problems accumulate as important tasks remain undone. All of these consequences deepen depression, which then makes activity feel even more difficult, creating a vicious downward spiral.

Behavioural activation reverses this cycle by systematically increasing activity despite low motivation and difficult feelings. This might sound like the unhelpful advice to 'just get on with it' that people with depression often receive. However, behavioural activation is systematic, structured, and compassionate. It does not involve forcing yourself to do everything at once or pushing through exhaustion recklessly. Rather, it involves carefully and gradually building activity back into life, starting small, planning specifically, monitoring progress, and celebrating achievements however modest they seem.

A crucial insight of behavioural activation is that action precedes motivation. People often believe they need to feel motivated before they can engage in activity, waiting for motivation to arrive before acting. Unfortunately, in depression, motivation rarely appears spontaneously. The relationship actually works in reverse: action generates motivation. When you engage in activity, even without feeling motivated initially, the activity itself begins to generate energy, interest, and motivation. This can feel counterintuitive and requires an act of faith to test the principle, but the evidence supporting it is robust.

Identifying Activities

The first step in behavioural activation is identifying activities to reintroduce into your life. Activities should be selected from several categories to ensure a balanced approach. Pleasurable activities are things you enjoy or used to enjoy before depression. These might include hobbies, entertainment, time with friends or family, being in nature, listening to music, reading, creative pursuits, or any activity that brings satisfaction or pleasure. The key principle is that these activities do not need to have any productive purpose beyond being enjoyable. Pleasure and enjoyment are valuable in themselves and are essential for recovery.

However, depression often involves anhedonia, where previously pleasurable activities no longer bring enjoyment. This creates a challenge: how do you identify pleasurable activities when nothing feels pleasurable? Several strategies help. First, think back to activities you enjoyed before depression. These activities might not feel appealing now, but they are strong candidates for reintroduction. Second, consider activities that other people find enjoyable, even if they do not currently interest you. Sometimes trying an activity can reignite interest. Third, be prepared to persist with activities even when they do not immediately produce pleasure. Often, the ability to experience pleasure returns gradually as depression lifts, and engaging in activities helps trigger this process even if enjoyment is muted initially.

Achievement-focused activities provide a sense of accomplishment and mastery. These include work tasks, household chores, self-care activities, completing errands, organising spaces, learning new skills, or making progress on projects. Achievement activities are important because they provide a sense of competence and effectiveness, countering the helplessness and inadequacy characteristic of depression. They also address practical aspects of life that might have become neglected during depression, reducing stress and creating conditions that support recovery.

When selecting achievement activities, it is important to choose tasks that are achievable given your current state. Setting yourself up to attempt things that are currently beyond your capacity creates failure experiences that worsen depression. Start with manageable tasks that you can complete successfully, building confidence and momentum gradually. A completed small task is far more valuable than an attempted but incomplete large task.

Social activities involve interaction with others. This might include meeting friends, calling family members, joining groups or clubs, attending community events, volunteering, or any activity involving social connection.

Social activities are particularly important given the central role of social isolation in maintaining depression. However, they are often particularly difficult for people with depression who feel they are not good company, worry about being judged, or find social interaction exhausting. Balancing the importance of social connection with the genuine difficulty of social activity when depressed requires careful planning and graduated approaches.

Physical activities and exercise deserve special attention. Physical activity has direct effects on mood through multiple biological mechanisms including effects on neurotransmitters, stress hormones, inflammation, and brain structure. Regular exercise has been shown in numerous studies to reduce depression, with effects comparable to antidepressant medication for some people. The type of exercise matters less than consistency; walking, swimming, dancing, team sports, gym-based exercise, or home-based activities can all be beneficial. For people who are currently very inactive, the initial goal might be as simple as a ten-minute walk, building up gradually from there.

Necessary routine activities, whilst not inherently enjoyable or achievement-oriented, are important for maintaining basic functioning and structure. These include personal hygiene, preparing meals, maintaining living spaces, managing finances, attending appointments, and other activities necessary for daily life. Depression often erodes these basic self-care activities, and their neglect then creates additional problems and reinforces feelings of inadequacy. Reestablishing routine activities creates structure, addresses practical needs, and provides a foundation for recovery.

Activity Scheduling and Planning

Once activities have been identified, the next step is scheduling and planning specific times to engage in them. Vague intentions to 'do more' or 'be more active' rarely translate into actual behaviour change. Specific, concrete plans are far more effective. Rather than 'I should see friends more,' an effective plan is 'I will call Sarah on Tuesday at 7pm to arrange coffee on Saturday morning.' Rather than 'I need to exercise more,' an effective plan is 'I will walk for 15 minutes on Monday, Wednesday, and Friday mornings before work.'

Using an activity schedule or diary to plan your week hour by hour creates structure and helps ensure a balance of different types of activities. The schedule should include pleasurable activities, achievement activities, social activities, physical activities, and routine activities. Initially, the schedule might look quite sparse, with only a few activities planned. This is entirely appropriate. The goal is gradual increase, not immediate return to pre-depression functioning.

When planning activities, several principles are helpful. Start small. It is better to plan modest activities that you can definitely complete than ambitious activities that prove overwhelming. Success breeds success, and each completed activity builds confidence and motivation. Be specific. Rather than 'tidy the house,' specify 'clear the kitchen table.' Rather than 'exercise,' specify 'walk around the block.' Break large tasks into small steps. A large, overwhelming task can often be approached through a series of small, manageable steps. Specify exactly when you will do each activity. 'Monday at 10am' is more effective than 'sometime this week.' Anticipate obstacles. Think about what might prevent you from completing the activity and plan how to overcome or work around obstacles.

After planning activities, it is crucial to review what actually happened. Did you complete the planned activity? If so, acknowledge and celebrate this achievement. It is easy to dismiss accomplishments as trivial, but completing activities despite depression is genuinely difficult and deserves recognition. If you did not complete the planned activity, examine what got in the way without harsh self-criticism. Was the activity too ambitious? Did an unexpected obstacle arise? Did you forget or get distracted? Understanding what prevented completion allows you to adjust future plans rather than concluding that you have failed.

Behavioural activation involves continual learning and adjustment. As you engage in activities and monitor your responses, you learn what activities are most helpful, what level of activity is manageable, what time of day works best for different activities, and what obstacles consistently arise. This learning allows increasingly effective planning. The process is gradual, requiring patience and persistence, but the cumulative effect of weeks of systematically increasing activity is typically substantial improvement in mood and functioning.

Overcoming Obstacles to Behavioural Activation

Numerous obstacles commonly arise when attempting behavioural activation. Recognising these obstacles and having strategies to address them improves the likelihood of success.

Overwhelming fatigue is perhaps the most common obstacle. Depression-related fatigue is profound and makes any activity feel exhausting. The key is not to wait for energy to arrive but to act despite fatigue, starting with very small activities and building gradually. Often, once you begin an activity, you find more energy than anticipated, or the activity itself generates energy. Physical activity, whilst feeling impossible to contemplate when exhausted, is particularly effective for improving energy levels through biological mechanisms. Starting extremely small – perhaps just five minutes of gentle activity – and building very gradually can overcome the fatigue barrier.

Lack of motivation is universal in depression. Motivation does not arrive spontaneously; it emerges through action. The strategy is to commit to engaging in the activity for a specified short period regardless of motivation, often just five or ten minutes. After that time, you can reassess. Often, you will find that once started, continuing becomes easier. Even if not, completing five minutes is an achievement.

Anhedonia, the inability to experience pleasure, makes it difficult to engage in pleasurable activities when they do not produce enjoyment. The strategy here is to engage in previously pleasurable activities regardless of current enjoyment, trusting that the capacity for pleasure will gradually return. Monitoring your experience carefully might reveal that whilst activities do not produce strong pleasure, they produce slightly less unpleasant feelings than inactivity, or moments of mild interest occur even if sustained enjoyment does not. These small responses are seeds from which greater enjoyment can grow.

Negative thoughts interfere with behavioural activation. Thoughts such as 'there's no point,' 'it won't help,' 'I can't do it,' 'I'll just fail,' or 'I don't deserve to feel better' undermine motivation and make activity feel impossible. The relationship between behavioural activation and cognitive work is complementary. Sometimes, examining and challenging negative thoughts is necessary before activity becomes possible. Other times, engaging in activity despite negative thoughts provides evidence that challenges the thoughts. A combined approach, working on both thoughts and behaviours simultaneously, is often most effective.

Perfectionism can be a significant obstacle. If activities must be done perfectly or completely, the threshold for attempting them becomes impossibly high. The antidote to perfectionism is explicitly giving yourself permission to engage in activities imperfectly, incompletely, or at a lower standard than you would prefer. A short walk counts even if you intended a longer walk. A partly tidied room is better than an untidied room even if not perfectly organised. Progress, not perfection, is the goal.

External circumstances can genuinely create obstacles. Caring responsibilities, work demands, financial constraints, physical health problems, or lack of access to resources can all make behavioural activation more difficult. The approach is to work within your constraints, identifying activities that are possible given your circumstances, adapting activities to fit your situation, and being creative about finding opportunities for activation. Even in severely constrained circumstances, some opportunities for activity usually exist if looked for creatively.

Chapter 5: Cognitive Restructuring: Changing Unhelpful Thinking Patterns

Cognitive restructuring, the systematic process of identifying and modifying unhelpful thinking patterns, is the second major component of cognitive behavioural therapy for depression. Whilst behavioural activation addresses the inactivity-depression cycle, cognitive restructuring addresses the thought-mood cycle, targeting the negative thinking patterns that maintain depression.

The Process of Cognitive Restructuring

Cognitive restructuring involves several steps that are learned sequentially and eventually become an integrated skill. The first step is becoming aware of automatic thoughts. As discussed earlier, automatic thoughts are the spontaneous thoughts that pop into our minds throughout the day, often so quickly and habitually that we barely notice them. In depression, these automatic thoughts are predominantly negative and are accepted as accurate reflections of reality rather than recognised as interpretations that might be examined.

Learning to identify automatic thoughts requires practise. A helpful strategy is to notice when your mood shifts or intensifies. When you notice feeling particularly sad, anxious, irritable, or hopeless, pause and ask yourself 'What just went through my mind?' The thought might be obvious, or it might require a moment's reflection to identify. The thought might be a sentence ('I'm useless'), a question ('What's the point?'), an image (picturing yourself failing at a task), or a memory (recalling a previous failure). Writing down automatic thoughts helps make them concrete and available for examination.

QUICK REFERENCE: Common Cognitive Distortions

• All-or-Nothing Thinking • Overgeneralisation • Mental Filter
• Disqualifying the Positive • Jumping to Conclusions
• Magnification/Catastrophising • Emotional Reasoning
• Should Statements • Labelling • Personalisation

Detailed explanations follow below. (Burns, 1980)

The second step is evaluating the accuracy and helpfulness of automatic thoughts. This involves stepping back from thoughts and examining them objectively rather than accepting them at face value. Several questions can help evaluate thoughts. What is the evidence for this thought? What facts support it? What is the evidence against this thought? What facts contradict it? Am I making any thinking errors such as all-or-nothing thinking, overgeneralisation, or mind reading? Am I confusing a feeling with a fact? What would I say to a friend who had this thought? Am I looking at the whole picture or just focusing on the negatives? What are alternative ways of looking at this situation? What is the most realistic, balanced way of viewing this situation?

The goal of evaluating thoughts is not forced positive thinking or denial of genuine problems. Rather, it is balanced thinking that acknowledges both positive and negative aspects of situations, recognises thinking errors, and develops realistic perspectives. Depression systematically biases thinking towards negative interpretations whilst filtering out positive information. Cognitive restructuring works to correct this bias, bringing thinking closer to reality.

The third step is generating alternative thoughts or balanced thoughts that are more accurate and helpful than the original negative automatic thoughts. Alternative thoughts should be believable and realistic rather than unrealistically positive. An automatic thought 'I'm a complete failure' might be countered not with 'I'm perfect at everything' (which would not be believable) but with 'I have succeeded at some things and failed at others, like everyone. This particular setback doesn't define my entire worth.' Alternative thoughts acknowledge the reality of the situation whilst correcting distortions and incorporating ignored positive information.

The fourth step is testing alternative thoughts through behavioural experiments. Beliefs maintained despite being inaccurate become particularly powerful when they have never been tested. Behavioural experiments involve setting up situations that test the validity of automatic thoughts versus alternative thoughts. If you believe 'If I make a mistake at work, everyone will think I'm incompetent,' you might deliberately make a minor mistake and observe people's actual reactions. If you believe 'No one wants to spend time with me,' you might invite someone to coffee and observe their response. Behavioural experiments provide powerful evidence that can shift beliefs more effectively than rational analysis alone.

Learning cognitive restructuring takes practise. Initially, the process feels effortful and artificial. Identifying thoughts requires deliberate attention. Evaluating thoughts requires conscious effort. Generating alternatives feels forced. However, with practise, the skill becomes more automatic. Eventually, you begin noticing and questioning negative thoughts spontaneously without needing to work through formal steps. The skill becomes a natural part of how you process information, providing lasting protection against future depression.

Common Negative Thought Patterns and How to Challenge Them

All-or-nothing thinking, also called black-and-white thinking or dichotomous thinking, involves viewing situations in absolute, extreme categories with no middle ground. Things are either perfect or terrible, success or complete failure, all good or all bad. For example, if you make a minor mistake at work, you might think 'I am completely incompetent' rather than acknowledging that everyone makes occasional mistakes while generally performing adequately. If you eat something not on your diet, you might think 'I have ruined everything' and give up entirely rather than recognising this as a minor lapse. All-or-nothing thinking is particularly problematic in depression because it prevents recognition of partial successes and incremental progress, both of which are essential to recovery.

Overgeneralisation involves drawing broad, sweeping conclusions based on a single incident or limited evidence. If one thing goes wrong, you assume everything will go wrong. If you experience one rejection, you conclude you will always be rejected. Overgeneralisation is often signalled by words like 'always', 'never', 'everyone', 'no one', 'everything', or 'nothing'. For instance, if a friend declines an invitation, you might think 'no one ever wants to spend time with me' rather than considering the many possible reasons for this single decline. If you have difficulty with one task, you might think, 'I never do anything right'. Overgeneralisation in depression creates a sense of pervasive, unchangeable negativity that maintains hopelessness.

Mental filtering, also called selective abstraction, involves focusing exclusively on negative aspects of a situation whilst filtering out or ignoring positive aspects. You might receive overwhelmingly positive feedback on a piece of work, but focus entirely on the one small criticism, discounting all the positive comments. You might have a day where many things go well, but remember only the one thing that went wrong. This filtering ensures that your experience confirms your negative beliefs, whilst positive information that contradicts those beliefs is dismissed as irrelevant, unimportant, or not genuine. Mental filtering maintains depression by ensuring you accumulate evidence supporting negative views, whilst evidence contradicting these views is not processed or retained.

Discounting the positive involves acknowledging positive experiences or qualities but immediately dismissing or minimising their significance. Unlike mental filtering, where positive aspects are not noticed, discounting the positive involves noticing them but explaining them away. If someone compliments you, you might think 'they are just being nice' or 'they do not really mean it'. If you succeed at something, you might attribute it to luck rather than ability or effort. If you have a good day, you might think 'this does not count' or 'it will not last'. Discounting the positive prevents positive experiences from challenging negative beliefs, maintaining the conviction that you are worthless, incompetent, or unlikeable despite evidence to the contrary.

Jumping to conclusions involves interpreting situations negatively without adequate evidence. This takes two main forms: mind reading and fortune telling. Mind reading involves assuming you know what others are thinking, typically assuming they are thinking negatively about you, without any evidence. If someone does not smile at you, you assume they dislike you. If a friend is quiet, you assume they are angry with you. Fortune telling involves predicting that things will turn out badly without evidence to support this prediction. You might avoid applying for a job because you are certain you will be rejected, or avoid a social event because you are certain you will not enjoy it. These negative predictions then become self-fulfilling prophecies as you avoid opportunities or approach them with such negativity that they do turn out badly.

Magnification and minimisation, sometimes called the binocular trick, involve exaggerating the importance of negative things whilst minimising the importance of positive things. You magnify your mistakes, flaws, or failures, seeing them as catastrophic or defining, whilst minimising your achievements, strengths, or successes, seeing them as trivial or meaningless. For example, you might view a minor error at work as proof that you are fundamentally incompetent (magnification) whilst dismissing years of good performance as 'not really mattering' or 'anyone could have done that' (minimisation). This distortion ensures that your self-evaluation remains predominantly negative despite a more balanced reality.

Emotional reasoning involves assuming that your emotional state reflects reality. If you feel worthless, you conclude you are worthless. If you feel hopeless, you conclude the situation is hopeless. If you feel anxious about something, you conclude it must be dangerous. In depression, because your emotional state is predominantly negative, emotional reasoning leads to systematically negative conclusions about yourself, your circumstances, and your future. The fact that these conclusions are based on feelings rather than evidence is not recognised. This is particularly problematic because emotions in depression are not reliable guides to reality; depression systematically biases emotional responses in negative directions.

Should statements involve rigid rules about how you, others, or the world 'should' or 'must' be. You have strict, inflexible standards that are often unrealistic or impossible to consistently meet. When these standards are not met, you experience guilt, anger, frustration, or disappointment. Examples include 'I should always be strong and never show weakness', 'I must never make mistakes', 'I should always be productive', 'other people should always be fair', 'life should not be difficult'. Should statements create a constant sense of falling short because reality inevitably fails to match these rigid expectations. Albert Ellis, founder of Rational Emotive Behaviour Therapy, called this pattern 'musturbation' and identified it as a core feature of emotional disturbance.

Labelling involves assigning a fixed, global label to yourself or others based on a single characteristic or incident. Rather than describing the specific behaviour or characteristic, you attach a negative label to your entire self. Instead of 'I made a mistake', you think 'I am a failure'. Instead of 'that was awkward', you think 'I am socially incompetent'. Labelling is an extreme form of overgeneralisation and is particularly damaging because labels are absolute and difficult to change. If you view yourself as 'a failure' rather than as 'someone who sometimes fails at things', it becomes much harder to see possibilities for change or to recognise successes when they occur.

Personalisation involves taking excessive responsibility for events, particularly negative events, that are not entirely or even primarily your fault. If something goes wrong, you automatically blame yourself even when other factors or other people contributed. If someone is in a bad mood, you assume it is because of something you did. If a social event is not enjoyable, you assume you ruined it. Personalisation is related to excessive guilt and can maintain depression by ensuring you repeatedly confirm the belief that you cause harm or are somehow defective. It prevents realistic appraisal of situations and can lead to unnecessary guilt and self-criticism.

Certain negative thought patterns are particularly common in depression. Understanding these patterns and specific strategies for addressing them is helpful.

Self-critical thoughts involve harsh judgment of oneself, often with much greater severity than one would direct at others. 'I'm useless,' 'I'm a failure,' 'I'm worthless,' 'I always mess things up,' 'I'm not good enough.' These thoughts are maintained by attention bias (focusing on failures whilst ignoring successes), unrealistic standards (expecting perfection), and underlying negative core beliefs about oneself. Strategies for addressing self-critical thoughts include asking yourself what you would say to a friend in the same situation (usually much kinder), examining the evidence for and against the self-critical statement, acknowledging that making mistakes or having difficulties does not make you worthless as a person, and practising self-compassion.

Hopeless thoughts involve negative predictions about the future and beliefs that things will never improve. 'Things will never get better,' 'I'll always feel this way,' 'There's no point trying,' 'Nothing will help.' These thoughts are maintained by the overgeneralisation thinking error (assuming the current state will continue forever), forgetting that feelings fluctuate, and lack of awareness that effective treatments exist. Strategies for addressing hopeless thoughts include examining whether the thought is a prediction or a feeling disguised as a fact, recalling times in the past when you have felt better, acknowledging that depression makes the future look bleak, but this does not mean the future will actually be bleak, and learning about the evidence that depression is treatable and that most people recover.

Helpless thoughts involve beliefs that you are powerless to influence your situation and that nothing you do will make a difference. 'I can't cope,' 'I have no control,' 'I'm powerless,' 'Nothing I do makes any difference.' These thoughts are maintained by the learned helplessness pattern discussed earlier, where past experiences of uncontrollability become generalised to all situations. Strategies for addressing helpless thoughts include identifying specific small actions you can take even in difficult circumstances, acknowledging that whilst you cannot control everything, you always have some choices about how to respond, examining evidence of times when you have coped or influenced outcomes, and distinguishing between situations you genuinely cannot control (requiring acceptance) versus situations where you have more influence than you recognise.

Social thoughts involve negative predictions and interpretations about how others perceive you or will respond to you. 'They think I'm boring,' 'They don't want to spend time with me,' 'If they really knew me, they wouldn't like me,' 'I'll be rejected.' These thoughts often involve mind-reading (assuming you know what others think) and fortune-telling (predicting negative outcomes without evidence). Strategies for addressing social thoughts include examining the evidence for your predictions (have people actually said or done things that indicate they dislike you, or are you assuming?), considering alternative explanations for people's behaviour, testing your predictions through behavioural experiments (actually engaging socially and observing what happens), and recognising that your view of yourself is likely more negative than how others view you.

Overwhelm thoughts involve feeling that demands exceed your capacity to cope and that everything is impossible. 'I can't handle this,' 'It's all too much,' 'I'll never get through everything,' 'I can't face it.' These thoughts are often accurate in that demands feel overwhelming, but they overgeneralise by treating all tasks as equally urgent and important, and they underestimate coping capacity. Strategies for addressing overwhelm include breaking large masses of demands into individual tasks, prioritising what actually needs doing versus what feels like it should be done, tackling one thing at a time rather than trying to hold everything in mind simultaneously, acknowledging that managing even small amounts when depressed demonstrates coping capacity, and recognising that feelings of overwhelm are symptoms of depression that will reduce as depression improves.

Using Thought Records

Thought records are structured tools for systematically working through the cognitive restructuring process. A thought record provides columns for recording different elements of cognitive work, creating a systematic way to identify and modify unhelpful thoughts. Whilst various formats exist, a typical thought record includes columns for situation, emotions, automatic thoughts, evidence for and against thoughts, alternative or balanced thoughts, and outcome.

When using a thought record, you begin by identifying a situation where you experienced a significant shift in mood. This might be a specific event ('Received an email from my manager'), an interaction ('Conversation with friend'), a task ('Starting to prepare dinner'), or even just a thought or memory that triggered distress. Being specific about the situation helps clarify what triggered the emotional response.

Next, you identify the emotions you experienced and rate their intensity on a scale from zero to 100. This might include sadness (85 per cent), anxiety (70 per cent), anger (40 per cent), or other emotions. Rating intensity helps track whether working on thoughts actually changes emotional intensity and helps identify which emotions are most prominent.

Then you identify the automatic thoughts that were present in the situation. What went through your mind? What were you thinking about yourself, the situation, others, or the future? You might identify several related thoughts. It is helpful to identify the 'hot thought,' the thought most strongly connected to the emotional distress. Rating how much you believe each thought (zero to 100 per cent) helps track changes in belief as you work on the thought.

The evidence column involves listing facts that support the automatic thought. Not feelings or interpretations, but actual observable facts. This column is often surprisingly sparse, as thoughts that feel obviously true often lack substantial factual support. You then list evidence that does not support the thought, including facts that contradict it, exceptions to the thought, alternative explanations, and balanced perspectives.

Based on examining the evidence, you develop an alternative or balanced thought that is more accurate and helpful than the original automatic thought. This is not fake positive thinking but a realistic appraisal based on all available evidence. The alternative thought should feel believable even if not yet fully convincing.

Finally, you re-rate belief in the original automatic thought and re-rate emotional intensity to see whether the cognitive work has produced any shift. Even small reductions in belief or emotion intensity represent progress. With practise, these shifts tend to become larger and more consistent.

Thought records are most effective when used regularly, ideally daily, working on real situations as they arise. Initially, completing thought records takes significant time and effort, perhaps 15 to 30 minutes per record. However, the process becomes faster with practise, and the skills learned through formal thought records gradually become integrated into spontaneous thinking. Eventually, you find yourself automatically catching and questioning negative thoughts without needing to write them down, though returning to written thought records during particularly difficult periods remains helpful.

Core Belief Work

Whilst working with automatic thoughts produces immediate benefits for mood and functioning, deeper and more lasting change often requires addressing underlying core beliefs. Core beliefs, as discussed earlier, are fundamental, absolute beliefs about oneself developed through early experiences and maintained through biased information processing. Because core beliefs operate below conscious awareness much of the time and are deeply ingrained, they require sustained work over time to modify.

The first step in core belief work is identifying your core beliefs. Several strategies help. Examining patterns in automatic thoughts often reveals themes that point to underlying core beliefs. If automatic thoughts frequently involve incompetence ('I can't do this,' 'I'll fail,' 'I'm not capable'), this might reflect a core belief 'I am inadequate.' If automatic thoughts frequently involve unlovability ('They won't like me,' 'I'll be rejected,' 'I don't fit in'), this might reflect a core belief 'I am unlovable.'

The downward arrow technique is particularly useful for identifying core beliefs. You start with an automatic thought and repeatedly ask 'If that were true, what would it mean about me?' or 'What's so bad about that?' Following the chain of meanings downwards typically reveals core beliefs. For example: Automatic thought: 'I made a mistake at work.' 'What does that mean?' 'It means I'm not doing my job properly.' 'And what does that mean?' 'It means I'm incompetent.' 'And what does being incompetent mean about you?' 'It means I'm worthless.' Here, 'I am worthless' might be the core belief.

Once core beliefs are identified, the next step is examining their development. Core beliefs typically develop in childhood and adolescence through experiences that seemed to teach these lessons. A child who was repeatedly criticised might develop the belief 'I am inadequate.' A child who experienced rejection or inconsistent care might develop the belief 'I am unlovable.' Understanding how core beliefs developed does not make them immediately disappear, but it helps contextualise them, recognising them as conclusions drawn by a child in difficult circumstances rather than fundamental truths about oneself.

Examining how core beliefs are maintained despite contradictory evidence is also important. Core beliefs operate like filters, letting in information that confirms the belief while screening out information that contradicts it. Someone who believes 'I am incompetent' might dwell on mistakes (confirmation) whilst dismissing successes as luck or not important (disconfirmation ignored). This biased processing maintains the core belief even when substantial evidence exists that contradicts it. Recognising this biased processing is the first step towards correcting it.

Developing a new, more adaptive core belief involves several strategies. Examining evidence for and against the negative core belief, similar to work with automatic thoughts but looking across your entire life rather than specific situations, can reveal that the belief is not supported by the full evidence. Identifying exceptions to the core belief, times when you have acted in ways inconsistent with it, provides evidence for alternative beliefs. Developing a more balanced, nuanced alternative belief that acknowledges both strengths and weaknesses, successes and failures, allows a more realistic self-view. For example, an alternative to 'I am incompetent' might be 'I have both strengths and weaknesses. I am competent in some areas and struggle in others. I am capable of learning and improving.'

Building evidence for the new core belief requires deliberate effort over time. A positive data log, where you record evidence supporting the new belief whilst actively looking for such evidence, helps counteract the automatic attention to negative information. Behavioural experiments testing the old versus new belief provide powerful evidence. For instance, if your old belief is 'I am unlovable' and new belief is 'I am worthy of love and capable of forming meaningful relationships,' experiments might involve reaching out to friends, being more authentic in relationships, or joining social groups, observing the responses you receive.

Core belief work is typically slower than work with automatic thoughts, requiring months of sustained effort rather than immediate shifts. However, modifying core beliefs produces lasting change, reducing vulnerability to future depression and improving overall psychological wellbeing beyond just treating the current episode. Core belief work is often most productive with support from a therapist who can help guide the process, though self-directed work is also valuable.

Chapter 6: Problem-Solving and Managing Sleep

Depression is often precipitated or maintained by practical problems and stressors. Relationship difficulties, financial pressures, work stress, health problems, caregiving demands, housing issues, or accumulated practical problems can all contribute to depression and make recovery difficult. Whilst depression itself is not simply a practical problem requiring practical solutions, effective problem-solving is an important component of recovery. Problem-solving therapy, a structured approach to identifying and addressing problems systematically, has good evidence for efficacy in depression.

When Problem-Solving Helps and When It Does Not

It is important to recognise that not all problems are amenable to problem-solving, and attempting to problem-solve situations that require acceptance rather than change can be frustrating and counterproductive. Effective problem-solving involves first assessing whether a problem is changeable or unchangeable. Changeable problems are those where specific actions can improve the situation. Examples include practical issues such as debt, unemployment, housing problems, or relationship difficulties, where communication could improve things. For changeable problems, systematic problem-solving is appropriate and helpful.

Unchangeable problems are those where the situation itself cannot be modified, at least not in the short term. Examples include chronic illness, death of a loved one, past events that cannot be undone, or other people's behaviour that we cannot control. For unchangeable problems, problem-solving efforts should focus on how to cope with or adapt to the situation rather than trying to change the unchangeable. This might involve managing emotions, adjusting expectations, finding meaning, or accepting reality whilst making the best of difficult circumstances.

Sometimes the distinction between changeable and unchangeable is unclear, or elements of a problem are changeable whilst others are not. For instance, you cannot control whether you have a chronic illness (unchangeable), but you might be able to influence how the illness is managed, how you cope with symptoms, and how the illness affects your life (changeable aspects). Breaking problems into components and identifying which aspects are changeable helps direct problem-solving efforts productively.

The Problem-Solving Process

Effective problem-solving follows a structured, systematic process that breaks down overwhelming difficulties into manageable steps. This structure is particularly important in depression, where problems feel insurmountable and the cognitive impairments associated with depression make it difficult to think clearly or generate solutions spontaneously. The problem-solving framework provides external scaffolding to support the problem-solving process when internal resources are depleted. Research demonstrates that structured problem-solving training reduces depression symptoms and improves functioning, with effects maintained over time.

The first step in effective problem-solving is problem definition and formulation. This involves clearly identifying and defining the specific problem you are trying to solve. Problems often present as vague, overwhelming entities: 'Everything is terrible', 'My life is a mess', 'I cannot cope'. These formulations, whilst capturing how things feel, are too broad and emotionally laden to solve. Effective problem definition involves breaking down these global statements into specific, concrete problems. For instance, 'My life is a mess' might break down into 'I am behind on bills', 'My flat is very untidy', 'I have missed several deadlines at work', and 'I am not seeing friends'. Each of these is a specific problem that can be addressed.

A good problem definition describes the problem in specific, observable terms, focuses on aspects you have some control over, avoids assuming the cause or solution, and distinguishes facts from interpretations or assumptions. For example, 'I am a failure' is a label, not a problem definition. A better formulation might be 'I did not meet the deadline for my report'. This is specific, observable, and focuses on behaviour rather than global self-evaluation. Once you have a clear problem definition, you can begin to work towards a solution. Without a clear definition, you remain stuck in vague distress without a clear target for problem-solving efforts.

The second step is goal setting: identifying what you want to achieve by solving this problem. Goals should be specific, measurable, achievable, relevant, and time-bound (SMART goals). For the problem 'My flat is very untidy', a goal might be 'To have my kitchen and living room clean and organised within one week'. This is specific (kitchen and living room, not entire flat), measurable (you can observe whether it is done), achievable (one week provides adequate time), relevant (addresses the problem), and time-bound (one-week deadline). SMART goals provide clear targets and allow you to determine when you have succeeded.

Goals should be broken down into small, manageable steps, particularly in depression when energy and motivation are limited. For the goal of having a clean kitchen and living room, steps might include: Day 1 – wash up dishes; Day 2 – clear surface clutter; Day 3 – clean kitchen surfaces; Day 4 – vacuum kitchen; Day 5 – clear living room clutter; Day 6 – dust living room; Day 7 – vacuum living room. Each individual step is much less overwhelming than 'clean the flat' and provides multiple opportunities for a sense of achievement as each step is completed. This successive approximation approach is crucial in depression.

The third step is brainstorming: generating as many potential solutions as possible without initially evaluating them. The key rule of brainstorming is quantity over quality. Allow yourself to think of any possible solution, however impractical, unusual, or imperfect it may seem. This might include asking for help, doing the task in small chunks, hiring someone to help, lowering standards temporarily, or any other approach that might address the problem. Brainstorming works best when you suspend judgment during the generation phase. Even ideas that seem silly or impractical may contain kernels of useful approaches or may trigger other ideas. Writing down all ideas, however preliminary, ensures they are not forgotten.

In depression, brainstorming can be particularly difficult because the negativity and hopelessness make it hard to imagine anything helping. Cognitive rigidity, difficulty concentrating, and reduced creativity all impair solution generation. If you are struggling to think of solutions, it can help to ask yourself what you would advise a friend with this problem, to think about how you have solved similar problems in the past, to research how others have addressed similar difficulties, or to ask trusted others for suggestions.

Even if brainstorming generates only two or three potential solutions, this provides options to consider, which is progress from the stuck feeling of having no solutions.

The fourth step is evaluating potential solutions. For each solution generated during brainstorming, consider its likely effectiveness (how likely is it to solve the problem?), its practicality (do you have the resources, time, and ability to implement it?), its acceptability (are you willing to do it?), and its potential negative consequences. Creating a simple table can help organise this evaluation, with solutions listed in rows and evaluation criteria in columns. Some solutions will quickly emerge as more promising than others. The goal is to identify the solution or combination of solutions most likely to be effective, practical, and acceptable.

The fifth step is developing an action plan: specifying exactly what you will do, when you will do it, where you will do it, and what resources or support you will need. Action plans should be as specific and concrete as possible. Rather than 'I will tackle the bills', an action plan might specify: 'On Saturday at 10 am, I will sit at the kitchen table with all my bills, my laptop, and my bank statements. I will make a list of all bills with due dates and amounts. Then I will set up online payments for the three most urgent bills. If I get stuck, I will phone my sister who offered to help. The specificity removes ambiguity and decision-making in the moment, making follow-through more likely.

The sixth step is implementation: actually carrying out the action plan. This is where intention translates into behaviour. It can be helpful to schedule implementation in your diary as you would an appointment, removing the need to rely on spontaneous motivation. If obstacles arise during implementation, mini problem-solving might be needed to address them. If you encounter a difficulty you did not anticipate, pause, define the problem, consider solutions, choose one, and continue. Flexibility is important; if your initial plan is not working, it is appropriate to revise it rather than persisting with an ineffective approach or giving up entirely.

The seventh step is evaluation: assessing whether your problem-solving efforts have been successful. Has the problem been solved or significantly improved? If yes, acknowledge this success and consider what you learned from the process that might be useful for future problems. If the problem has not improved adequately, consider why. Was the solution chosen not effective? Were there implementation difficulties? Do you need to try a different solution from your brainstormed list? Problem-solving is often iterative, requiring multiple attempts and adjustments. Partial success is still success and provides information about what works and what needs modification.

Structured problem-solving involves several steps that are worked through systematically. The first step is defining the problem clearly and specifically. Vague problem definitions, such as 'my life is a mess' or 'everything is going wrong' are difficult to address. Specific problem definitions such as 'I am £2,000 in debt on my credit card and cannot meet the minimum payments' or 'I am not speaking to my sister following an argument three months ago and I miss her' are much more workable. A well-defined problem statement describes the problem concretely, specifies what is happening that should not be happening or what is not happening that should be, and identifies who is involved and what the obstacles or constraints are.

Breaking large, overwhelming problems into smaller, more manageable sub-problems often helps. Rather than trying to solve 'I hate my job and my life feels meaningless,' you might break this into separate problems: 'I need to identify what aspects of my job I find most problematic,' 'I need to consider whether changes within my current job could improve things,' 'I need to explore whether a different job would be better,' and 'I need to develop sources of meaning outside work.' Each smaller problem is more approachable than the large, amorphous whole.

The second step is generating multiple possible solutions without immediately evaluating them. This is a brainstorming stage where quantity matters more than quality. The goal is to generate as many potential solutions as possible, including solutions that might seem impractical, unusual, or only partial. Deferring judgment during this stage allows creative solutions to emerge that might otherwise be dismissed too quickly. Even outlandish solutions can sometimes spark ideas for workable approaches. Generating solutions is often more productive when done with another person who can contribute perspectives you might not consider yourself.

Once a range of potential solutions has been generated, the third step is evaluating each solution systematically. For each potential solution, consider the advantages and disadvantages, the practical feasibility, the resources required, the likely effectiveness, potential obstacles, and the acceptability of the solution. This evaluation allows comparing solutions and identifying which seem most promising. Often, no solution is perfect, but some are clearly preferable to others. Sometimes, combining elements of multiple solutions produces the best approach.

The fourth step is selecting a solution and developing a specific action plan for implementing it. The action plan should specify exactly what will be done, when it will be done, who will do it, and what resources or support are needed. Detailed, specific plans are more likely to be implemented than vague intentions. Anticipating obstacles and planning how to overcome them improves the likelihood of following through. Breaking the solution into small, manageable steps creates a roadmap for implementation.

The fifth step is implementing the solution and monitoring the outcome. Follow through on the action plan, adjusting as needed based on what you learn through implementation. After sufficient time for the solution to have an effect, evaluate whether it improved the problem. If the problem is resolved or substantially improved, problem-solving was successful. If the problem persists, review the problem-solving process. Was the problem adequately defined? Were enough solutions generated? Was the selected solution implemented as planned? Was sufficient time allowed? Based on this review, you might refine the problem definition, generate additional solutions, select a different solution, or modify your implementation approach.

Common Obstacles to Effective Problem-Solving

Several obstacles commonly interfere with effective problem-solving, particularly in depression. Cognitive impairments associated with depression, including difficulty concentrating, impaired decision-making, memory problems, and slowed thinking, make the problem-solving process more difficult. Working through problem-solving systematically using written tools rather than trying to hold everything in mind can help compensate for these cognitive difficulties. Working with another person who can help guide the process also helps.

Negative thinking biases problem-solving in depression. Problems seem overwhelming and insurmountable. Solutions seem unlikely to work. Potential obstacles appear insurmountable. Oneself appears incapable of implementing solutions effectively. These cognitive biases interfere with generating solutions, evaluating solutions accurately, and following through on implementation. Recognising and challenging these biases using cognitive restructuring techniques helps. Additionally, starting with smaller, more manageable problems where success is likely builds confidence in problem-solving abilities.

Avoidance of problems is extremely common in depression. Problems feel overwhelming, and facing them directly increases distress in the short term. Avoidance provides temporary relief but allows problems to worsen over time. Breaking problems into small steps, committing to working on problems for brief specified periods rather than trying to solve everything at once, and using support from others to make problem-solving less isolating can help overcome avoidance.

Perfectionism interferes with problem-solving by creating unrealistic expectations that solutions must be perfect and problems must be completely resolved. This makes any solution that does not completely eliminate the problem seem like failure, leading to abandoning problem-solving attempts prematurely. Adjusting expectations to recognise that partial improvements are valuable, that most problems require iterative solutions rather than perfect first-time fixes, and that any progress is better than no progress, makes problem-solving more effective and sustainable.

Emotional overwhelm can make it difficult to engage with problem-solving. When emotions are very intense, the cognitive resources needed for systematic problem-solving are not available. In these situations, emotion regulation strategies such as grounding techniques, distraction, or self-soothing might need to precede problem-solving. Addressing the emotional intensity first creates the mental space needed for effective problem-solving.

Managing Sleep Problems

Sleep problems are among the most common and distressing symptoms of depression, affecting approximately seventy-five to ninety per cent of people with depression. The relationship between sleep and depression is bidirectional: depression disrupts sleep, whilst poor sleep maintains and worsens depression. This creates a vicious cycle that must be addressed for successful recovery. Understanding the nature of sleep disturbance in depression and learning evidence-based strategies for improving sleep is therefore a crucial component of depression treatment. Sleep improvement often produces rapid benefits for mood, energy, and cognitive function, making sleep a high-priority target for intervention.

Normal sleep architecture involves cycling through distinct sleep stages approximately every ninety minutes throughout the night. Non-rapid eye movement (NREM) sleep includes light sleep (stages N1 and N2) and deep sleep (stage N3 or slow-wave sleep). Deep sleep is particularly restorative, crucial for physical recovery, immune function, and clearing metabolic waste from the brain. Rapid eye movement (REM) sleep is when most vivid dreaming occurs and is important for emotional processing, memory consolidation, and learning. A typical night involves four to six sleep cycles, with more deep sleep occurring in the first half of the night and more REM sleep in the second half.

Depression disrupts normal sleep architecture in characteristic ways. Sleep onset latency, the time taken to fall asleep, is often prolonged, with people lying awake for an hour or more unable to quiet their minds. Sleep maintenance is impaired, with frequent awakenings throughout the night and difficulty returning to sleep. Early morning awakening, waking two to three hours before desired wake time and being unable to return to sleep, is particularly characteristic of depression. Total sleep time is usually reduced. Subjective sleep quality is poor; even when sleep duration is adequate, it does not feel refreshing. These difficulties are exhausting and demoralising.

Polysomnography studies reveal that depression alters the microarchitecture of sleep. Slow-wave sleep (deep sleep) is reduced in amount and intensity. REM sleep occurs earlier in the night than normal (reduced REM latency) and is more intense (increased REM density). The normal distribution of sleep stages across the night is disrupted. These changes are thought to be related to the neurobiological abnormalities in depression, including alterations in neurotransmitter function, HPA axis dysregulation, and circadian rhythm disturbance. Successful treatment of depression typically normalises sleep architecture, though sleep disturbance may persist even after other symptoms improve, creating vulnerability to relapse if not addressed.

Sleep deprivation, whether due to depression or other causes, has profound effects on mood, cognition, and functioning. Even a single night of poor sleep impairs attention, memory, decision-making, and emotional regulation. Chronic sleep restriction, sleeping less than six to seven hours per night consistently, accumulates sleep debt that cannot be fully repaid by occasional longer sleep. This chronic sleep deprivation increases the risk of depression onset, worsens existing depression, impairs response to treatment, and increases relapse risk. The cognitive impairments from sleep deprivation overlap considerably with the cognitive symptoms of depression, meaning poor sleep both contributes to and mimics depression.

Sleep hygiene refers to behavioural and environmental practices that promote consistent, good-quality sleep. Whilst sleep hygiene alone may be insufficient to resolve severe sleep problems, it provides the foundation for all other sleep interventions. Key sleep hygiene principles include maintaining a consistent sleep-wake schedule seven days a week, creating a bedroom environment conducive to sleep (dark, quiet, cool, comfortable), avoiding screens (television, computer, smartphone) for at least one hour before bed as the blue light they emit suppresses melatonin production, avoiding large meals, vigorous exercise, and stimulating activities close to bedtime, limiting daytime napping or keeping naps brief (twenty to thirty minutes) and not too late in the day, and getting regular exposure to natural daylight, particularly in the morning.

Stimulus control instructions aim to strengthen the association between the bed and sleep whilst weakening associations between the bed and wakefulness. The bed should be used only for sleep and sexual activity, not for watching television, using computers or phones, eating, or engaging in worry or problem-solving. If you cannot fall asleep within approximately twenty minutes, or if you wake during the night and cannot return to sleep within twenty minutes, get out of bed and go to another room. Engage in a quiet, non-stimulating activity such as reading a book (not on a screen) until you feel sleepy, then return to bed. Repeat this as often as necessary. This prevents lying in bed awake from becoming a habit and reconditions the association between bed and sleep.

Sleep restriction therapy paradoxically improves sleep by initially reducing time in bed to match actual sleep time, then gradually increasing it as sleep efficiency improves. For example, if you are in bed for eight hours but sleeping only five hours, sleep restriction would involve being in bed only five hours initially. This creates mild sleep deprivation that strengthens sleep drive, making falling asleep easier and sleep more consolidated. As sleep efficiency (the percentage of time in bed spent asleep) improves to eighty-five to ninety per cent, time in bed is gradually increased. Sleep restriction is highly effective but should be done under professional guidance as it requires careful monitoring and adjustment. (Edinger & Means, 2005)

Cognitive factors maintain insomnia and sleep difficulties in depression. Worry about sleep, particularly performance anxiety about whether you will sleep, is counterproductive because anxiety and sleep are incompatible states. Catastrophic thinking about the consequences of poor sleep ('If I don't sleep tonight, tomorrow will be ruined', 'I cannot function without eight hours of sleep') increases anxiety that prevents sleep. Monitoring how long you have been awake, watching the clock, and calculating remaining sleep opportunity all increase anxiety and arousal. Unhelpful beliefs about sleep ('I must have eight hours', 'I must fall asleep within ten minutes', 'any wakening means bad sleep') create unrealistic standards that are rarely met. Cognitive therapy for insomnia addresses these cognitive patterns through psychoeducation, challenging unhelpful beliefs, and practising acceptance of sleep variability.

Relaxation techniques can facilitate the transition to sleep by reducing physiological and psychological arousal. Progressive muscle relaxation involves systematically tensing and releasing muscle groups throughout the body, promoting physical relaxation whilst focusing attention away from racing thoughts. Diaphragmatic breathing, slow deep breathing using the diaphragm rather than shallow chest breathing, activates the parasympathetic nervous system, promoting calm. Imagery techniques involve visualising peaceful, pleasant scenes, occupying the mind with soothing content rather than worries. Autogenic training involves repeating phrases related to feelings of heaviness and warmth, promoting deep relaxation. These techniques require regular practice to become effective; practising during the day builds skill that can then be applied at bedtime.

Mindfulness approaches to sleep difficulties involve accepting rather than fighting sleeplessness. When you cannot sleep, instead of struggling against wakefulness or worrying about sleep, you observe the present-moment experience with curiosity and acceptance. You notice thoughts, feelings, and bodily sensations without trying to change them or judging them as good or bad. This paradoxically reduces arousal because the struggle against sleeplessness and the sleep anxiety are often more distressing than simple wakefulness. Acceptance and commitment therapy for insomnia explicitly works with this paradox, helping people unhook from the struggle with sleep whilst committing to behaviours that support good sleep.

Medications for sleep include various classes of drugs with different mechanisms of action and risk-benefit profiles. Benzodiazepines and related Z-drugs (zolpidem, zopiclone) work on GABA receptors to induce sedation. They can be effective short-term but carry risks of tolerance, dependence, rebound insomnia when discontinued, and cognitive side effects, particularly in older adults. They are generally recommended only for short-term use. Sedating antidepressants such as mirtazapine, trazodone, or amitriptyline are often prescribed for depression-related insomnia. They address both depression and sleep, though sedating side effects can persist into the day. Melatonin supplements support circadian rhythm regulation and may help with sleep onset, particularly in circadian rhythm disorders, though effects are modest. Over-the-counter antihistamines cause sedation but are not recommended for regular use due to tolerance and anticholinergic side effects.

Addressing mental health conditions that affect sleep is crucial. Depression itself causes sleep disturbance, and treating the depression improves sleep. However, sleep problems may persist even when other depression symptoms improve, requiring specific attention. Anxiety commonly coexists with depression and substantially affects sleep through worry, physiological arousal, and hypervigilance. Addressing anxiety through psychological therapy or medication often improves sleep. Post-traumatic stress disorder causes nightmares and hyperarousal, affecting sleep. Bipolar disorder involves marked sleep disruption, particularly during manic phases.

Careful diagnostic assessment ensures all relevant conditions are identified and treated.

Physical health conditions affecting sleep must be evaluated and treated. Obstructive sleep apnoea involves repeated breathing interruptions during sleep, causing fragmented sleep and daytime fatigue. It is more common in people who are overweight, snore loudly, or have thick necks. If suspected, sleep study assessment and treatment with continuous positive airway pressure (CPAP) is required. Restless legs syndrome causes unpleasant sensations in the legs and an irresistible urge to move them, particularly at bedtime, delaying sleep onset. Periodic limb movement disorder involves repeated leg movements during sleep causing arousals. Chronic pain conditions disrupt sleep. Treating underlying physical health problems is essential for resolving sleep difficulties they cause.

When to seek specialist help for sleep problems is an important consideration. If sleep difficulties persist despite consistent application of sleep hygiene, stimulus control, and other self-help strategies, or if you suspect a sleep disorder such as sleep apnoea or restless legs, referral to sleep medicine is appropriate. Cognitive behavioural therapy for insomnia (CBT-I) delivered by a trained therapist is the gold-standard treatment for chronic insomnia and is more effective long-term than medication. CBT-I is increasingly available through NHS services and privately. Sleep clinics can provide a comprehensive assessment, including polysomnography if needed, diagnose specific sleep disorders, and provide specialised treatment. Sleep problems should not be accepted as inevitable; effective treatments are available. (Trauer et al., 2015)

Sleep disturbance is one of the most common and distressing symptoms of depression, affecting over 80 per cent of people with depression. The relationship between sleep and depression is bidirectional: depression disrupts sleep, but poor sleep also worsens depression, creating another vicious cycle that must be broken for recovery to occur. Addressing sleep problems systematically using evidence-based approaches is an important component of treating depression.

Understanding Sleep and Sleep Problems in Depression

Normal sleep involves cycling through different sleep stages throughout the night, including light sleep, deep sleep, and rapid eye movement (REM) sleep, with each stage serving important functions for physical and mental health. Sleep is regulated by two main processes: the circadian rhythm, the internal biological clock that creates a roughly 24-hour cycle of alertness and sleepiness, and sleep homeostasis, the drive to sleep that builds during waking hours and is discharged during sleep. Multiple factors influence these processes, including light exposure, timing of activity and meals, stress, medications, and mood.

Depression disrupts sleep through several mechanisms. Changes in neurotransmitter systems that regulate both mood and sleep lead to difficulty falling asleep, frequent waking, early morning waking, or excessive sleep. Circadian rhythm disturbances can shift the timing of sleep or reduce the amplitude of circadian signals. Rumination and worry make it difficult to switch off mentally and fall asleep. Physical symptoms of depression, such as agitation or restlessness, interfere with sleep. Behavioural changes such as irregular sleep schedules, excessive daytime sleeping, or reduced daytime activity worsen sleep quality.

The pattern of sleep disturbance varies between individuals. Insomnia, difficulty falling asleep or staying asleep, is very common. People might lie awake for hours before falling asleep, wake frequently during the night with difficulty returning to sleep, or wake in the early morning hours unable to fall back asleep. Hypersomnia, excessive sleepiness and extended sleep duration, is less common but occurs particularly in atypical depression. People might sleep 10, 12, or more hours per day yet still feel unrefreshed and fatigued. Some people experience both insomnia and hypersomnia at different times or have disrupted sleep with frequent waking but extended time in bed. Any of these patterns interfere with daytime functioning and worsen depression symptoms.

Sleep Hygiene Principles

Sleep hygiene refers to behaviours and environmental factors that promote good sleep. Whilst sleep hygiene alone is often insufficient to resolve sleep problems in depression, it provides a foundation that supports other sleep interventions and is a necessary component of managing sleep effectively.

Maintaining a consistent sleep schedule is fundamental. Going to bed and waking up at approximately the same time every day, including weekends, helps stabilise circadian rhythms. The body becomes trained to expect sleep at particular times, making falling asleep easier. Whilst the temptation to stay in bed longer when you have had a poor night's sleep is understandable, maintaining wake time consistency is important for re-establishing normal sleep patterns.

Creating a sleep-conducive bedroom environment supports better sleep. The bedroom should be dark, as light suppresses melatonin production and signals to the body that it is time to be awake. Heavy curtains or blackout blinds help. The bedroom should be cool, as body temperature naturally drops during sleep and cooler temperatures facilitate this process. Temperatures around 16 to 18 degrees Celsius are generally optimal, though individual preferences vary. The bedroom should be quiet, as noise disrupts sleep. If environmental noise cannot be eliminated, earplugs or white noise machines help. The bed and pillows should be comfortable, as discomfort interferes with sleep.

Limiting exposure to blue light from electronic screens in the evening helps because blue light suppresses melatonin production, signalling to the body that it is daytime. Televisions, computers, tablets, and smartphones all emit blue light. Ideally, screen use should be discontinued an hour or two before bedtime. If this is not practical, reducing screen brightness, using night mode settings that reduce blue light, or wearing blue-light-blocking glasses helps.

Avoiding caffeine, alcohol, and nicotine near bedtime is important. Caffeine is a stimulant with effects that can last six to eight hours, interfering with falling asleep. Caffeine is found not only in coffee but also in tea, many soft drinks, chocolate, and some medications. For people with sleep difficulties, avoiding caffeine after early afternoon or eliminating it entirely might be necessary. Alcohol, whilst initially sedating, disrupts sleep quality and architecture, leading to fragmented sleep and early waking. Nicotine is also a stimulant that interferes with sleep.

Regular physical activity promotes better sleep through multiple mechanisms, but the timing of exercise matters. Exercise too close to bedtime can be alerting and make falling asleep difficult. Exercising earlier in the day, ideally in the morning or afternoon, promotes better sleep at night.

Being mindful of food intake around bedtime is helpful. Going to bed very hungry can make falling asleep difficult, but heavy meals too close to bedtime can cause discomfort and interfere with sleep. A light snack if hungry, avoiding rich, heavy, or spicy foods near bedtime, and finishing dinner several hours before bed is ideal.

Developing a relaxing pre-sleep routine signals to the body that sleep is approaching and helps transition from wakefulness to sleep. This might include activities such as reading, listening to calming music, gentle stretching, a warm bath, or relaxation exercises. The specific activities matter less than having a consistent, relaxing routine that becomes associated with sleep preparation.

Stimulus Control and Sleep Restriction

Stimulus control is a behavioural technique based on the principle that the bed and bedroom should become strongly associated with sleep rather than with wakefulness and frustration. When people spend extended periods lying in bed awake, worrying, tossing and turning, or engaging in wakeful activities, the bed becomes associated with being awake rather than with sleeping. This association then makes falling asleep more difficult, as the bed itself becomes a cue for wakefulness. Stimulus control works to re-establish the bed as a strong cue for sleep.

The core principles of stimulus control include using the bed only for sleep and intimacy, not for other activities such as watching television, using devices, eating, or working. Go to bed only when sleepy, not just because it is a particular time. If you have not fallen asleep within approximately 20 minutes, get out of bed and do a quiet, relaxing activity in another room until you feel sleepy, then return to bed. Repeat this process as many times as needed throughout the night. The key is to avoid lying in bed awake for extended periods. Get up at the same time every morning regardless of how much sleep you obtained. Avoid daytime napping, as it reduces sleep drive at night.

A crucial point: you should not watch the clock to determine when this time has elapsed. Clock-watching itself increases anxiety and makes sleep more difficult. Instead, judge the passage of time by how you feel. If you find yourself feeling awake, frustrated, or your mind racing, this is your signal to get up, regardless of whether precisely fifteen or twenty minutes have passed.

These instructions can feel counterintuitive and difficult to follow, particularly when you are exhausted and desperately want to stay in bed hoping sleep will arrive. However, consistently following stimulus control principles typically produces improvement in sleep quality within a few weeks. The bed becomes strongly associated with sleep again, and falling asleep becomes progressively easier.

Sleep restriction is another behavioural technique that might seem paradoxical but is highly effective. Sleep restriction involves initially limiting time in bed to approximately the amount of time you are actually sleeping currently. For example, if you are spending eight hours in bed but only sleeping five hours, you would initially limit time in bed to five hours. This creates some sleep deprivation, which serves to consolidate sleep by increasing sleep drive and reducing time spent lying awake in bed.

Sleep restriction is implemented by setting a specific wake time and then calculating bedtime based on the sleep restriction schedule. If you are restricting time in bed to five hours and need to wake at 7 am, your bedtime would be 2 am. You must get up at 7 am regardless of how much sleep you got. Daytime napping is not permitted. After maintaining this schedule for several days and achieving good sleep efficiency (actually sleeping for most of the time in bed), the time in bed is gradually extended by 15 to 30 minutes, continuing to extend as long as sleep efficiency remains high, until you reach an optimal amount of sleep.

Sleep restriction should not be attempted by people with certain conditions including bipolar disorder (as sleep deprivation can trigger mania), epilepsy, or occupations where sleepiness could be dangerous. For others, sleep restriction is typically very effective but challenging, as the initial period of restricted sleep time creates fatigue. Working with a healthcare professional is advisable when implementing sleep restriction.

Managing Racing Thoughts and Rumination at Bedtime

For many people with depression, the primary obstacle to sleep is not the physical environment or sleep schedule but rather racing thoughts, rumination, and worry that prevent the mind from settling enough to fall asleep. Lying in bed provides an opportunity for all the worries, regrets, problems, and distressing thoughts to flood consciousness, keeping the person alert and distressed rather than relaxed and ready for sleep.

Several strategies help manage nighttime rumination. Setting aside a designated worry time earlier in the day allows you to deliberately attend to worries and concerns during waking hours, which can reduce their intrusion at bedtime. During worry time, you write down worries and concerns, consider potential solutions if appropriate, or simply acknowledge the worries without trying to solve them. By scheduling this time, you give yourself permission to postpone worries that arise at bedtime, reminding yourself that you will address them during tomorrow's worry time.

A worry list or thought dump involves keeping paper and pen by your bed and, if worries or thoughts arise when trying to sleep, briefly noting them down. This externalises the thoughts, reducing the need to keep rehearsing them mentally to avoid forgetting them. The act of writing often also reduces the urgency and power of thoughts. You can review the list the following day during your designated worry time or use it to inform problem-solving work.

Cognitive techniques such as challenging anxious predictions that arise at night can help. Thoughts such as 'I won't be able to function tomorrow if I don't sleep,' 'I'll never fall asleep,' or ''This is unbearable' increase arousal and prevent sleep. Examining and modifying these thoughts using cognitive restructuring techniques reduces their intensity. More balanced thoughts, such as 'I might be tired tomorrow, but I will cope as I have before,' 'I will eventually fall asleep, I always do,' or 'This is unpleasant but not dangerous' are less arousing and allow the mind to settle.

Distraction techniques provide an alternative to rumination. Thinking about something neutral or mildly engaging provides something for the mind to focus on other than worries. Some people find visualisation helpful, imagining a peaceful scene in detail. Others find mental games engaging enough to prevent rumination but boring enough not to prevent sleep, such as counting backwards from 300 by threes, listing items in alphabetical order, or mentally redecorating a room. Audio books or podcasts played quietly can provide a distraction, though content should be interesting enough to engage attention but not so exciting as to prevent sleep.

Relaxation exercises are specifically designed to reduce physical arousal and prepare the body for sleep. Progressive muscle relaxation involves systematically tensing and then releasing different muscle groups throughout the body, creating physical relaxation. Breathing exercises such as slow, deep breathing or the 4-7-8 technique (breathe in for four counts, hold for seven counts, breathe out for eight counts) activate the parasympathetic nervous system, promoting relaxation. Body scan meditations guide attention through different body parts, releasing tension and promoting awareness without engagement with thought content.

Mindfulness meditation, where attention is focused on the present moment, observing thoughts and sensations without engaging with them or trying to change them, can be particularly effective for managing nighttime rumination. Rather than trying to stop thoughts or solve problems, you simply notice thoughts arising and passing without pursuing them, gently returning attention to the breath or body sensations. This reduces engagement with thought content, allowing the mind to settle. Mindfulness is a skill that improves with practise, so regular daytime practise enhances its effectiveness at bedtime.

When to Seek Additional Help for Sleep Problems

Whilst the strategies outlined above are effective for many people, sometimes additional help is needed. If sleep problems persist despite consistently implementing good sleep hygiene, stimulus control, and cognitive-behavioural strategies, consultation with your GP or a sleep specialist is advisable. There might be underlying sleep disorders requiring specific treatment, such as sleep apnoea, restless legs syndrome, or periodic limb movement disorder, which require medical assessment and intervention.

Cognitive behavioural therapy specifically for insomnia (CBT-I) is a structured programme typically delivered over six to eight sessions, which systematically implements the techniques described in this chapter with professional guidance. CBT-I has strong evidence for efficacy and produces lasting improvements in sleep. It is considered first-line treatment for chronic insomnia. CBT-I programmes are available through some NHS services and through private therapists.

Medication for sleep is sometimes considered when behavioural approaches have been insufficient. However, sleeping medications are generally recommended only for short-term use due to concerns about dependency, tolerance, side effects, and limited evidence for long-term efficacy. Decisions about sleep medication should be made in consultation with your doctor, weighing benefits and risks. If sleeping medication is used, it works best in combination with behavioural strategies rather than as a substitute for them.

Physical Activity, Exercise, and Nutrition

Physical activity and nutrition significantly influence mood and recovery from depression through multiple biological, psychological, and social mechanisms. Whilst neither exercise nor diet alone is sufficient treatment for depression, both are valuable components of a comprehensive recovery plan. This chapter explores the evidence for their effects on depression and provides practical guidance for incorporating physical activity and nutritional improvements into your recovery journey.

Chapter 7: Physical Activity, Exercise, and Nutrition

A large body of research evidence demonstrates that physical activity and exercise reduce depressive symptoms and can prevent depression onset. Meta-analyses examining multiple studies consistently find that exercise produces significant antidepressant effects, with effect sizes comparable to those of psychotherapy or medication for mild to moderate depression. Exercise appears to work through several mechanisms including effects on neurotransmitters such as serotonin and dopamine, reduction in inflammation and stress hormones, promotion of neurogenesis (growth of new neurons) and neuroplasticity, improvement in sleep quality, and provision of behavioural activation, structure, and achievement.

Importantly, the antidepressant effects of exercise appear to be dose-dependent, with more exercise generally producing greater benefits up to a point. However, even modest amounts of activity produce measurable improvements. Studies suggest that as little as 20 to 30 minutes of moderate-intensity activity several times per week can produce significant mood benefits. This is encouraging because it means that substantial exercise programmes are not necessary; even moderate, achievable amounts of activity can help.

The type of exercise appears less important than consistency. Aerobic exercise, such as walking, running, cycling, or swimming, has been most extensively studied and has clear benefits. Resistance training with weights also has demonstrated antidepressant effects. Flexibility and balance exercises, such as yoga or tai chi, have benefits. Team sports, outdoor activities, and gym-based exercise can all be effective. The best exercise is the exercise you will actually do consistently, so personal preference and enjoyment should guide exercise selection.

Exercise also has important preventive effects. Longitudinal studies following people over time find that those who engage in regular physical activity have lower risk of developing depression. For people who have recovered from depression, maintaining regular exercise reduces the risk of relapse. This suggests that exercise is not only a treatment but also a protective factor that can be maintained long-term to support ongoing mental health.

Barriers to Exercise in Depression and How to Overcome Them

Whilst the benefits of exercise are clear, depression creates substantial barriers to engaging in physical activity. Understanding and addressing these barriers is essential for successfully incorporating exercise into your recovery plan.

Fatigue and lack of energy are perhaps the most significant barriers. Depression-related fatigue is profound, making even thinking about exercise feel exhausting. The paradox is that whilst exercise initially requires expenditure of energy you feel you do not have, it ultimately increases energy levels through biological effects on sleep, metabolism, and neurochemistry. The strategy is to start with very small amounts of activity that feel manageable despite fatigue, even just five or ten minutes of gentle walking, and to persist with regular activity despite it feeling effortful initially. As depression improves and fitness increases, energy levels typically rise, making exercise progressively less difficult.

Lack of motivation is universal in depression. Waiting for motivation to arrive before exercising rarely works, as motivation in depression is typically absent or minimal. The principle, as with all behavioural activation, is that action precedes motivation. You schedule exercise as a non-negotiable part of your routine, commit to a specific minimum duration that feels achievable, and engage in the activity regardless of how motivated you feel. Motivation follows action, not the reverse.

Anhedonia means that exercise does not feel enjoyable. Previously pleasurable activities no longer bring pleasure, and exercise might never have been particularly enjoyable even before depression. The approach here is similar to other behavioural activation: engaging in activity despite a lack of enjoyment, trusting that the capacity for enjoyment will return as depression improves. Additionally, recognising that exercise does not need to be fun to be worthwhile helps. Exercise can be valued for its effects on mood, energy, health, and recovery, even if not enjoyed in the moment.

Negative thoughts about exercise create barriers. Thoughts such as 'exercise won't help,' 'I'm too unfit,' 'people will judge me,' 'I don't have time,' or 'I'll fail' undermine motivation and prevent starting. Identifying and challenging these thoughts using cognitive restructuring techniques helps. Testing predictions through behavioural experiments (actually trying exercise and observing what happens) provides evidence that often disconfirms negative predictions. Starting with private, low-pressure forms of exercise such as walking near home reduces social anxiety about exercise.

Practical barriers, including cost, lack of time, absence of facilities, physical health limitations, or competing demands, need to be acknowledged and addressed. Exercise does not require gym membership or special equipment; walking is free and accessible to most people. Short bursts of activity throughout the day, such as walking during lunch breaks or taking stairs, can accumulate benefits without requiring large blocks of time. Home-based exercise using online videos or apps removes the need for facilities. Consulting with your GP about any physical health concerns before starting exercise provides reassurance and guidance about appropriate activities.

Starting and Maintaining an Exercise Routine

Starting exercise when depressed requires careful planning and realistic goal-setting. The most common mistake is setting overly ambitious initial goals that prove unsustainable, leading to discouragement and abandonment of exercise attempts. Starting small, building gradually, and focusing on consistency over intensity produces better outcomes.

Begin by assessing your current activity level honestly. If you are currently completely inactive, your initial goal might be as modest as a ten-minute walk three times per week. If you are somewhat active, you might aim for 20 to 30 minutes of moderate activity most days. Whatever starting point you select, it should feel genuinely achievable given your current state. Success builds confidence and motivation, making subsequent increases easier.

Choosing activities you find tolerable, if not enjoyable, increases the likelihood of consistency. If you hate running, do not set a goal to run. Walking, swimming, cycling, dancing, sports, exercise videos, or gym workouts all provide options. Experimenting with different activities helps identify what suits you. Variety can prevent boredom. Some people prefer solitary exercise, whilst others find group activities more motivating.

Scheduling exercise at specific times creates structure and increases adherence. Rather than vague intentions to 'exercise more,' commit to specific days and times. Morning exercise, whilst difficult to contemplate when you are tired, often works well because it is completed before the demands and fatigue of the day accumulate. However, any time you consistently exercise is the right time. Building exercise into existing routines, such as walking after dinner or doing stretches after waking, helps establish habits.

Having a backup plan for when obstacles arise increases resilience. If you plan to walk outside but the weather is poor, have a home-based backup activity. If you feel especially unwell, commit to a minimal amount of activity rather than all-or-nothing thinking. Even five minutes is better than nothing and maintains the habit. Flexibility within consistency allows you to adapt to circumstances whilst maintaining forward momentum.

Tracking your activity helps maintain motivation and provides objective evidence of progress. A simple log recording what activity you did and for how long, along with mood ratings before and after exercise, helps you observe the mood benefits of exercise even when they are not immediately dramatic. Seeing progress over weeks in terms of increased activity, improved mood, or greater ease of exercising provides encouragement. Fitness trackers or apps can facilitate tracking if helpful, though simple written records work equally well.

Finding ways to make exercise more enjoyable or at least less unpleasant supports adherence. Listening to music, podcasts, or audiobooks whilst exercising provides distraction and entertainment. Exercising with a friend or joining a class provides social contact and accountability. Exercising in pleasant environments such as parks or natural settings might be more enjoyable than indoor exercise. Rewarding yourself after exercise, even just with acknowledgment of your accomplishment, reinforces the behaviour.

As your fitness and mood improve, gradually increasing activity maintains progress. Increases might involve longer duration, higher intensity, more frequent sessions, or trying new activities. Progression should be gradual, perhaps increasing by 10 per cent per week, to allow adaptation and prevent injury or exhaustion. However, plateaus where activity level remains steady are also entirely acceptable. Maintaining consistent regular activity is valuable even without constant progression.

Nutrition and Depression

The relationship between nutrition and mental health, including depression, is increasingly recognised as significant and bidirectional. What you eat affects your brain function and mood, whilst depression affects eating patterns and nutritional status. The brain is a metabolically active organ consuming approximately twenty per cent of the body's energy despite representing only two per cent of body weight. It requires a constant supply of nutrients, including glucose, amino acids, essential fatty acids, vitamins, and minerals, to function optimally. Nutritional deficiencies or excesses can affect neurotransmitter production, inflammation, oxidative stress, and numerous other processes relevant to mood regulation.

The gut-brain axis represents a complex bidirectional communication system between the gastrointestinal tract and the central nervous system. This communication occurs through neural pathways (particularly the vagus nerve), hormonal signalling, and immune system interactions. The gut microbiome, the trillions of bacteria and other microorganisms living in the digestive tract, plays a crucial role in this communication. These microbes produce neurotransmitters including serotonin (approximately ninety per cent of the body's serotonin is produced in the gut), affect immune function and inflammation, influence the hypothalamic-pituitary-adrenal axis, and produce various metabolites that affect brain function.

Research demonstrates that people with depression often have different gut microbiome compositions compared to people without depression, with reduced diversity and altered proportions of specific bacterial species. Whilst we cannot yet conclude that microbiome changes cause depression, the associations are intriguing and suggest that interventions affecting the microbiome, including dietary changes and potentially probiotic supplementation, may influence mood. The emerging field of nutritional psychiatry investigates how diet affects mental health and how dietary interventions might treat or prevent mental health conditions including depression.

Several dietary patterns have been associated with reduced depression risk in observational studies. The Mediterranean diet, characterised by high intake of vegetables, fruits, legumes, nuts, whole grains, fish, and olive oil with moderate wine consumption and low intake of meat and dairy, has been most consistently associated with better mental health outcomes. Large prospective studies demonstrate that people who adhere closely to a Mediterranean dietary pattern have lower rates of depression than those following other dietary patterns. Whilst observational studies cannot prove causation, randomised controlled trials providing dietary intervention have begun to demonstrate that improving diet quality can reduce depression symptoms.

The SMILES trial, published in 2017 in the journal BMC Medicine, was the first randomised controlled trial to demonstrate that dietary intervention could treat depression. Participants with major depression were randomised to receive either dietary support to improve diet quality or social support (control condition). The dietary intervention group received individualised dietary counselling promoting a modified Mediterranean diet. After twelve weeks, approximately one third of participants in the dietary group achieved remission from depression compared to eight per cent in the control group. Subsequent trials have replicated these findings, establishing dietary intervention as a legitimate treatment approach for depression, though it should complement rather than replace other evidence-based treatments.

Specific nutrients have been investigated for their potential roles in depression. Omega-3 fatty acids, particularly eicosapentaenoic acid (EPA) and docosahexaenoic acid (DHA), are essential fats that cannot be synthesised by the body and must be obtained from diet. They are crucial components of neuronal cell membranes, affect neurotransmitter function, and have anti-inflammatory properties. People with depression often have lower levels of omega-3 fatty acids. Meta-analyses of randomised controlled trials suggest that omega-3 supplementation, particularly preparations high in EPA, may have modest antidepressant effects, though results are mixed and omega-3s are not as effective as standard antidepressant medications. Dietary sources of omega-3s include oily fish (salmon, mackerel, sardines), walnuts, flaxseeds, and chia seeds. (Grosso et al., 2014)

B vitamins, particularly folate (vitamin B9), vitamin B12, and vitamin B6, are involved in neurotransmitter synthesis and function. Deficiencies in these vitamins are associated with increased depression risk, and some people with depression have low levels. Folate is required for synthesis of serotonin, noradrenaline, and dopamine. Vitamin B12 is necessary for maintaining the myelin sheath that insulates nerve cells. Vitamin B6 is a cofactor in the conversion of tryptophan to serotonin. Some research suggests that supplementation with folate or a bioactive form of folate called methylfolate may enhance antidepressant response, particularly in people with low baseline folate levels. Dietary sources of B vitamins include leafy green vegetables, legumes, whole grains, eggs, dairy products, and fortified cereals.

Vitamin D deficiency is common, particularly in northern latitudes and during winter months, and is associated with increased depression risk. Vitamin D receptors are widespread in the brain, and vitamin D affects neurotransmitter synthesis, neuroprotection, and inflammation. Whilst observational studies consistently show associations between low vitamin D levels and depression, randomised controlled trials of vitamin D supplementation have produced mixed results. Some studies show benefit, particularly in people with very low baseline levels, whilst others show no effect. Given that vitamin D deficiency has numerous other health consequences beyond mental health, checking vitamin D levels and correcting deficiency if present is reasonable. Vitamin D is obtained from sun exposure (skin synthesis), oily fish, egg yolks, and fortified foods.

Iron deficiency, common particularly in menstruating women, causes fatigue and can affect mood. Iron is necessary for oxygen transport and is involved in neurotransmitter synthesis. Iron deficiency anaemia produces fatigue that can be difficult to distinguish from depression-related fatigue. If fatigue is prominent, checking iron status through blood tests is worthwhile. Iron supplementation should only be undertaken if deficiency is demonstrated, as excess iron can be harmful. Dietary iron is found in red meat, poultry, fish, legumes, spinach, and fortified cereals. Plant-based iron sources are less efficiently absorbed than animal sources, but absorption can be enhanced by consuming vitamin C-rich foods alongside iron-rich plant foods.

Magnesium is involved in hundreds of enzymatic reactions in the body including those relevant to brain function and stress response. Some research suggests magnesium supplementation may have mild antidepressant effects, though evidence is limited. Magnesium-rich foods include dark leafy greens, nuts, seeds, whole grains, legumes, and dark chocolate. Zinc is another mineral involved in neurotransmitter function and stress response. Zinc deficiency is more common in depression, and some studies suggest zinc supplementation may enhance antidepressant effects. Dietary sources include meat, shellfish, legumes, seeds, nuts, and dairy products.

The amino acid tryptophan is the precursor to serotonin. Some research has investigated whether increasing dietary tryptophan or supplementing with tryptophan or its metabolite 5-hydroxytryptophan (5-HTP) might alleviate depression. Results are mixed, with some studies showing modest benefits whilst others show no effect. Tryptophan supplementation alone is unlikely to be as effective as standard antidepressants. Dietary sources of tryptophan include turkey, chicken, cheese, eggs, tofu, salmon, nuts, and seeds. However, simply eating tryptophan-rich foods does not necessarily increase brain serotonin levels due to competition with other amino acids for transport across the blood-brain barrier.

Sugar and refined carbohydrates have complex relationships with mood. In the short term, consuming sugar can provide a temporary mood boost through effects on blood glucose and possibly serotonin. However, this is followed by a crash as blood glucose drops, which can worsen mood. High consumption of sugar and refined carbohydrates is associated with increased depression risk in observational studies, though causality is unclear. Possible mechanisms include effects on inflammation, blood glucose regulation, and gut microbiome. Whilst there is no need to eliminate sugar entirely, reducing consumption of sugary drinks, sweets, and refined carbohydrates whilst emphasising whole grains, fruits, and vegetables supports both physical and mental health.

Caffeine affects mood and arousal. Moderate caffeine consumption (one to four cups of coffee daily) is associated with reduced depression risk in some studies, possibly through effects on adenosine receptors and dopamine function. However, excessive caffeine can increase anxiety, disrupt sleep, and cause withdrawal symptoms including low mood when consumption is reduced. Individual sensitivity to caffeine varies. If you experience anxiety alongside depression, or if caffeine affects your sleep, reducing intake may be beneficial. If you consume large amounts and want to cut down, do so gradually to avoid withdrawal symptoms.

Alcohol, whilst providing temporary mood elevation, is a central nervous system depressant that worsens depression with regular or heavy use. Alcohol disrupts sleep architecture, interferes with antidepressant medication effectiveness, impairs judgment and problem-solving, and creates additional life problems. The risk of harmful alcohol use is elevated in depression, creating a vicious cycle. Limiting alcohol consumption to moderate levels (as defined by health authorities) or abstaining entirely supports recovery from depression. If you find it difficult to moderate alcohol use despite wanting to, seeking specific support for alcohol problems alongside depression treatment is important.

The relationship between nutrition and mental health is complex and bidirectional. Diet influences mood and mental well-being through multiple mechanisms, whilst depression affects eating behaviours, appetite, and nutritional status. Whilst nutrition alone is not sufficient treatment for depression, dietary factors can influence symptom severity, recovery trajectory, and overall well-being.

Research examining the relationship between diet and depression has identified several patterns. Mediterranean-style diets, characterised by high intake of vegetables, fruits, legumes, nuts, whole grains, fish, and olive oil, with moderate intake of poultry and dairy and low intake of red meat and sweets, are associated with reduced depression risk. Conversely, Western-style diets high in processed foods, refined carbohydrates, sugar, and unhealthy fats are associated with increased depression risk. Intervention studies where people are supported to improve their diet quality show reductions in depressive symptoms, suggesting a causal relationship rather than simply correlation.

Several mechanisms link diet and depression. Nutritional deficiencies can affect brain function and mood. Omega-3 fatty acids, found in oily fish, play important roles in brain structure and function, and low omega-3 intake is associated with depression. B vitamins, particularly folate, B6, and B12, are involved in neurotransmitter synthesis and metabolism, and deficiencies are linked with depression. Vitamin D deficiency, common in the UK particularly during winter, is associated with depression. Iron deficiency causes fatigue and can exacerbate depression symptoms. Whilst taking supplements to correct identified deficiencies can be helpful, obtaining nutrients from whole foods within a balanced diet is generally preferable to relying on supplements.

The gut-brain axis represents another mechanism linking diet and mood. The gut contains trillions of bacteria that influence brain function through multiple pathways including production of neurotransmitters, regulation of inflammation, and effects on the stress response system. Diet affects the composition and function of gut bacteria, and emerging research suggests that gut bacteria influence mood and mental health. Diets high in fibre from vegetables, fruits, legumes, and whole grains promote healthy gut bacteria, whilst diets high in processed foods and sugar may promote unhealthy gut bacteria patterns.

Inflammation has been implicated in depression, and diet influences inflammation. Pro-inflammatory diets high in refined carbohydrates, sugar, processed foods, and unhealthy fats increase inflammation, whilst anti-inflammatory diets rich in vegetables, fruits, whole grains, fish, nuts, and healthy oils reduce inflammation. Blood sugar regulation is also relevant, as diets causing rapid spikes and crashes in blood sugar can affect mood and energy, whilst diets that stabilise blood sugar support steadier mood and energy.

Practical Dietary Changes to Support Recovery

Making dietary changes when depressed is challenging, as depression affects appetite, motivation to prepare food, and the ability to engage in planning and shopping. The approach is gradual, starting with small, manageable changes rather than attempting a complete dietary overhaul, which would likely feel overwhelming and unsustainable.

Increasing intake of vegetables and fruits is one of the most important dietary changes. Vegetables and fruits provide vitamins, minerals, fibre, and phytonutrients that support brain health and mood. Aim for variety in colours, as different colours indicate different beneficial compounds. Practical strategies for increasing vegetable and fruit intake include adding vegetables to meals you already eat (adding spinach to pasta sauce, adding peppers to omelettes, having a side salad), choosing fruit as snacks instead of processed snacks, batch cooking vegetable-based soups or stews that can be reheated easily, and buying frozen vegetables which are nutritious, convenient, and economical.

Increasing intake of omega-3 fatty acids supports brain health. Oily fish such as salmon, mackerel, sardines, and trout are the best sources. Aim for two portions of fish per week, with at least one being oily fish. For people who do not eat fish, plant sources of omega-3 include walnuts, flaxseeds, chia seeds, and hemp seeds, though the type of omega-3 from plant sources is less efficiently converted to the forms used by the brain. Omega-3 supplements might be considered if dietary intake is insufficient, though evidence for supplementation in the absence of deficiency is mixed.

Choosing whole grains instead of refined carbohydrates provides more stable energy and supports gut health. Whole grains include wholemeal bread, brown rice, wholemeal pasta, oats, barley, and quinoa. They contain fibre, vitamins, and minerals that are removed during refining. Whole grains are digested more slowly than refined carbohydrates, leading to more stable blood sugar levels and more sustained energy. Practical changes include swapping white bread for wholemeal, choosing brown rice instead of white, and eating porridge for breakfast.

Reducing intake of processed foods, sugary foods, and unhealthy fats supports mood and health. Processed foods often contain high levels of sugar, salt, unhealthy fats, and additives whilst being low in nutrients. Whilst complete elimination is neither necessary nor realistic, reducing consumption is beneficial. Practical strategies include cooking meals from basic ingredients more often rather than relying on ready meals, choosing water or unsweetened drinks instead of sugary beverages, limiting cakes, biscuits, and sweets, and choosing healthier snacks such as nuts, fruit, or yoghurt.

Maintaining regular meal patterns supports stable energy and mood. Depression often disrupts eating patterns, with people either skipping meals entirely or eating erratically. Going for long periods without eating causes blood sugar to drop, which can worsen mood, energy, and concentration. Aim for three meals per day at roughly regular times, with healthy snacks if needed. Even when appetite is poor, eating something is better than nothing. If large meals feel overwhelming, smaller, more frequent meals might be more manageable.

Staying adequately hydrated is important, as even mild dehydration can affect mood, energy, and concentration. Aim for approximately six to eight glasses of fluid per day, with water being the healthiest choice. Tea and coffee count towards fluid intake but should be consumed in moderation due to caffeine content. If plain water feels unappealing, adding slices of fruit, cucumber, or herbs can make it more palatable.

Being mindful of alcohol consumption is important. Whilst alcohol might seem to provide temporary relief from depression symptoms, it is actually a depressant that worsens mood, disrupts sleep, interferes with medication effectiveness, and can contribute to development or worsening of depression. UK guidelines recommend no more than 14 units of alcohol per week spread over at least three days, with several alcohol-free days. If you are using alcohol to cope with depression, this should be addressed as part of your treatment plan.

Overcoming Barriers to Healthy Eating

Several barriers commonly interfere with healthy eating when depressed. Lack of appetite is common, making eating feel like a chore. Strategies include choosing nutrient-dense foods so that even small amounts provide good nutrition, eating with others when possible as social context can stimulate appetite, choosing foods you find palatable even if they are not perfect nutritionally (eating something is better than nothing), and eating at regular times even when not hungry to maintain energy levels.

Overwhelming increased appetite or comfort eating, particularly of high-sugar or high-fat foods, occurs in some people with depression. Emotional eating provides temporary comfort but often leads to guilt and weight gain, worsening depression. Strategies include identifying triggers for emotional eating, finding alternative ways to manage emotions such as talking to someone, engaging in activities, or using relaxation techniques, keeping less healthy foods out of the house or harder to access, planning meals and snacks in advance, and being compassionate with yourself when emotional eating occurs whilst recommitting to healthier patterns.

Lack of energy and motivation to shop, prepare, and cook food is a major barrier. Depression makes these tasks feel exhausting. Strategies include keeping convenient, healthy options available such as frozen vegetables, tinned fish, eggs, and wholemeal bread which require minimal preparation, batch cooking when you have more energy and freezing portions for later, accepting help from others with shopping or meal preparation if available, using online shopping with home delivery to reduce the effort of shopping, and lowering standards about meal complexity (simple meals are perfectly adequate).

Financial constraints limit food choices for many people. Healthy eating can be achieved on a budget with planning. Strategies include buying seasonal produce which is cheaper, choosing frozen or tinned vegetables and fish which are nutritious and economical, buying larger bags of basics such as rice, pasta, oats, and lentils which are cheap and nutritious, reducing food waste by planning meals and using leftovers, and reducing spending on processed foods, takeaways, and sugary drinks, reallocating that budget to healthier ingredients.

Chapter 8: Mindfulness and Acceptance-Based Approaches

Whilst cognitive behavioural therapy focuses on changing unhelpful thoughts and behaviours, mindfulness and acceptance-based approaches offer complementary strategies that involve changing one's relationship to thoughts and feelings rather than changing their content. These approaches have strong evidence for efficacy in preventing depression relapse and can be valuable components of recovery from acute depression.

What Is Mindfulness?

Mindfulness is the practise of paying attention to present moment experience with an attitude of openness, curiosity, and acceptance, without judgment or attempts to change what is being experienced. This involves deliberately noticing what is happening in the present moment, including thoughts, feelings, physical sensations, and the surrounding environment, rather than being lost in thoughts about the past or future, and relating to present experience with acceptance rather than fighting against it or judging it as good or bad.

This definition highlights several key elements. Present moment focus means bringing attention back to what is actually happening right now rather than ruminating about the past or worrying about the future. Both past and future focus are common in depression, with rumination about past failures and worry about future difficulties consuming mental resources. Mindfulness practise trains the ability to disengage from these thought patterns and anchor attention in the present.

Non-judgmental awareness means observing experience without labelling it as good or bad, right or wrong, or engaging in self-criticism. Depression involves harsh self-judgment and constant evaluation. Mindfulness offers a different mode of relating to experience, simply noticing what is present without adding layers of judgment. This does not mean approving of everything or believing nothing should change, but rather means observing reality as it is before responding.

Acceptance in mindfulness does not mean resignation or passive tolerance of unacceptable situations. Rather, it means acknowledging what is actually present in the current moment rather than denying it, fighting against it, or insisting it should be different. Paradoxically, acceptance is often the first step toward effective change, as it allows clear seeing of the situation rather than distorted perception through the lens of what we wish were true.

Mindfulness differs from the usual mode of mind, often called 'doing mode,' where attention is on goals, problems to solve, gaps between how things are and how we want them to be, and action to close those gaps. Doing mode is essential and adaptive for many life tasks. However, in depression, doing mode becomes problematic when applied to mood itself, as attempts to 'fix' depression through rumination and self-criticism often worsen it. Mindfulness offers an alternative 'being mode' where experience is simply observed without constant evaluation and problem-solving.

How Mindfulness Helps with Depression

Mindfulness helps with depression through multiple interconnected mechanisms operating at cognitive, emotional, physiological, and behavioural levels. Understanding these mechanisms can enhance motivation to practise mindfulness and can help you recognise the changes occurring as you develop mindfulness skills. The benefits of mindfulness are cumulative, building gradually through regular practice rather than appearing immediately or dramatically. Patience and consistency are required, but the evidence supporting mindfulness as an effective intervention for depression is compelling.

At a cognitive level, mindfulness addresses rumination, which is a key maintaining factor in depression. Rumination involves repetitive, passive focus on symptoms, problems, and their causes and consequences without moving towards solutions. Research by Susan Nolen-Hoeksema demonstrated that rumination predicts onset, duration, and severity of depressive episodes. Mindfulness interrupts rumination by redirecting attention away from past regrets and future worries to present-moment experience. When you notice your mind has wandered into rumination, you gently bring attention back to the breath or other anchor in the present. This repeated practice weakens the habit of rumination and strengthens the capacity to redirect attention.

Mindfulness also changes the relationship to thoughts. In depression, thoughts are typically experienced as facts, as accurate reflections of reality. The thought 'I am worthless' is experienced as a true statement about yourself rather than as a mental event that may or may not accurately reflect reality. Mindfulness cultivates metacognitive awareness, the ability to observe thoughts as thoughts rather than identifying with their content. You learn to notice 'I am having the thought that I am worthless' rather than 'I am worthless'. This subtle shift creates distance from thoughts, reducing their power to drive emotion and behaviour. You recognise thoughts as transient mental events that arise and pass rather than as enduring truths.

Mindfulness enhances emotional regulation, the ability to manage and respond skilfully to emotions. Through mindfulness practice, you develop greater awareness of emotions as they arise, before they become overwhelming. You learn to notice early signs of emotional change in thoughts, bodily sensations, and impulses to act. This early awareness creates an opportunity for choice about how to respond. You might notice sadness beginning to rise and choose to engage in an activity that provides support or distraction rather than withdrawing and allowing the sadness to intensify unchecked. You develop the capacity to experience emotions without being overwhelmed by them or needing to immediately escape them.

The principle of 'turning towards' rather than 'turning away from' difficult experiences is central to mindfulness-based approaches. In depression, there is a strong tendency to avoid, suppress, or try to eliminate negative emotions and thoughts. This avoidance is understandable but problematic. Attempted suppression of thoughts and emotions paradoxically increases their frequency and intensity. Avoidance of difficult experiences limits life and maintains depression by preventing exposure to situations where positive experiences might occur. Mindfulness teaches a different approach: acknowledging and allowing difficult thoughts and emotions to be present without struggling against them.

This acceptance does not mean resignation or passivity. It means acknowledging reality as it is in the present moment, including the presence of difficult thoughts and emotions, without adding struggle, self-criticism, or attempts to force things to be different. The paradox is that acceptance of present-moment reality, including emotional pain, often reduces suffering more effectively than fighting against it. The suffering in depression comes not only from painful emotions themselves but from the struggle against them, the belief that we should not feel this way, the fear that we will feel this way forever. Mindfulness addresses this secondary suffering by teaching non-judgmental acceptance of present-moment experience.

Physiologically, mindfulness practice affects the body's stress response system. Regular mindfulness practice has been shown to reduce activity in the amygdala, the brain structure involved in fear and stress responses, and to increase activity in the prefrontal cortex, which is involved in emotional regulation and executive function. Mindfulness reduces levels of cortisol, the primary stress hormone. It activates the parasympathetic nervous system, promoting physiological calm and counteracting the chronic stress arousal often present in depression. These physiological changes contribute to improved mood, better sleep, and reduced physical symptoms of depression and anxiety.

Mindfulness enhances awareness of the body, which is important in depression where disconnection from the body is common. You might not notice hunger, fullness, tension, or fatigue until they have reached extreme levels. Mindfulness cultivates the ability to notice bodily sensations as they arise, allowing you to respond to your body's needs more effectively. This might include eating when genuinely hungry, resting when tired, or addressing muscle tension before it becomes painful. Body awareness also provides early warning signals of emotional changes, as emotions are accompanied by characteristic bodily sensations. Noticing these bodily sensations allows earlier recognition of emotional shifts.

Behaviourally, mindfulness supports valued action by helping you identify what truly matters to you and by providing skills for managing the obstacles that arise when pursuing valued directions. Depression often involves loss of connection with values, with what makes life meaningful. Mindfulness practices can help clarify values by bringing awareness to moments of meaning, connection, and satisfaction when they occur. Mindfulness also provides skills for managing the difficult thoughts and emotions that inevitably arise when pursuing valued activities, allowing you to persist even when things are difficult. The willingness to experience discomfort in the service of what matters is central to both mindfulness and values-based action.

The cultivation of self-compassion through mindfulness is particularly important in depression. Depression involves harsh self-criticism, shame, and feelings of worthlessness. Self-compassion, treating yourself with the same kindness and understanding you would offer a good friend, counteracts these patterns. Mindfulness-based self-compassion practices explicitly teach this kinder relationship with yourself. Research by Kristin Neff demonstrates that self-compassion is strongly protective against depression and promotes resilience. Self-compassion does not mean self-indulgence or lowering standards. It means acknowledging your suffering, recognising it as part of shared human experience, and responding with kindness rather than judgment.

Mindfulness helps with depression through several mechanisms. It disrupts rumination by providing an alternative to repetitive negative thinking. When you notice you are ruminating and bring attention back to the present sensory experience, such as the breath, the body, or sounds, the rumination cycle is interrupted. With practise, this becomes easier and more automatic, reducing the time spent ruminating and its negative effects on mood.

Mindfulness creates distance from thoughts, allowing you to observe thoughts as mental events rather than as facts about reality. A thought such as 'I am worthless' can be noticed as simply a thought that the mind has produced, rather than a truth about oneself. This cognitive defusion, as it is termed in acceptance and commitment therapy, reduces the power of thoughts to control mood and behaviour. You recognise 'I am having the thought that I am worthless' rather than accepting 'I am worthless' as reality.

Mindfulness reduces experiential avoidance, the tendency to avoid or escape from uncomfortable thoughts, feelings, and sensations. Whilst avoidance provides short-term relief, it is counterproductive in the longer term, as it prevents processing of emotions, limits life engagement, and often increases the intensity of what is being avoided through suppression effects. Mindfulness involves turning toward difficult experiences with acceptance and curiosity, which paradoxically often reduces their intensity and makes them more manageable.

Mindfulness enhances awareness of pleasant experiences that might otherwise go unnoticed when attention is consumed by negative thoughts and feelings. In depression, positive experiences occur but often pass unnoticed because attention is elsewhere. Deliberately bringing mindful attention to pleasant moments, however small, increases their impact on mood. This might include savouring the taste of food, noticing beauty in nature, enjoying the warmth of sunshine, or appreciating moments of connection with others.

Mindfulness promotes self-compassion, a kind and understanding attitude toward oneself, particularly during difficult times. This contrasts sharply with the harsh self-criticism characteristic of depression. Mindfulness helps recognise self-critical thoughts as thoughts rather than truths and creates space for alternative, more compassionate responses. Self-compassion, which will be discussed further shortly, is associated with reduced depression and greater resilience.

Research on mindfulness-based interventions for depression shows clear benefits. Mindfulness-based cognitive therapy (MBCT), an eight-week programme combining mindfulness meditation practices with cognitive therapy elements, significantly reduces risk of relapse in people who have recovered from depression. For people with a history of three or more depressive episodes, MBCT reduces relapse risk by approximately 40 to 50 per cent, an effect comparable to maintenance antidepressant medication. MBCT is recommended by NICE (National Institute for Health and Care Excellence) as a relapse prevention intervention for recurrent depression. (Kuyken et al., 2016)

Basic Mindfulness Practices

Learning mindfulness involves regular practise of formal mindfulness exercises alongside informal integration of mindful awareness into daily activities. Formal practices are structured exercises where you set aside time specifically for mindfulness practise. Informal practices involve bringing mindful attention to everyday activities such as eating, walking, or washing.

Mindful breathing is a foundational practise. Find a comfortable position, sitting or lying down. Bring your attention to the physical sensations of breathing. You might notice the sensation of air moving through your nostrils, the rise and fall of your chest or abdomen, or the slight pause between in-breath and out-breath. You are not trying to change your breathing, simply observing it. When your attention wanders, which it inevitably will, gently notice that it has wandered and bring it back to the breath. The wandering itself is not failure; noticing the wandering and bringing attention back is the practise.

Initially, your mind might wander dozens of times within a few minutes. This is normal. Each time you notice wandering and return attention to the breath, you are strengthening the attention regulation skills that mindfulness develops. With practise, you might be able to sustain attention on the breath for longer periods, though even experienced meditators experience mind wandering. Start with brief periods, perhaps five minutes, and gradually extend the duration as you feel comfortable.

Body scan meditation involves systematically bringing attention to different parts of the body. Lie down in a comfortable position. Begin by bringing attention to your feet, noticing any sensations present, which might include tingling, warmth, pressure, tension, or perhaps numbness. There are no right or wrong sensations. Simply notice what is there. After spending time with the feet, move attention gradually up through the body, including legs, pelvis, abdomen, chest, back, hands, arms, shoulders, neck, and head. If you notice areas of tension or discomfort, bring gentle, accepting awareness to them without trying to change them. When attention wanders, gently guide it back to the body part you are focusing on.

Body scan practise serves several functions. It develops the ability to notice physical sensations, which is important because depression involves disconnection from the body. It provides practise bringing attention to the present moment. It often reveals areas of physical tension connected to stress or emotion, and the gentle, accepting attention sometimes allows tension to release. Recordings that guide you through body scan meditation are widely available and can be helpful when learning the practise.

Mindful walking involves bringing full attention to the experience of walking. This can be done as a formal practise, walking slowly back and forth in a quiet space, or informally during normal daily walking. Notice the sensations in your feet and legs as you walk. Feel the contact of your feet with the ground. Notice the movement of your body through space. You might notice your breath, the position of your arms, sensations of air on your skin, or sounds around you. When attention wanders to thoughts, gently return it to the sensations of walking. Mindful walking can be particularly useful for people who find sitting meditation difficult or who feel the need for movement.

Loving-kindness meditation involves deliberately cultivating feelings of warmth and goodwill, initially toward oneself and then progressively toward others. Find a comfortable position and bring to mind a phrase or series of phrases expressing goodwill, such as 'May I be happy, may I be healthy, may I be safe, may I be at ease.' Repeat these phrases gently whilst holding yourself in awareness with kindness. If this feels difficult or false initially, which is common for people with depression, simply notice that difficulty with acceptance. After some time focusing on yourself, bring to mind someone you care about and direct the phrases toward them. Then progressively extend to neutral people, difficult people, and ultimately all beings.

Loving-kindness practise directly addresses the harsh self-criticism and feelings of disconnection from others common in depression. Research shows it increases positive emotions, enhances social connection, and reduces depressive symptoms. The practise can feel uncomfortable initially, particularly when directed toward oneself, but typically becomes easier and more natural with repetition.

Informal Mindfulness practise

Whilst formal practices are important for developing mindfulness skills, informal practise integrates mindfulness into daily life and makes the benefits more accessible throughout the day. Informal practise involves bringing full attention to everyday activities that are normally done automatically or whilst thinking about something else.

Mindful eating is an accessible introduction to informal practise. Choose a meal or snack to eat mindfully. Before eating, take a moment to actually look at the food, noticing colours, shapes, and arrangement. As you bring food to your mouth, notice the movement of your hand and arm. Notice the smell. As you take a bite, notice the texture, temperature, and flavour. Chew slowly, paying attention to how the taste and texture change. Notice the sensations of swallowing. Throughout, when your mind wanders to thoughts, gently return attention to the sensory experience of eating.

Most people rarely eat with full attention, instead eating whilst working, watching television, or lost in thought. Mindful eating reveals the richness of sensory experience that normally goes unnoticed. It often increases the enjoyment of food. It can help with emotional eating by creating a pause where you can notice emotions driving eating rather than responding automatically. Even eating one meal or snack per day mindfully provides regular practise.

Mindful daily activities can include any routine activity: showering, washing dishes, making tea, brushing teeth, or cleaning. Choose an activity and commit to doing it with full attention. Notice the sensations, sounds, and visual aspects of the activity. When attention wanders to planning, worrying, or ruminating, gently return it to the sensory experience of what you are doing. These practices develop the habit of present moment awareness and provide numerous brief opportunities throughout each day to step out of automatic mode and into mindful awareness.

Three-step breathing space is a brief practise that can be used at any time during the day, particularly when you notice difficulty with emotions, stressful situations, or unhelpful thinking. The first step involves becoming aware of your present moment experience, asking 'What am I experiencing right now?' and noticing thoughts, feelings, and body sensations. The second step involves gathering attention and focusing it on breathing, following the breath in and out. The third step involves expanding attention to include awareness of the whole body, breathing, and the space around you. This practise takes just a few minutes and provides a way to step back from difficult experiences and re-centre.

Developing Self-Compassion

Self-compassion, treating yourself with the same kindness and understanding you would offer a good friend who was struggling, is a powerful antidote to the harsh self-criticism characteristic of depression. Research by Kristin Neff and others demonstrates that self-compassion is associated with reduced depression, reduced anxiety, greater psychological resilience, and greater life satisfaction. Importantly, self-compassion can be learned and strengthened through practise.

Self-compassion involves three key components. Self-kindness means being warm and understanding toward yourself when you suffer, fail, or feel inadequate, rather than harshly criticising yourself. Common humanity involves recognising that suffering, failure, and imperfection are part of the shared human experience rather than signs of personal inadequacy or isolation. Mindfulness involves holding painful thoughts and feelings in balanced awareness rather than over-identifying with them or suppressing them.

Depression makes self-compassion particularly difficult. The negative self-view central to depression creates beliefs that you do not deserve kindness or compassion. Self-criticism feels natural and justified. The isolation of depression makes the universal nature of human struggle harder to recognise. Intense emotions make balanced awareness challenging. However, these difficulties make self-compassion even more important to cultivate, as it directly counters the processes maintaining depression.

Developing self-compassion involves several practices. Noticing self-critical thoughts is the first step. Throughout the day, pay attention to how you speak to yourself internally. Would you speak to a friend the way you speak to yourself? For many people with depression, the answer reveals striking harshness toward oneself that would never be directed at others. Simply noticing this discrepancy can motivate change.

When you notice self-criticism, pause and ask yourself what you might say to a close friend in the same situation. How would you express understanding and support? What would you want them to know? Then, deliberately direct these compassionate responses toward yourself. This might feel awkward or false initially, but with practise becomes more natural. You might write compassionate letters to yourself, expressing understanding and support for difficulties you face.

Developing a compassionate self-talk habit involves practising phrases you can use during difficult moments. 'This is really hard right now, and it makes sense that I am struggling,' 'I am doing the best I can with the resources I have,' 'Everyone makes mistakes; this does not make me worthless,' 'I deserve kindness and understanding, especially when things are difficult.' Find phrases that resonate with you and practise them regularly.

Practising self-compassion meditation, similar to loving-kindness meditation but specifically focused on self-compassion, strengthens these skills. You might bring to mind a difficulty you face and then offer yourself expressions of kindness and understanding, acknowledge the common humanity of struggle, and hold your pain with mindful awareness.

Chapter 9: Depression and Relationships

Depression does not occur in isolation but profoundly affects relationships with partners, family members, friends, and colleagues. Understanding how depression impacts relationships, how relationships impact depression, and how to navigate these challenges is crucial for recovery. Relationships can be sources of support that facilitate recovery, but they can also become strained by depression in ways that worsen symptoms. This chapter and the following chapters explore these dynamics and provide strategies for protecting and strengthening relationships during depression.

How Depression Affects Relationships

Depression profoundly affects all types of relationships, from intimate partnerships to family relationships, friendships, and professional relationships. The impact is bidirectional: depression affects how you relate to others, and relationship difficulties can maintain or worsen depression. Understanding these reciprocal influences is important for addressing both depression and relationship difficulties effectively. Research consistently demonstrates that relationship quality is strongly associated with depression outcomes, with supportive relationships protecting against depression and conflictual relationships increasing risk and maintaining symptoms.

The emotional symptoms of depression directly affect relationships. Persistent sadness, irritability, and emotional numbing reduce your capacity for warmth, responsiveness, and connection. You may struggle to experience or express positive emotions towards loved ones, even when you care deeply about them. This can be confusing and hurtful for others who may misinterpret your emotional flatness as not caring. Increased irritability can lead to more frequent conflicts over minor issues. The emptiness and lack of pleasure in depression can make it difficult to enjoy time with others, even during activities you previously shared happily. This loss of shared enjoyment can create distance in relationships.

The cognitive symptoms of depression shape how you interpret interactions and perceive relationships. Negative thinking biases lead you to focus on negative aspects of relationships whilst overlooking positive aspects. You might ruminate on past conflicts or interpret neutral comments as criticism. Difficulty concentrating makes it hard to be fully present in conversations, leading to misunderstandings or making others feel you are not interested in what they are saying. Negative automatic thoughts about being a burden, being unlovable, or deserving rejection create anxiety and defensiveness in relationships. You might withdraw to spare others from having to deal with you, which then creates the very rejection or abandonment you fear.

Behavioural changes in depression affect relationship functioning in numerous ways. Social withdrawal and reduced initiation of contact mean you spend less time with others and may not respond to their attempts to connect. Reduced energy and motivation make it difficult to maintain household responsibilities or contribute to shared activities, potentially creating resentment or increased burden on others. Loss of interest in activities means you may no longer participate in things you previously did together, which can feel like rejection to partners or friends. Reduced self-care might concern others or affect physical intimacy in romantic relationships. Changes in communication patterns, such as speaking less or being less responsive, can leave others feeling shut out.

Depression affects communication in specific ways that can create or worsen relationship difficulties. You may have difficulty expressing needs or feelings clearly, either due to cognitive difficulties or because you fear being a burden. You might become more critical or demanding of others due to irritability or high emotional distress. Alternatively, you might become excessively accommodating and passive, agreeing to things you do not want to avoid conflict. Depression impairs the ability to engage in constructive conflict resolution, making disagreements more likely to escalate or remain unresolved. The combination of withdrawal, poor communication, and negative interpretation of interactions creates a pattern that strains even strong relationships.

Depression influences relationships through multiple pathways, creating challenges that strain even strong, supportive relationships. Understanding these effects helps both people with depression and their loved ones make sense of relationship difficulties and respond constructively.

Social withdrawal is one of the most prominent ways depression affects relationships. People with depression often isolate themselves, avoiding social contact, declining invitations, and withdrawing from previously enjoyed social activities. This withdrawal stems from multiple factors: fatigue makes social interaction feel exhausting, anhedonia means social activities no longer bring pleasure, concentration difficulties make following conversations difficult, feelings of worthlessness create beliefs that one is not good company, and social anxiety emerges around being with others. Whilst understandable, this withdrawal deprives people of social support precisely when they need it most, and friends and family often feel hurt, confused, or rejected by the withdrawal. (Gariepy et al., 2016)

Communication difficulties arise in depression. Cognitive slowing makes conversation more effortful. Difficulty concentrating means attention wanders during interactions. Flat affect, where emotional expression becomes muted, can make people seem uninterested or distant. Reduced verbal output means conversations become one-sided. These changes make communication less rewarding for both parties, potentially leading to reduced interaction and increased misunderstanding.

Emotional unavailability and reduced intimacy affect close relationships particularly. When you are consumed by depression, there is little emotional capacity left to attend to others' needs or to engage emotionally in relationships. You might be physically present but emotionally absent. In romantic relationships, reduced interest in sex due to depression itself or medication side effects creates additional strain. Partners often feel lonely, unloved, or neglected, even whilst understanding intellectually that these changes reflect depression rather than lack of care.

Irritability and increased conflict commonly occur in depression. The persistent low mood, frustration with one's own symptoms, reduced tolerance for stress, and sleep deprivation all contribute to shorter temper and increased irritability. Small annoyances that would normally be shrugged off become major irritations. Patience with others decreases. This can lead to increased arguments, criticism, or tension, damaging relationship quality and creating additional stress that worsens depression.

Increased dependency and reassurance-seeking can strain relationships. Depression undermines confidence and increases need for support, validation, and reassurance from others. Whilst some need for support is healthy and appropriate, excessive dependency where others are constantly required to provide reassurance, make decisions, or take responsibility can exhaust caregivers and create resentment. Additionally, reassurance-seeking often provides only temporary relief, with doubts and anxieties returning quickly, leading to repetitive patterns that frustrate both parties.

Role functioning difficulties affect practical aspects of relationships. Depression interferes with work performance, household responsibilities, childcare, financial management, and other practical contributions to family life. Partners, family members, or housemates often take on additional responsibilities to compensate, which can create practical burden and resentment, particularly if the depression and its effects are not understood or acknowledged.

The impact on children deserves particular attention when parents experience depression. Children are acutely sensitive to parents' emotional states and might not understand what is happening. They might blame themselves for the parent's unhappiness, develop their own emotional or behavioural difficulties in response to the altered family atmosphere, or take on inappropriate caring responsibilities. Parental depression is a significant risk factor for children developing mental health difficulties themselves. However, these risks can be substantially mitigated through appropriate treatment of the parent's depression, open age-appropriate communication with children, maintaining structure and routines, and ensuring children have additional support if needed.

How Relationships Affect Depression

Just as depression affects relationships, relationship factors significantly influence the course of depression. Understanding these bidirectional effects is important for addressing both depression and relationship difficulties.

Relationship conflict and discord are powerful triggers for depression onset and maintenance. Chronic relationship conflict, whether with partners, family members, or others, creates ongoing stress that contributes to depression development and maintenance. Critical, hostile, or emotionally over-involved family environments, sometimes termed 'high expressed emotion,' predict worse outcomes in depression. Conversely, warm, supportive, low-conflict relationships predict better outcomes.

Particular relationship events such as separation, divorce, or significant betrayal are among the most powerful triggers for depression episodes. The loss, rejection, humiliation, and practical disruption associated with relationship breakdown often precipitate depression in vulnerable individuals. Even in ongoing relationships, specific conflicts or disappointments can trigger depression episodes, particularly if they activate underlying beliefs about being unlovable or worthless.

Lack of intimacy and emotional connection in relationships, even in the absence of overt conflict, contributes to depression. Feeling lonely within a relationship, experiencing emotional distance from a partner, or having no close confiding relationships creates vulnerability to depression. Humans have fundamental needs for connection, belonging, and intimacy, and unmet needs in these areas affect mental health.

Certain relationship patterns are particularly problematic. Criticism and blame from partners or family members, whether about the depression itself or other matters, worsen depression and undermine recovery. Messages that the person should 'snap out of it,' 'try harder,' or 'stop being selfish' are particularly damaging, invalidating the person's experience and increasing guilt and shame. Conversely, excessive accommodation where others take over all responsibilities without supporting the person's own coping efforts can inadvertently reinforce helplessness and dependence.

The quality of support offered by relationships matters enormously. Effective support is responsive to the person's needs, validating without being overwhelming, practical without being controlling, and balanced between supporting recovery and accepting current limitations. Ineffective support might be intrusive, controlling, invalidating, or inconsistently available. Understanding what constitutes helpful versus unhelpful support is important for both people with depression and their loved ones.

Depression in Romantic Relationships

Romantic relationships face particular challenges when one or both partners experience depression. The intimacy, interdependence, and expectations inherent in romantic partnerships mean that depression significantly impacts the relationship, whilst relationship dynamics significantly influence the depression. Understanding these dynamics and developing strategies to support both the individual's recovery and the relationship's health is essential.

Understanding Your Partner's Experience

When your partner is depressed, understanding their experience helps you respond effectively and maintain your own wellbeing. Depression changes how people think, feel, and behave in ways that are often confusing or hurtful to partners who do not understand what is happening.

Your partner's withdrawal, emotional unavailability, or irritability are symptoms of their illness, not reflections of their feelings toward you. Depression makes connection feel difficult or impossible, not because the person does not care about you, but because depression consumes emotional resources. Recognising that these behaviours stem from depression rather than relationship problems or lack of love helps reduce personalising their symptoms, though this understanding does not eliminate the pain of feeling disconnected from your partner.

The changes you observe are temporary, though depression duration varies. Your partner has not permanently transformed into a different person. The person you knew is still there, even if currently obscured by depression. With effective treatment and support, most people recover and relationships can heal. Maintaining this long-term perspective helps during difficult periods when change feels impossible.

Your partner needs different things at different times. Sometimes they need practical help with tasks that feel overwhelming. Sometimes they need emotional support and validation. Sometimes they need space. Sometimes they need gentle encouragement to engage in helpful activities. Sometimes they need acceptance of their current limitations without pressure to change. Learning to read what is needed in each moment, asking directly what would help, and accepting that your efforts will not always have the desired effect, are all important aspects of supporting a depressed partner.

Understanding that you cannot fix your partner's depression is crucial. Love and support are important but insufficient. Depression is a health condition requiring professional treatment. Your role is to support your partner whilst they engage in treatment, not to be their therapist or to be solely responsible for their recovery. Accepting this limitation reduces frustration and self-blame when your efforts do not immediately resolve the depression.

Communication Strategies

Maintaining and improving communication despite depression's interference is essential for relationship health. Depression disrupts communication in multiple ways, but deliberate strategies can help maintain connection and understanding.

Creating regular times to talk, even briefly, maintains connection despite depression's tendency to reduce interaction. This might be a daily check-in over breakfast, a walk together after work, or time set aside in the evening. The structure ensures that communication continues even when it feels difficult. These conversations need not always be deep or about the depression; simply maintaining the habit of talking together is valuable.

Being direct and specific about needs and feelings helps overcome communication difficulties. Depression makes reading subtle cues more difficult. Assumptions about what the other person needs or feels often prove inaccurate. Instead, stating directly 'I need some reassurance that you still love me' or 'I am feeling overwhelmed and need some help with household tasks' or 'I need some time alone this evening' reduces misunderstanding and allows more effective responses.

Expressing appreciation and positive feelings, even for small things, helps counteract the negativity of depression. When you are not depressed, you might tell your partner you appreciate them cooking dinner, or you notice them making an effort despite their low mood. When you are depressed, you might need your partner's expressions of love and appreciation because your own negative thinking makes you doubt their feelings. These positive expressions cost little but provide significant benefit for relationship quality.

Avoiding criticism, even when frustrated, is important. Criticism worsens depression, damages self-esteem, and creates conflict. When problems need addressing, using 'I' statements that express your feelings rather than blaming helps. 'I feel lonely when we do not spend time together' is more constructive than 'You never make any effort with me.' 'I am worried about our finances and would like us to look at our budget together' is better than 'You are being irresponsible about money.'

Validating feelings rather than immediately trying to fix or minimise them is a fundamental communication skill. When your partner expresses distress, responding with validation such as 'That sounds really difficult' or 'I can see how much this is affecting you' is often more helpful than immediately jumping to solutions or reassurances such as 'I am sure it is not that bad' or 'Just try to think positively.' Validation acknowledges the person's experience and helps them feel heard and understood.

Negotiating around difficult topics helps manage conflicts constructively. Depression lowers stress tolerance, making conflict more likely and harder to manage. Agreeing on how to handle disagreements helps. This might include taking breaks when emotions escalate, agreeing to discuss difficult topics at particular times rather than in the moment, or establishing that certain topics are temporarily off-limits if they consistently trigger severe distress with no productive resolution.

Maintaining Intimacy and Connection

Sexual intimacy is often affected by depression, with reduced libido being a core symptom for many people. Additionally, antidepressant medications, particularly SSRIs, commonly cause sexual side effects, including reduced desire, difficulty with arousal, or difficulty achieving orgasm. These changes create strain in romantic relationships where sexual connection is an important component of intimacy.

Open communication about sexual difficulties is essential, though often uncomfortable. Avoiding the topic typically worsens relationship strain, with both partners feeling anxious and rejected. Discussing changes in sexual desire or function, acknowledging the difficulty, and problem-solving together are important. Solutions might include adjusting timing or method of sexual activity, exploring non-penetrative intimacy, discussing medication changes with your doctor if side effects are problematic, focusing on emotional and physical closeness through non-sexual touch, or temporarily accepting reduced sexual frequency whilst working on recovery.

Emotional intimacy and connection can be maintained through non-sexual means. Physical affection such as hugging, holding hands, cuddling on the sofa, or massage maintains physical connection without pressure for sexual activity. Shared activities, even quiet ones such as watching a film together or going for a walk, provide togetherness. Small acts of care and kindness such as making tea, leaving notes, or checking in during the day express love and maintain connection.

Accepting that intimacy might look different during the depression episode, whilst maintaining hope that it will improve with recovery, helps both partners adjust expectations without abandoning connection entirely. Flexibility and creativity in finding ways to stay connected that work within current limitations supports the relationship through a difficult period.

Managing Practical Responsibilities

Depression significantly impairs the ability to manage practical responsibilities, including household tasks, childcare, work obligations, and financial management. This creates a practical burden on partners and potential resentment, whilst also creating guilt and inadequacy for the person with depression.

Acknowledging the reality of impairment without blame helps frame conversations about practical responsibilities. 'Depression makes it difficult for you to manage everything right now, and we need to figure out how to distribute tasks differently temporarily' is more constructive than 'You are not pulling your weight.' Recognising this as a health-related difficulty rather than laziness or lack of care reduces blame and facilitates problem-solving.

Redistributing responsibilities temporarily whilst maintaining some engagement for the depressed person supports both practical management and recovery. Completely taking over all responsibilities can reinforce helplessness and reduce self-efficacy, whilst maintaining unrealistic expectations creates overwhelm. Finding a middle ground where the depressed person continues contributing in ways that are manageable whilst the partner or others take on additional load temporarily often works best. As recovery progresses, responsibilities can gradually shift back.

Being specific about what needs doing and breaking tasks into manageable steps helps. Rather than 'The house is a mess,' specify 'Could you load the dishwasher this evening?' Rather than expecting the depressed person to initiate and complete complex tasks, provide structure and support. This reduces cognitive load and increases likelihood of follow-through.

Seeking additional support when needed prevents exhaustion. This might include accepting help from extended family or friends, hiring help for tasks such as cleaning if financially possible, using online shopping and delivery services, reducing standards about how things are done temporarily, or accessing professional support services. Partners supporting someone with depression need support themselves and should not attempt to shoulder everything alone.

When to Seek Relationship Support

Sometimes the combination of depression and relationship difficulties requires professional help beyond individual treatment for depression. Couple therapy or relationship counselling can be valuable in several situations.

If relationship conflict is severe, frequent, or escalating, couples therapy provides a structured setting for addressing difficulties with professional support. Relationship conflict both contributes to depression and is worsened by depression, creating a cycle that is difficult to interrupt without help. A couple therapist can help improve communication, reduce conflict, increase mutual understanding, and develop more effective ways of supporting each other.

If you are considering separation but are uncertain whether difficulties stem from depression or from fundamental relationship incompatibility, couples therapy provides space to explore these questions. Depression can make relationships seem hopeless when they might recover with treatment and support. Conversely, sometimes depression obscures genuine relationship problems that need addressing. Professional help clarifies these issues and supports better decision-making.

If the non-depressed partner is struggling significantly with caring burden, resentment, or their own mental health difficulties, couple therapy validates these experiences and develops strategies to better support both partners. Sometimes partners suppress their own needs to avoid burdening the depressed person, creating their own distress. Therapy creates space to address both partners' needs.

Couple therapy should not replace individual treatment for depression but can complement it. The optimal approach is often individual therapy and medication for the depressed person combined with couple therapy addressing relationship dynamics. This addresses both individual symptoms and relationship patterns that might be maintaining or worsening depression.

Depression and Family Relationships

Family relationships, whether with parents, adult children, siblings, or extended family, are profoundly affected by depression. These relationships often carry long histories, complex dynamics, and strong emotions that influence both the experience of depression and the recovery process. Understanding how depression affects family relationships and how to navigate these challenges is important for maintaining family connections whilst managing your mental health.

Adult Children and Parents

The relationship between adult children and their parents can be complicated by depression on either side. When adult children experience depression, parents often feel a combination of concern, worry, helplessness, and sometimes guilt, wondering if they contributed to their child's difficulties. Parents might struggle to know how to help, oscillating between being overprotective and giving too much space. They might not understand depression, leading to unhelpful comments or advice. Conversely, they might be the most consistent source of practical and emotional support available.

If you are an adult with depression whose parents are involved in your life, communicating with them about what is helpful and what is not can improve the quality of support you receive. Many parents want to help but do not know how. Providing specific guidance such as 'It helps when you check in regularly but do not push me to do things I am not ready for' or 'I need practical help with shopping rather than advice about what I should be doing' allows them to support you more effectively. Setting boundaries when necessary, such as limiting contact if interactions consistently worsen your mood, is also important, though this can be difficult when parents mean well.

When parents experience depression, adult children often feel responsible for their wellbeing, particularly if the parent is elderly or has limited support. This can create significant caregiver burden, particularly if you are also managing your own mental health, work, and family responsibilities. Finding balance between supporting your parent appropriately and maintaining your own wellbeing is essential. This might involve encouraging your parent to access professional help, coordinating support from other family members, accessing carer support services, and being clear about your own limits.

Sibling Relationships

Sibling relationships in adulthood vary enormously, from very close and supportive to distant or conflicted. When you experience depression, some siblings might be important sources of support, understanding your family background and history in ways that others cannot. Other siblings might be unhelpful or unsupportive, minimising your difficulties, competing for family resources or attention, or bringing up old conflicts.

If you have supportive siblings, maintaining and utilising these relationships during depression is valuable. Siblings who understand your family dynamics, who know you well, and who care about you can provide both practical help and emotional support. They might help with caring for parents, understanding family patterns that contribute to your depression, or simply being there during difficult times.

If sibling relationships are strained, depression might exacerbate existing conflicts or create new ones. Siblings might have different understandings of or beliefs about mental health. They might judge you for your difficulties or compare their ability to cope with yours unfavourably. Family gatherings might become sources of stress rather than support. In these situations, it is important to protect yourself by limiting exposure to unhelpful interactions, being selective about what you share, and seeking support primarily from other sources.

Extended Family Relationships

An extended family including grandparents, aunts, uncles, and cousins might play varying roles depending on family culture and closeness. In some families, extended family members are central to daily life and important sources of support. In others, relationships are more distant. Depression might bring you closer to some extended family members while distancing you from others.

Stigma about mental health can be particularly pronounced in extended family, especially in older generations or in cultural contexts where mental health difficulties are poorly understood. You might face unhelpful comments, minimisation of your difficulties, or pressure to hide your depression from extended family. Deciding what to share with extended family, setting boundaries around unhelpful comments, and seeking support from those who are understanding whilst limiting engagement with those who are not, helps protect your wellbeing.

Family Patterns and Depression

Family patterns and dynamics often contribute to depression development and maintenance. Understanding these patterns can inform your recovery work and help you make decisions about family relationships.

Critical family environments where criticism, judgment, and high expectations are prevalent create stress and undermine self-esteem. If your family is characterised by frequent criticism, where achievements are dismissed and failures are emphasised, this contributes to the negative self-view central to depression. Managing criticism involves setting boundaries, limiting exposure when necessary, working on not internalising critical messages through cognitive work, and seeking validation and support from other sources.

Enmeshed families where boundaries between family members are unclear and emotional independence is discouraged can make it difficult to develop a secure sense of self separate from family. If your wellbeing is excessively dependent on family approval, if you feel responsible for family members' emotions, or if you struggle to make decisions independently of family opinion, these patterns might contribute to depression. Developing appropriate boundaries, building identity and self-worth independent of family, and sometimes physically distancing yourself from family can support recovery.

Emotionally distant families where emotional expression is discouraged, where practical care is provided but emotional needs are unmet, and where vulnerability is seen as weakness, create deficits in emotional skills and self-understanding that increase depression vulnerability. If you grew up in such a family, you might struggle to identify or express emotions, might dismiss your own emotional needs, or might lack models for healthy emotional intimacy. Therapy can help develop these skills, as can building close relationships with people who do provide emotional connection.

Family communication patterns characterised by avoidance of conflict, indirectness, or the opposite extreme of constant conflict without resolution, interfere with healthy problem-solving and relationship maintenance. Learning direct, assertive communication, developing conflict resolution skills, and sometimes accepting that certain family relationships will remain dysfunctional despite your efforts, all support better outcomes.

Depression and Friendships

Friendships provide vital social support, companionship, and sense of belonging that protect against depression and support recovery. However, depression significantly affects friendships through social withdrawal, reduced reciprocity, and changes in one's ability to engage socially. Understanding these effects and actively working to maintain friendships despite depression's interference is important.

How Depression Affects Friendships

Social withdrawal is perhaps the most damaging effect of depression on friendships. When you consistently decline invitations, cancel plans, or withdraw from social contact, friends eventually stop reaching out, leading to social isolation precisely when support is most needed. Friends might feel hurt or rejected by your withdrawal, interpreting it as lack of interest in the friendship rather than symptom of illness. Some friends, not understanding depression, might give up on the friendship, whilst others persist but feel increasingly frustrated or worried.

Reduced reciprocity in friendships occurs when depression consumes your emotional and practical resources, leaving little capacity to attend to friends' needs, provide support to them, or contribute to the friendship's give-and-take. Friendships require mutual care and support. When depression makes you unable to fulfil your side of this reciprocity, friendships become imbalanced, which can feel unfair to friends and create guilt for you. Acknowledging this imbalance and expressing appreciation for friends' continued support despite your limited capacity to reciprocate helps maintain goodwill.

Changes in interests and ability to enjoy social activities mean that activities you previously enjoyed with friends no longer appeal. This makes it harder to find common ground for spending time together. If friendships were built primarily around particular activities that you can no longer engage in, maintaining connection becomes more difficult.

Communication difficulties arising from cognitive symptoms, flat affect, reduced verbal output, and difficulty following conversations make social interaction less rewarding for both parties. Conversations might feel stilted or one-sided. Friends might feel they are doing all the work to maintain the interaction. This can lead to reduced contact and weakening of the friendship bond.

Maintaining Friendships During Depression

Actively working to maintain key friendships despite depression's interference requires effort but is worthwhile for both social support benefits and long-term relationship preservation. Several strategies help.

Being honest with close friends about your depression, explaining that your withdrawal or changed behaviour reflects illness rather than lack of care about them, helps maintain understanding and reduces hurt feelings. You need not share all details if you prefer privacy, but acknowledging that you are going through a difficult period and that this affects your availability helps frame your behaviour appropriately. Many friends will be relieved to understand what is happening and will want to support you once they know.

Setting realistic expectations for social engagement allows you to maintain some contact without overwhelming yourself. Rather than trying to maintain pre-depression levels of social activity, which would be impossible, commit to smaller, manageable amounts of contact. This might mean shorter visits, phone calls instead of in-person meetings, one-to-one contact instead of group gatherings, or activities that require less energy, such as watching a film together instead of going out. Some contact is better than complete withdrawal.

Communicating clearly about what support is helpful allows friends to help effectively. If you need practical help, emotional support, distraction, or simply someone to sit with you without expectation of conversation, letting friends know enables them to provide what you actually need rather than guessing. Similarly, being clear about whether you need space prevents friends from feeling rejected if you decline invitations.

Expressing appreciation for friends' support, even when you cannot reciprocate fully, maintains the positive aspects of the friendship and acknowledges their efforts. A simple 'Thank you for checking in, it means a lot even though I cannot talk properly right now' or 'I appreciate you being patient with me' helps friends feel valued despite the current imbalance in the relationship.

Gradually increasing social contact as your mood improves, actively reaching out to friends as you become more able, and working to restore reciprocity demonstrates that you value the friendship and are working toward recovery. Friends who have stood by you during depression deserve acknowledgment and efforts to rebuild the relationship as you recover.

When Friendships End

Despite best efforts, some friendships might not survive depression. Friends who do not understand mental health difficulties, who take your withdrawal personally despite explanations, or who are unwilling or unable to adjust the friendship to accommodate your current needs, might drift away or actively end the friendship. This is painful, particularly when you are already vulnerable and in need of support.

Whilst the loss of friendships during depression is difficult, it is important to recognise that friendships which cannot accommodate you during difficult times might not be the supportive relationships you need. True friends remain supportive through difficult periods, even if the friendship looks different temporarily. Friendships that end might have been more superficial than you realised, might have been based on particular activities that no longer work, or might involve people who lack the capacity for supporting others through difficulties.

Grieving friendship losses is appropriate and important. Allow yourself to feel the sadness and hurt without harsh self-blame. Recognise that some relationship loss might be due to depression's effects on your behaviour, some might be due to others' limitations in understanding or supporting mental health difficulties, and often it is a combination of both. Learning from these experiences about what you need from friendships and what type of friends you want to invest in going forward informs future relationship choices.

Recovery provides opportunities to rebuild existing friendships and develop new ones. As your mood improves and you become more able to engage socially, you can reach out to friends who remained supportive, work to restore friendships that became strained, and pursue new friendships based on current interests and values. Many people find that recovery involves both restoring old relationships and developing new, healthier relationship patterns.

Chapter 10: Depression in the Workplace

Work is a major part of life for most adults, and depression significantly affects work performance, satisfaction, and relationships with colleagues. Understanding how depression affects work, managing work demands whilst depressed, and navigating decisions about disclosure and workplace accommodations are important for protecting both your mental health and your career.

How Depression Affects Work Performance

Managing work demands whilst experiencing depression presents significant challenges. The cognitive symptoms of depression, including difficulty concentrating, reduced working memory, slowed processing speed, and impaired decision-making, directly interfere with work performance. Tasks that previously required little effort now demand intense concentration you cannot sustain. You may read emails or documents multiple times without absorbing their content. Meetings feel overwhelming as you struggle to follow complex discussions or multiple threads of conversation. Decision-making becomes paralysed, even for routine work choices. These cognitive difficulties are not simply a matter of trying harder or being more motivated; they reflect genuine neurobiological impairments associated with depression that improve as depression is treated.

The physical symptoms of depression affect work capacity substantially. Fatigue makes it difficult to sustain energy throughout the workday. You may function adequately for brief periods but find sustained effort impossible. Sleep disturbance means you arrive at work already exhausted, making concentration and productivity even more difficult. Psychomotor slowing affects how quickly you can complete tasks. What previously took one hour might now take two or three hours. Physical symptoms such as headaches, muscle aches, or digestive problems create additional discomfort and distraction. The combination of cognitive and physical symptoms can reduce work productivity by fifty per cent or more in moderate to severe depression.

Emotional symptoms of depression profoundly affect workplace functioning and relationships. Irritability can lead to conflicts with colleagues or supervisiveness responses to feedback. Emotional numbing reduces your capacity for enthusiasm, creativity, or connection with colleagues. Anxiety, which commonly accompanies depression, creates fear of evaluation, avoidance of presentations or meetings, and heightened sensitivity to perceived criticism. Feelings of worthlessness and self-doubt undermine confidence in your abilities and contributions. You may become convinced you are incompetent or about to be fired, even when your performance, whilst reduced from your usual standard, remains acceptable. These emotional difficulties can be as impairing as the cognitive and physical symptoms.

Behavioural changes in depression affect work attendance, punctuality, and engagement. You may struggle to get out of bed in the morning, leading to lateness or absence. Procrastination and avoidance increase as tasks feel overwhelming. You may avoid colleagues, declining lunch invitations or working through breaks to avoid interaction. Reduced initiative means you complete only assigned tasks without the additional contributions or proactive problem-solving you might normally offer. These behavioural changes, whilst understandable symptoms of depression, can be interpreted by others as a lack of commitment or a poor work ethic, particularly if your depression is not disclosed or recognised.

The impact of depression on work performance creates secondary stressors that can worsen depression. Falling behind on work generates anxiety and additional stress. Making mistakes or missing deadlines leads to criticism or disciplinary action, which compounds feelings of worthlessness and failure. Conflict with colleagues or supervisors damages relationships and creates a more stressful work environment. Fear of job loss creates financial anxiety. These secondary consequences of depression-related work difficulties can create a vicious cycle in which work problems worsen depression, which then further impairs work performance. Breaking this cycle often requires addressing both the depression itself and the practical work difficulties it has created.

Workplace culture and environment significantly influence how depression affects work and how manageable it is to continue working whilst depressed. Supportive workplaces with understanding managers, flexible working arrangements, manageable workloads, and cultures that accept mental health difficulties as legitimate health issues make it more feasible to continue working during depression. Hostile or unsupportive workplaces with rigid requirements, excessive workloads, cultures of presenteeism (expectation that employees work even when ill), or stigma around mental health make continuing to work much more difficult and stressful. The workplace environment can either support recovery or maintain and worsen depression.

Reasonable adjustments at work can significantly help manage the impact on work performance. Under the Equality Act 2010, depression can be considered a disability if it has substantial and long-term adverse effects on your ability to carry out normal day-to-day activities. Employers have a legal duty to make reasonable adjustments for disabled employees. Adjustments might include a temporary reduction in hours or workload, flexible working hours to accommodate treatment appointments or difficulty with mornings, working from home some days, modified duties temporarily avoiding the most stressful aspects of the role, additional supervision or support, or allowing more frequent breaks. The adjustments needed will depend on your specific symptoms and circumstances, and should be discussed collaboratively with your employer.

Disclosure of depression to your employer is a significant decision with potential benefits and risks. Benefits of disclosure include accessing workplace support and reasonable adjustments, explaining performance difficulties that might otherwise be misinterpreted, protection under disability discrimination legislation, and potentially reduced stress from hiding your difficulties. Risks include potential discrimination despite legal protections, changed perceptions of your capabilities or reliability, reduced opportunities for promotion or challenging assignments, and concerns about confidentiality. The decision whether to disclose is personal and depends on factors including severity of symptoms, impact on work, relationship with your manager, workplace culture, and your own preferences. There is no single right answer.

If you choose to disclose depression, careful consideration of how, when, and to whom enhances the likelihood of a positive outcome. Disclosing to your immediate line manager first is usually appropriate, though some organisations have dedicated HR staff or occupational health services who may be contacted initially. Preparing for the disclosure conversation by writing down key points ensures you communicate important information clearly despite potential anxiety. Being specific about what you are experiencing and its impact on work, what treatment you are receiving, and what support or adjustments would be helpful provides your manager with clear information to work with. Following up the conversation in writing creates a record and ensures shared understanding.

Occupational health services, available in many larger organisations, provide expert assessment of how health conditions, including depression, affect work capacity and can recommend appropriate adjustments. Occupational health physicians and nurses understand both medical conditions and workplace demands, allowing them to bridge the gap between your health needs and work requirements. They can assess your current capability, recommend reasonable adjustments, advise on fitness for work, and facilitate communication between you, your employer, and your treating clinicians whilst maintaining appropriate confidentiality. Engaging with occupational health, if available, can be valuable in managing the interface between depression and work.

Sick leave is sometimes necessary when depression becomes too severe to work safely or effectively. Continuing to work when severely depressed can worsen symptoms, delay recovery, and increase the risk of serious mistakes or safety incidents. Knowing when to take sick leave involves assessing whether you can perform your role safely and to a minimum acceptable standard whilst managing your health. If depression is so severe that you cannot concentrate, are making serious errors, cannot manage safety-critical tasks, are experiencing acute suicidality, or are simply becoming more ill despite trying to continue working, sick leave may be necessary. Sick leave is not a failure; it is appropriate medical management of a disabling illness.

Returning to work after sick leave for depression requires planning and often benefits from a phased approach. A phased return involves initially working reduced hours or modified duties, gradually increasing over several weeks to full duties. This allows you to rebuild stamina and confidence whilst managing the transition from being off work to full work demands. Maintaining therapeutic activities and support during the return to work is important; returning to work should not mean abandoning the self-care practices, therapy, and support that helped you recover. Clear communication with your employer about your capacity and needs during the return supports a successful transition.

Work-life balance becomes particularly important when managing depression. Long hours, excessive workload, inadequate rest, and work encroaching on personal time all contribute to stress and can trigger or maintain depression. Setting boundaries around work, protecting time for rest and recovery, ensuring adequate sleep, maintaining activities and relationships outside work, and being willing to say no to unreasonable demands all support recovery and prevent relapse. Work is important, but it is not the only important thing. Rebuilding life outside work is an essential part of recovery from depression and creation of a life worth living.

Depression impairs multiple aspects of work performance. Concentration difficulties make complex tasks requiring sustained attention particularly challenging. You might read documents multiple times without retaining information, lose track during meetings, or make errors you would normally catch. Decision-making difficulties interfere with tasks requiring judgment or choices. Memory problems mean you forget tasks, appointments, or conversations, potentially creating problems with colleagues or clients.

Reduced motivation and initiative mean you do the minimum requirements rather than going beyond expectations, you procrastinate on tasks, and you struggle to start work without external pressure. Energy and fatigue problems mean you tire quickly, accomplish less in a day than previously, and may need more breaks or experience reduced productivity, particularly later in the day. These changes are often noticeable to colleagues and supervisors, potentially raising concerns about your performance.

Interpersonal difficulties at work arise from irritability, reduced tolerance for stress, withdrawal from colleagues, difficulty engaging in workplace socialising, and reduced ability to read social cues appropriately. This can strain workplace relationships, reduce teamwork effectiveness, and create reputation problems if colleagues or supervisors interpret these changes as attitude problems rather than symptoms of illness.

Attendance problems commonly occur, including increased sick leave, arriving late or leaving early, or reduced productivity when at work despite physical presence (presenteeism). Whilst taking necessary sick leave is appropriate, excessive absence creates practical problems, might threaten job security, and often worsens depression through guilt and worry about work piling up.

Managing Work Demands

Balancing work responsibilities with mental health needs requires careful judgment. Complete withdrawal from work through extended sick leave is sometimes necessary for severe depression but has its own costs, including financial stress, loss of structure and purpose, potential job loss, and the difficulty of returning to work after a long absence. Conversely, attempting to maintain full performance despite severe depression can worsen symptoms, delay recovery, and lead to breakdown or errors with serious consequences. Finding the right balance depends on depression severity, the nature of your work, and available support.

For many people with moderate depression, continuing work with modifications provides the best balance. Work provides structure, purpose, social contact, and income, all of which support wellbeing, whilst modifications reduce demands to manageable levels. Possible modifications include temporarily reducing hours or workload, adjusting deadlines, shifting to less demanding tasks temporarily, working from home if possible, taking regular short breaks, or adjusting start times to accommodate sleep problems.

Prioritising and simplifying work tasks helps manage cognitive difficulties and reduce energy. Focus on essential tasks, defer non-urgent work, break large tasks into smaller steps, use lists and reminders to compensate for memory problems, and accept that your work might be adequate rather than excellent during this period. Letting go of perfectionism and accepting 'good enough' reduces stress and allows you to maintain work despite depression.

Using available support at work, if comfortable doing so, provides practical and emotional assistance. This might include discussing difficulties with a trusted supervisor or HR representative, accessing employee assistance programmes offering counselling or advice, requesting reasonable adjustments under disability discrimination legislation, or accepting help from colleagues with workload when appropriate. The decision about disclosure is personal and depends on workplace culture, relationships with supervisors, and your assessment of risks versus benefits.

Disclosure Decisions

Deciding whether to disclose depression at work is complex and personal. Disclosure has potential benefits and risks that must be weighed carefully based on your specific circumstances.

Potential benefits of disclosure include access to workplace accommodations and support that might make continuing work more manageable, legal protections under the Equality Act 2010, which considers depression a disability if it has substantial and long-term effects on the ability to carry out normal activities, reduced stress from hiding difficulties, and the possibility of understanding and support from supervisors and colleagues. Some workplaces have supportive cultures around mental health where disclosure is well-received and helpful.

Potential risks include stigma and discrimination, where, despite legal protections, some supervisors or colleagues hold prejudiced views about mental health that might affect how they treat you or assess your performance. Career implications might arise, with concerns about being passed over for promotions or opportunities, or being informally labelled as unreliable. Relationship changes might occur, where colleagues or supervisors interact with you differently after disclosure, either through excessive concern and reduced expectations or through awkwardness and distance. Loss of privacy occurs, as once disclosed, you cannot control who learns about your depression or how that information is used.

Factors to consider when deciding about disclosure include your assessment of workplace culture and likely response, the severity of your symptoms and degree of work impairment, whether accommodations are necessary for you to continue working, your relationship with and trust in your supervisor, legal protections available in your jurisdiction and workplace, and whether you have energy to manage potential negative responses. There is no universally correct answer; the decision depends on your specific situation.

If you decide to disclose, being strategic about how, when, and to whom you disclose provides some control. You might choose to disclose to HR or occupational health rather than your direct supervisor initially. You might disclose the need for accommodations without providing detailed information about your diagnosis. You might disclose selectively to trusted individuals. You can provide only information necessary for getting the support you need rather than full details. Preparing what you will say in advance and considering likely questions helps the conversation go more smoothly.

If you decide not to disclose, you forfeit access to formal workplace supports but maintain privacy and control over information. You might still access support confidentially through employee assistance programmes. You will need to manage symptoms and work demands without workplace accommodations, which might be possible for mild to moderate depression but difficult for severe depression.

Chapter 11: Relapse Prevention and Building Resilience

Recovery from depression is a significant achievement, but for many people, depression has a recurrent pattern. Understanding relapse risk, recognising warning signs, developing a relapse prevention plan, and building long-term resilience help maintain recovery and manage future difficulties more effectively. This chapter focuses on staying well after recovery and responding effectively if symptoms return.

Understanding Relapse Risk

Understanding your personal relapse risk involves examining factors that increase vulnerability to depression recurrence. People who have experienced one episode of major depression have approximately a fifty per cent risk of experiencing another episode at some point in their life. After two episodes, the risk of a third episode increases to approximately seventy per cent. After three or more episodes, the risk of further episodes is approximately ninety per cent. This does not mean recurrence is inevitable, but it does mean that ongoing attention to relapse prevention is important. Understanding your specific risk factors allows you to target prevention efforts appropriately. (Hardeveld et al., 2010)

Residual symptoms following treatment of a depressive episode are one of the strongest predictors of relapse. If you still experience some symptoms of depression even though you are significantly better than at your worst, these persistent symptoms create vulnerability to full relapse. Residual symptoms might include low-level persistent low mood, reduced interest in activities, though not complete anhedonia, fatigue, sleep difficulties, or negative thinking patterns that are improved but not fully resolved. Research demonstrates that achieving full remission, meaning a virtual absence of symptoms, significantly reduces relapse risk compared to achieving only partial response. This is why continuing treatment until symptoms have fully resolved, rather than stopping as soon as you feel somewhat better, is important.

Life stress and adverse events increase the risk of depression onset and recurrence. Major stressful life events such as bereavement, relationship breakdown, job loss, serious illness, or significant financial difficulties can trigger depressive episodes in vulnerable individuals. However, the relationship between stress and depression is complex. Not everyone exposed to stress becomes depressed, and depression can occur in the absence of obvious stressors. The impact of stress depends on how it is perceived and coped with, the resources available to manage it, and individual vulnerability based on previous experiences, genetic factors, and current circumstances. Building stress management skills and resilience reduces the likelihood that stress will trigger depression.

Poor sleep is both a symptom and a risk factor for depression. Sleep disturbance often persists after other symptoms of depression have improved and can trigger relapse if not addressed. Chronic insufficient sleep impairs emotional regulation, reduces cognitive function, affects appetite and metabolism, and increases stress hormone levels. All of these effects increase vulnerability to depression. Prioritising good sleep hygiene, maintaining consistent sleep-wake times, addressing sleep disorders if present, and seeking help for persistent sleep problems are important aspects of relapse prevention. Sleep is not a luxury; it is a fundamental requirement for mental health.

Substance use, particularly alcohol, increases depression risk and relapse risk. Whilst alcohol may provide temporary relief from distress, it is a central nervous system depressant that worsens mood over time. Heavy drinking disrupts sleep, interferes with medication effectiveness if you are taking antidepressants, impairs judgment and problem-solving, creates additional life problems, and can trigger depressive episodes. Other substances, including cannabis, stimulants, and sedatives, also affect mood and brain function in ways that increase depression vulnerability. Moderating alcohol use and avoiding other recreational drugs supports a stable mood and reduces relapse risk.

Discontinuing antidepressant medication prematurely is a significant risk factor for relapse. Antidepressants should generally be continued for at least six to twelve months after full recovery from a depressive episode, and longer-term or indefinite treatment may be recommended for people with recurrent depression. Stopping medication abruptly or too soon after recovery leads to high rates of relapse. When the time comes to discontinue medication, this should be done very gradually over several months under medical supervision. Some people benefit from indefinite antidepressant treatment to prevent recurrence, just as people with other chronic conditions take medication long-term to prevent relapse.

Dropping psychological therapy or self-help practices as soon as you feel better is another common path to relapse. The skills and strategies learned in therapy need to become integrated into ongoing life, not abandoned once you feel better. Regular practice of behavioural activation, cognitive restructuring, mindfulness, or other skills that helped you recover maintains their benefits and provides ongoing protection against relapse. Many people find it helpful to have occasional booster sessions with their therapist after the main course of therapy has ended, particularly during stressful periods or when they notice early warning signs of depression returning.

Social isolation and relationship difficulties both predict depression relapse. Humans are social beings; we need connection, support, and belonging for well-being. Depression creates a tendency towards withdrawal and isolation, which then maintains depression and increases relapse risk. Maintaining and building social connections, working on important relationships, seeking social support when needed, and participating in social or group activities all protect against relapse. Relationships do not need to be numerous to be protective; a few close, supportive relationships are more beneficial than many superficial connections. Quality of relationships matters more than quantity.

Neglecting physical health increases vulnerability to depression relapse. Regular physical activity, adequate nutrition, consistent sleep, management of chronic health conditions, attending to medical and dental needs, and avoiding excessive alcohol or substance use all support mood stability. Physical and mental health are interconnected; neglecting one undermines the other. Physical health may feel like a low priority when you are busy or stressed, but it is foundational to resilience and wellbeing. Building physical health into routine life through sustainable, enjoyable habits is more effective than periodic, intense but unsustainable efforts.

Returning to environments, situations, or patterns that contributed to previous depression without adequate support or coping strategies increases relapse risk. If work stress contributed to your depression, returning to the same overwhelming workload without changes creates risk. If relationship problems were a factor, remaining in the same problematic relationship patterns without addressing them maintains vulnerability. If social isolation was a problem, falling back into isolated patterns recreates risk. This does not mean you must change everything in your life, but it does mean identifying what contributed to depression and making changes where possible or developing better ways of managing unchangeable difficulties.

Perfectionism and self-criticism are personality traits that predict depression onset and recurrence. Holding unrealistically high standards for yourself, being unable to accept good enough, engaging in harsh self-criticism, deriving self-worth primarily from achievement, and difficulty accepting imperfection or failure all create vulnerability. Working on these patterns through therapy, particularly schema-focused therapy or compassion-focused therapy, can reduce relapse risk. Developing self-compassion, accepting your humanity, including imperfection and limitation, deriving worth from your inherent value as a person rather than from achievements, and learning to be kind to yourself are protective factors.

Rumination, the tendency to repetitively focus on symptoms, problems, and their causes without moving towards solutions, is a strong predictor of depression onset and persistence. People who ruminate in response to low mood are more likely to develop full depressive episodes and to experience longer episodes. Breaking the rumination habit through mindfulness, deliberately redirecting attention, engaging in absorbing activities, and learning to recognise and interrupt rumination reduces risk. Rumination feels like it should be helpful, like you are working through problems, but research shows it actually maintains distress without producing solutions. Recognising rumination as unhelpful rather than necessary is an important insight.

Depression commonly recurs. After a first episode of depression, approximately 50 per cent of people experience at least one further episode. After two episodes, the risk of further episodes increases to around 70 to 80 per cent. After three or more episodes, the risk approaches 90 per cent. These statistics highlight that maintaining vigilance and having relapse prevention strategies is important for most people who have experienced depression.

Several factors affect relapse risk. The number of previous episodes is the strongest predictor, with each episode increasing the risk of future episodes. This might reflect biological changes, psychological vulnerabilities, or life circumstances, but practically, it means that people with recurrent depression need particularly robust relapse prevention plans. Incomplete recovery from the most recent episode, where residual symptoms persist, substantially increases relapse risk. Achieving full symptom resolution and maintaining it for several months provides a more stable foundation.

Discontinuing treatment too soon is a major relapse risk. Both antidepressant medication and psychological therapy should be continued for a sufficient duration after symptoms resolve. For medication, this typically means continuing for at least six to twelve months after recovery, or longer for recurrent depression. For psychological therapy, completing a full course even after feeling better and potentially engaging in maintenance or booster sessions provides ongoing benefit. The temptation to stop treatment once feeling better is understandable, but it often leads to relapse.

Stressful life events, particularly those involving loss, humiliation, or entrapment, can trigger depression recurrence just as they can trigger initial episodes. Whilst you cannot prevent all stressful events, developing effective coping strategies, maintaining social support, and recognising vulnerability during stressful periods allows for more effective management. Accumulated minor stressors can also contribute to relapse risk, highlighting the importance of ongoing stress management.

Failure to maintain helpful behaviours learned during treatment is common after recovery. When symptoms resolve, people often gradually discontinue behaviours that supported recovery, such as regular exercise, behavioural activation, sleep hygiene practices, or cognitive monitoring. This gradual drift away from helpful practices increases vulnerability. Making these practices permanent lifestyle changes rather than temporary interventions reduces relapse risk.

Recognising Warning Signs

Early recognition of warning signs that depression might be returning allows intervention before a full relapse occurs. Each person has somewhat unique warning signs, though common patterns exist. Identifying your personal warning signs through reflection on previous episodes and ongoing self-monitoring is important.

Common early warning signs include changes in sleep patterns, which are often among the first signs of returning depression. This might be difficulty falling asleep, waking during the night, early morning waking, or sleeping more than usual. Whilst occasional sleep problems are normal, persistent changes over several days warrant attention. Similarly, subtle mood changes such as increased sadness, irritability, anxiety, or loss of enjoyment that persist over days to weeks might signal emerging depression. These changes might be mild initially but represent movement away from the recovered baseline.

Behavioural warning signs include gradual withdrawal from activities, declining social invitations more frequently, procrastination increasing, exercise or other healthy routines slipping, or self-care declining. These behavioural changes both signal emerging depression and contribute to it, making intervention particularly important. Cognitive warning signs include increased negative thinking, self-criticism returning, rumination increasing, difficulty concentrating emerging, or decision-making becoming harder. Noticing these thought patterns allows cognitive strategies to be re-implemented before they become entrenched.

Physical warning signs beyond sleep changes might include energy declining, appetite changes, physical tension increasing, or unexplained aches and pains. Social warning signs include relationship conflicts increasing, feeling increasingly distant from others, or support systems deteriorating. Stress warning signs include feeling overwhelmed by demands that previously felt manageable, minor problems feeling like major crises, or coping strategies feeling less effective.

Keeping a symptom monitoring log or using mood tracking apps provides objective information about patterns that might otherwise be missed. Weekly check-ins where you systematically review symptoms, activities, sleep, social contact, and stress levels help detect gradual changes. Having trusted others who know your warning signs and can provide feedback if they notice changes offers additional monitoring, as we are not always the best judges of our own state.

Developing a Relapse Prevention Plan

A relapse prevention plan is a written document outlining your warning signs, coping strategies, and specific actions to take if you notice signs of returning depression. Creating this plan whilst you are well, when thinking clearly and able to plan effectively, provides a resource you can turn to if symptoms begin returning, when clear thinking might be compromised.

Your relapse prevention plan should begin by listing your personal warning signs in detail. Include behavioural changes, cognitive changes, emotional changes, physical changes, and social changes that typically signal emerging depression for you. Be specific rather than vague. For example, 'declining invitations to the weekly book club more than twice in a month' is more useful than 'social withdrawal.' You might organise warning signs by urgency, distinguishing between early subtle signs and more serious indicators requiring immediate action.

The plan should list specific coping strategies that have helped you in the past, organised by domain. For behavioural strategies, list specific activities you should increase or maintain, such as 'go for a 30-minute walk at least four times per week' or 'schedule one social activity per week.' For cognitive strategies, note techniques that help, such as 'complete thought record when notice increased self-criticism' or 'review list of cognitive distortions.' For self-care strategies, specify sleep hygiene practices, nutrition goals, or stress management techniques. For social strategies, identify who you should reach out to and how.

Include clear action steps matched to warning signs. For mild warning signs, actions might include reinstating behavioural activation strategies, increasing monitoring of symptoms, reviewing materials from therapy, or practising relaxation techniques more regularly. For moderate warning signs, actions might include contacting your GP or therapist for an appointment, implementing more intensive coping strategies, reducing workload temporarily, or increasing support from friends and family. For severe warning signs or crises, include emergency contacts and clear instructions for accessing immediate help.

Specify what help you need from others and from whom. Identify trusted friends, family members, or colleagues whom you can ask for support, specifying what type of support each person can best provide. Include contact information for professional supports including your GP, therapist, crisis services, and emergency contacts. Give key people copies of your relapse prevention plan if you are comfortable doing so, enabling them to help you recognise and respond to warning signs.

Include information about medication, including names, doses, prescriber contact information, and plans for what to do if symptoms return. This might include instructions to restart medication you have discontinued, contact your GP to discuss medication adjustment, or take medication more regularly if you have been somewhat inconsistent. Note any previous medication side effects or problems so these can be avoided in future.

Review and update your relapse prevention plan regularly, perhaps every six months, or after any significant change in circumstances or symptoms. Plans developed after a first episode might need updating after experiencing subsequent episodes and learning more about your pattern. Changes in life circumstances, available supports, or treatment options should be reflected in plan updates. Periodic review keeps the plan current and keeps relapse prevention active in your awareness.

Maintaining Recovery

Maintaining recovery requires ongoing attention and effort rather than assuming that once recovered, no further work is needed. Several strategies help maintain well-being and prevent relapse over the long term.

Continue treatment for an appropriate duration even after symptoms resolve. For medication, this typically means at least six to twelve months after recovery, and longer for recurrent depression or high relapse risk. Many people with recurrent depression benefit from longer-term or even indefinite maintenance medication. The decision about treatment duration should be made collaboratively with your prescriber, weighing relapse risk against medication burden. If discontinuing medication, do so gradually under medical supervision rather than abruptly, as sudden discontinuation increases relapse risk.

For psychological therapy, completing a full course even after symptoms improve consolidates skills and addresses underlying vulnerabilities. Booster sessions at intervals after the main treatment ends provide ongoing support and allow early intervention if difficulties emerge. Some people benefit from ongoing therapy at reduced frequency for continued monitoring and skill refinement.

Integrate helpful behaviours into permanent lifestyle patterns rather than discontinuing them once recovered. Regular exercise, behavioural activation principles, sleep hygiene practices, mindfulness, cognitive monitoring, social engagement, and stress management should become ongoing habits. Whilst the intensity might reduce compared to acute treatment phase, maintaining these practices provides ongoing protective benefits. Consider which practices are most important for your wellbeing and commit to maintaining them permanently.

Continue monitoring your mood and functioning, even when well. This need not be intensive daily monitoring but regular check-ins, perhaps weekly, where you assess mood, sleep, activity levels, social engagement, and stress. Noticing gradual deterioration early allows intervention before full relapse. Various apps facilitate mood tracking, though simple written logs work equally well.

Maintain and strengthen social connections. Social isolation is a major depression risk factor, so deliberately maintaining relationships, engaging socially regularly even when tempted to withdraw, and building new relationships provides ongoing protective benefit. Invest in relationships that provide genuine support and reciprocity. Address relationship difficulties proactively rather than allowing conflicts to accumulate.

Develop and maintain meaning and purpose in life. Depression often involves loss of meaning and purpose. Recovery involves rediscovering or developing engagement with valued activities, relationships, goals, and commitments that provide life with direction and significance. This might involve work that feels meaningful, volunteering, creative pursuits, spiritual or religious engagement, political or social activism, deep relationships, or the pursuit of personal growth. Having reasons to engage with life beyond just the absence of depression supports sustained wellbeing.

Continue developing skills and self-understanding. Recovery is not just a return to pre-depression functioning but an opportunity for growth, learning about yourself, developing new skills, and building greater resilience. Ongoing learning about mental health, self-reflection about patterns and triggers, development of emotional intelligence, and cultivation of psychological flexibility all contribute to long-term wellbeing beyond just preventing relapse.

If Depression Returns

Despite best efforts at prevention, depression might return. This is not failure. It reflects the recurrent nature of depression for many people. How you respond to returning symptoms significantly affects the severity and duration of the episode.

Recognise and acknowledge returning symptoms promptly rather than denying them or hoping they will spontaneously resolve. Early intervention when symptoms are mild is far more effective than waiting until symptoms are severe. Use your relapse prevention plan to guide your response. Review your warning signs and match your current symptoms to the actions you have specified.

Seek professional help early. Contact your GP, therapist, or psychiatrist as soon as you recognise returning symptoms rather than waiting to see if things improve on their own. If you have discontinued medication, this might be restarted. If you are on medication, the dose might be adjusted. If you have finished therapy, you might restart or have booster sessions. Early professional involvement prevents escalation.

Reinstate coping strategies that helped previously. Return to behavioural activation, reinstate helpful routines, increase physical activity, improve sleep hygiene, practise cognitive strategies, use mindfulness techniques, increase social engagement, and reduce unnecessary stress. You know what helps because you have been through this before. Draw on that knowledge systematically.

Be compassionate with yourself rather than self-critical about experiencing relapse. Harsh self-judgment worsens depression and is not helpful. Recognise that depression sometimes recurs despite best efforts, that this does not negate your previous recovery or mean you are failing, and that you have successfully recovered before and can do so again. Self-compassion supports recovery more effectively than self-criticism.

Adjust expectations and demands temporarily. Just as during initial depression, you might need to reduce workload, simplify responsibilities, increase support from others, and lower standards for what you accomplish. Accepting these temporary adjustments rather than maintaining unrealistic expectations reduces stress and allows focus on recovery.

Use the supports available to you. Reach out to friends and family you have identified as helpful. Access workplace accommodations if needed. Contact support services. Having experienced depression before, you likely have a better understanding of what helps and can mobilise support more effectively.

Remember that you have recovered before and can recover again. Previous recovery demonstrates that recovery is possible for you. Even if this episode feels as difficult as previous ones, your experience of coming through depression successfully provides hope and confidence that recovery will occur again. Draw on this knowledge during difficult moments.

Building Long-Term Resilience

Resilience, the ability to adapt to and recover from adversity, stress, and difficult experiences, can be developed and strengthened over time. Building resilience does not eliminate the risk of future depression, but reduces risk and supports more effective coping when difficulties arise.

Developing flexible thinking patterns enhances resilience. This involves recognising that thoughts are interpretations rather than facts, being able to generate alternative perspectives on situations, avoiding all-or-nothing thinking, and accepting uncertainty and ambiguity. Psychological flexibility, the ability to be present in the moment, open to experience, and to take valued action even in the presence of difficult thoughts and feelings, is a core component of resilience developed through acceptance and mindfulness practices.

Building self-efficacy, the belief in your own ability to cope with challenges and influence outcomes, is central to resilience. This develops through successfully managing difficulties, setting achievable goals and accomplishing them, recognising your own competence and contributions, and learning from setbacks rather than being defeated by them. Each time you successfully cope with a challenge, even a small one, your self-efficacy grows.

Maintaining physical health supports mental health resilience. Regular exercise, adequate sleep, good nutrition, and management of chronic health conditions all contribute to the capacity to cope with stress. Whilst perfect health is not possible for everyone, working within your capacities to support physical wellbeing provides a foundation for mental resilience.

Nurturing relationships and social connections provides social support that buffers against stress. Investing in relationships, being available to support others as well as receiving support, resolving conflicts constructively, and building a network of supportive relationships creates social resources you can draw on during difficult times. Loneliness increases vulnerability, whilst connection promotes resilience.

Engaging in valued activities and pursuing meaningful goals provides purpose and direction that sustains motivation during difficult periods. When life feels meaningful and you are engaged in activities you value, you are more resilient in the face of setbacks. This might involve work, family, hobbies, creative pursuits, helping others, spiritual or religious engagement, or personal development. What matters is that activities feel personally significant.

Developing effective coping strategies and knowing when to use them is central to resilience. This includes problem-solving for changeable difficulties, acceptance for unchangeable situations, emotional regulation skills, stress management techniques, and knowing when to seek help. The skills you have learned through treatment for depression are skills for life, applicable to future challenges beyond just preventing depression.

Maintaining perspective during difficulties involves recognising that most difficulties are temporary, that you have survived difficult times before, that this difficult period does not define your entire life, and that growth often emerges from adversity. Whilst perspective alone does not eliminate suffering, it prevents catastrophising and maintains hope during difficult periods.

Practising gratitude, taking time to notice and appreciate positive aspects of life even during difficult periods, has been shown to improve wellbeing and resilience. This is not about denying difficulties or forcing positivity, but about balancing attention to problems with attention to the good things in your life, however small. Regular gratitude practise, such as noting three things you are grateful for each day, can shift attention patterns in helpful ways.

Chapter 12: Depression in Specific Life Circumstances

Whilst the core features and treatment approaches for depression are consistent across situations, specific life circumstances create unique challenges and considerations. This section addresses depression as it manifests in particular contexts, providing tailored guidance for these situations.

Managing Depression with Chronic Physical Health Conditions

The relationship between depression and physical health conditions is bidirectional and complex. Chronic physical health conditions substantially increase depression risk, with rates of depression in people with chronic illness approximately three times higher than in the general population. Conversely, depression adversely affects physical health through multiple pathways. Understanding this relationship and managing both conditions effectively is crucial for wellbeing.

Chronic physical health conditions contribute to depression through several mechanisms. Chronic pain, fatigue, disability, and physical symptoms are inherently distressing and limit activities that provide pleasure and meaning. Loss of function and independence affects self-concept and requires adaptation to changed capabilities. Uncertainty about disease course and prognosis creates anxiety. Physical limitations might reduce work capacity, affecting financial security and sense of purpose. Treatment burdens, including frequent appointments, medication regimens, and medical procedures, create stress. Social isolation might increase if illness limits mobility or if others withdraw due to discomfort with illness. Biological processes of illness, including inflammation and effects on stress hormones, directly influence mood regulation.

Depression, in turn, worsens physical health outcomes. Depression increases pain perception and pain-related disability. It reduces treatment adherence, with depressed people less likely to take medications consistently, attend appointments, or follow treatment recommendations. Depression impairs immune function, potentially affecting disease course. It increases inflammation, relevant for multiple chronic conditions. Depression reduces engagement in health-promoting behaviours, including exercise, healthy eating, and smoking cessation. The combination of depression and chronic illness creates worse outcomes than either condition alone.

Treatment of depression in the context of chronic physical illness follows standard evidence-based approaches but requires integration with physical health management. Antidepressant medication can be used safely with most chronic physical conditions, though attention to drug interactions with medications for physical health is necessary. Some physical health conditions or their treatments might limit medication choices. For instance, some pain medications interact with certain antidepressants, some physical conditions might be worsened by particular antidepressant side effects, and dose adjustments might be needed for kidney or liver impairment. These considerations require close collaboration between mental health prescribers and physical health physicians.

Psychological therapy for depression with comorbid physical illness addresses both standard depression symptoms and illness-specific challenges. Cognitive work might focus on thoughts about the physical condition, its implications, and one's capacity to cope. Behavioural activation must be adapted to physical limitations, identifying activities that are meaningful and enjoyable whilst being physically achievable. Problem-solving addresses challenges specific to managing chronic illness. Acceptance and mindfulness approaches help with tolerating unpleasant physical symptoms and uncertainty. Grief work might be necessary when illness involves significant losses of function, role, or life plans.

Several cognitive themes are common when depression accompanies chronic illness. Beliefs about being damaged, diminished, or less valuable due to illness are frequent. 'I am not the person I used to be' or 'I have nothing to offer anymore' reflect difficulty adjusting to changed circumstances and maintaining a sense of worth despite limitations. Cognitive work involves recognising that whilst circumstances have changed, core worth and identity persist, and that value exists beyond what you can physically do. Identifying ways to continue expressing values and engaging meaningfully within current constraints supports adjustment.

Anger and resentment about the unfairness of illness, particularly if the illness onset was early or the disease is progressive, are common and valid. However, ruminating on unfairness maintains distress without leading to resolution. Acceptance work, distinguishing between accepting the reality of illness versus resigning to poor quality of life, and focusing energy on aspects of life that can be influenced rather than dwelling on what cannot be changed, supports better adjustment. This does not mean you must be happy about illness or pretend limitations do not matter, but rather involves acknowledging reality whilst still finding meaningful engagement with life.

Guilt about burden on others, particularly family members who provide care or take on additional responsibilities, is common and contributes to depression. Whilst recognising the impact on others is appropriate, excessive guilt is unhelpful. Cognitive work examines whether illness is truly your fault (it is not), whether others' willingness to help indicates their care for you (it does), and whether you would judge someone else as harshly for needing help (you would not). Expressing appreciation for support, contributing in ways you can, and accepting help with graciousness rather than excessive guilt maintains relationships whilst acknowledging your needs.

Catastrophic thinking about disease progression, worst-case scenarios, and future deterioration is common and understandable, but increases distress without improving outcomes. Cognitive restructuring examines whether predictions are facts or fears, whether worst-case scenarios are the only possibilities or if better outcomes are also possible, and whether focusing on frightening possibilities helps or hinders coping. Shifting focus to managing current challenges rather than dwelling on uncertain future scenarios reduces anxiety whilst still allowing appropriate planning for realistic possibilities.

Behavioural activation with chronic physical conditions requires creativity and flexibility. Physical limitations might prevent previous activities, necessitating the identification of new activities that provide similar psychological benefits within current capabilities. If you previously exercised through running but can no longer do so, swimming, chair exercises, or gentle walking might provide similar physical and mood benefits. If social activities previously involved going out but mobility is now limited, hosting friends at home, video calls, or online social participation maintains connection. The psychological functions of activities matter more than the specific forms they take.

Pacing becomes particularly important when physical conditions involve fatigue or pain. This involves balancing activity with rest, breaking tasks into smaller chunks, prioritising the most important activities, and accepting that you might accomplish less in a day than previously. Learning your energy envelope, the amount of activity sustainable without triggering symptom flares, and working consistently within that envelope prevents the boom-bust cycle of overexertion followed by extended recovery periods. Pacing is not laziness but intelligent management of limited energy resources.

Pain management integrates with depression treatment when chronic pain is present. Pain and depression have overlapping neurobiological mechanisms and mutually reinforce each other. Addressing both simultaneously produces better outcomes than treating either alone. Cognitive approaches help modify catastrophic thinking about pain, reduce pain-related fear and avoidance, and improve sense of control. Behavioural approaches, including graduated activity despite pain, pain-reduction techniques such as relaxation and distraction, and pacing, reduce pain-related disability. Mindfulness helps change the relationship to pain sensations, observing pain without constant resistance and distress. These psychological approaches complement medical pain management.

Collaborating with your healthcare team to optimise management of your physical condition supports both physical and mental health. This might include ensuring medications are optimised, exploring additional treatment options that might reduce symptoms or improve functioning, accessing rehabilitation services such as physiotherapy or occupational therapy, or consulting specialists for particular aspects of your condition. Physical symptom control provides the foundation on which psychological recovery becomes more possible.

Connect with others managing similar physical health conditions through support groups or online communities. Shared experience reduces isolation, provides practical tips for managing both the physical condition and emotional challenges, and offers understanding from people who truly comprehend your situation. However, be selective about groups, as some might reinforce helplessness or negative thinking. Seek groups that balance acknowledging difficulties with maintaining hope and focusing on effective coping.

Depression and Anxiety: Managing Co-occurring Conditions

Depression and anxiety commonly co-occur, with approximately 50 to 60 per cent of people with depression also meeting criteria for an anxiety disorder. This comorbidity is the rule rather than the exception and creates particular challenges for treatment and recovery. Understanding how depression and anxiety interact and how to address both conditions simultaneously is important for effective management.

Depression and anxiety share substantial overlap in symptoms, neurobiology, and psychological processes. Both involve negative thinking patterns, though with different content and focus. Both involve behavioural avoidance, though for different reasons. Both are associated with alterations in similar neurotransmitter systems. Both respond to similar treatments including cognitive behavioural therapy and particular classes of medication. This overlap means that treatments addressing one condition often benefit the other, though specific attention to each is also necessary.

The negative thinking in depression focuses predominantly on the past and present, involving rumination about losses, failures, and current deficits. The negative thinking in anxiety focuses predominantly on the future, involving worry about potential threats, dangers, and negative outcomes. When depression and anxiety coexist, thinking becomes negatively biased across all time perspectives: regrets about the past, dissatisfaction with the present, and dread about the future. This comprehensive negative thinking is particularly distressing and requires systematic cognitive work across all three temporal domains.

Behavioural avoidance, central to both conditions, operates through different mechanisms but creates similar consequences. In anxiety, avoidance is driven by fear of particular situations, activities, or sensations, with avoidance providing short-term anxiety relief whilst maintaining fear in the long term by preventing discovery that feared outcomes do not occur. In depression, avoidance is driven by lack of motivation, energy, and pleasure, with avoidance providing short-term relief from effort whilst maintaining depression by removing sources of pleasure, achievement, and activation. When conditions coexist, avoidance is overdetermined by both mechanisms, making it particularly entrenched.

Treatment of comorbid depression and anxiety requires integrated approaches addressing both conditions. Cognitive behavioural therapy, effective for both depression and anxiety, provides an ideal framework. Behavioural activation addresses depressive withdrawal whilst graduated exposure addresses anxious avoidance. These approaches complement each other, with behavioural activation increasing general activity levels and exposure systematically addressing specific feared situations. Cognitive restructuring addresses both depressive and anxious thinking, identifying and modifying characteristic thinking patterns of each condition.

For behavioural activation with comorbid anxiety, attention to anxiety triggers and anxious avoidance is important. Your activity schedule should include not only activities that provide pleasure and achievement but also activities you have been avoiding due to anxiety. These anxiety-related activities should be approached gradually, starting with less anxiety-provoking situations and building toward more challenging ones as confidence increases. Each approach to anxiety-provoking situations represents both behavioural activation for depression and exposure for anxiety, creating synergistic benefits.

For cognitive work with both conditions, it helps to identify whether particular negative thoughts reflect primarily depressive or anxious thinking. 'I will fail' reflects anxious prediction, whilst 'I am a failure' reflects depressive interpretation. 'Something terrible will happen' reflects anxiety, whilst 'Nothing good ever happens' reflects depression. Identifying the nature of thoughts guides the most appropriate restructuring approach. For anxious predictions, examining likelihood and evidence for predictions, considering alternative outcomes, and behaviourally testing predictions through exposure are effective. For depressive interpretations, examining evidence for and against beliefs about self, situation, and world, identifying thinking errors, and developing more balanced perspectives are central.

Worry and rumination, whilst distinct, share the feature of repetitive, perseverative thinking that maintains distress. Worry involves anxious anticipation of future threats, whilst rumination involves depressive focus on past losses and current problems. Both are attempts to solve problems mentally, but rarely lead to resolution or constructive action. Addressing both through similar strategies is effective. These strategies include scheduled worry or rumination time that contains these processes to limited periods rather than allowing them to dominate the day, mindfulness practices that create distance from thought content, and shifting from passive repetitive thinking to active problem-solving when problems are actually addressable.

Medication for comorbid depression and anxiety often involves selective serotonin reuptake inhibitors (SSRIs), which are effective for both conditions. Serotonin-noradrenaline reuptake inhibitors (SNRIs) are also used. These medications typically require several weeks to produce a full effect and might cause a temporary increase in anxiety symptoms during the first couple of weeks, which should be anticipated and managed rather than leading to premature discontinuation. Benzodiazepines might provide short-term relief of severe anxiety, but are not appropriate for long-term use due to dependence risk, and should not be considered a solution to comorbid depression and anxiety.

Physical anxiety symptoms, including rapid heartbeat, shortness of breath, muscle tension, sweating, and trembling, require specific management. These symptoms often maintain anxiety through creating fear of the symptoms themselves and through being misinterpreted as signs of serious physical danger. Learning that these symptoms, whilst uncomfortable, are not dangerous, are understandable physiological responses to perceived threat, and can be tolerated without catastrophic consequences, reduces fear of symptoms. Techniques including controlled breathing, progressive muscle relaxation, and mindfulness of body sensations help manage physical anxiety symptoms whilst reducing their capacity to trigger fear.

Sleep disturbance, common in both depression and anxiety, requires particular attention when conditions coexist. Anxiety often causes difficulty falling asleep due to worry and physical tension, whilst depression often causes early morning waking or hypersomnia. The sleep management strategies discussed earlier in this book apply, with particular emphasis on wind-down routines that reduce anxiety before bed, management of racing thoughts and worry, and careful sleep hygiene. Adequate sleep supports recovery from both conditions and reduces vulnerability to symptom worsening.

When both depression and anxiety are present, determining which to prioritise in treatment can be challenging. In general, addressing them simultaneously through integrated CBT approaches is most effective. However, if one condition is substantially more severe or functionally impairing, initial emphasis on that condition whilst maintaining attention to the other might be appropriate. As each condition improves, the other often improves as well due to shared mechanisms. Consultation with a therapist helps establish appropriate treatment priorities for your specific situation.

Seasonal Patterns and Environmental Factors in Depression Management

Beyond seasonal affective disorder specifically, many people with depression notice that symptoms fluctuate with seasons or are influenced by environmental factors such as weather, light exposure, and outdoor versus indoor time. Understanding and working with these patterns supports recovery and ongoing management.

Daylight exposure influences mood through multiple mechanisms including effects on circadian rhythms, melatonin suppression, and possibly direct effects on mood-regulating brain systems. Reduced daylight exposure during winter, whether due to shorter days or due to indoor lifestyle, can worsen depression symptoms. Maximising natural light exposure throughout the year supports mood regulation. This involves spending time outdoors during daylight hours when possible, sitting near windows when indoors, keeping curtains and blinds open to allow natural light in, and arranging workspaces to maximise natural light exposure.

During winter months or during extended periods of poor weather, deliberate strategies to maintain light exposure and activity levels counteract mood worsening. This might include scheduling outdoor walks even in poor weather, using bright indoor lighting, particularly in the morning, considering a light therapy box if significant winter mood worsening is a pattern, maintaining exercise despite less appealing weather, and planning enjoyable indoor activities that provide pleasure and achievement when outdoor activities are less accessible.

Seasonal changes in activity patterns affect mood. Summer naturally facilitates outdoor activity, social engagement, and varied activities, all of which support mood. Winter reduces these activities, partly due to weather making them less appealing and partly due to cultural patterns around winter activity. Consciously maintaining activity levels and variety throughout the year rather than allowing winter to become a period of reduced engagement supports a more stable mood. This requires deliberate planning and effort to counteract natural tendencies to reduce activity when the weather is poor.

Some people notice mood worsening during particular seasons for psychological reasons beyond light and activity. If significant negative events occurred during particular months or seasons, anniversary reactions might occur where mood declines at those times without conscious awareness of the connection. Identifying such patterns through mood monitoring over the years and preparing for vulnerable periods with increased self-care and coping strategies helps manage these predictable difficulties.

Time spent in natural environments, sometimes called nature exposure or green time, has demonstrated benefits for mood and mental health. Time in parks, gardens, the countryside, near water, or other natural settings reduces stress, improves mood, and supports recovery from mental fatigue. This benefits people with depression even when their mood is too low to notice or appreciate the positive effects consciously. Building regular nature exposure into your routine, whether through walks in parks, gardening, or simply sitting in green spaces, provides a simple, accessible intervention with no downside.

For people living in urban environments with limited access to nature, small doses matter. Even a brief time in small green spaces, bringing plants into your home, looking at natural scenes, or spending time near water features provides some benefit. Using outdoor spaces available to you regularly, even if not ideal natural environments, is better than avoiding outdoor time entirely because perfect nature exposure is not accessible.

Weather conditions beyond seasonal patterns affect mood and activity for many people. Prolonged periods of grey, rainy weather can lower mood, whilst sunny weather tends to improve mood. Extreme heat or cold might limit outdoor activity and affect sleep. Whilst you cannot control the weather, you can prepare for its effects. On particularly grey days, increase indoor activities that support mood, use bright indoor lighting, engage in social contact, and avoid assuming low mood is permanent rather than weather-influenced. On hot days that disrupt sleep, implement cooling strategies for sleep environments, adjust activity timing to cooler parts of the day, and maintain hydration.

Substance Use and Depression: Complex Interactions

Alcohol and drug use frequently coexist with depression, creating complex, bidirectional relationships. Substances might be used to cope with depressive symptoms, to temporarily elevate mood, to facilitate sleep, to reduce anxiety, or to escape from painful thoughts and feelings. However, substance use ultimately worsens depression through direct pharmacological effects, behavioural consequences, and perpetuation of unhelpful coping patterns. Understanding these relationships and addressing both depression and substance use is essential for recovery.

Alcohol is a depressant that directly affects brain chemistry in ways that worsen depression. Whilst alcohol might provide temporary relief from psychological pain and initial euphoria or relaxation, these effects are short-lived and followed by mood deterioration. Alcohol disrupts sleep architecture, reducing sleep quality despite potentially facilitating falling asleep. Alcohol interferes with the effectiveness of antidepressant medications. Alcohol impairs judgment, increasing risky behaviours and potentially creating additional problems that worsen depression. Regular alcohol use can independently cause depressive symptoms even in people without primary depression. The combination of depression and alcohol use creates a downward spiral where each condition worsens the other.

Cannabis use, sometimes perceived as benign or even therapeutic, also has concerning interactions with depression. Whilst some people report short-term anxiety reduction or mood improvement from cannabis, research links regular cannabis use with increased depression risk, particularly in young people. Cannabis can impair motivation and initiative, worsening the inactivity characteristic of depression. Cannabis use can trigger anxiety and paranoia in some people. Heavy cannabis use might reflect avoidance of addressing underlying difficulties. Cannabis affects memory and concentration, potentially worsening these cognitive symptoms of depression.

Stimulants, including cocaine, amphetamines, or excessive caffeine, might be used to combat the fatigue and low energy of depression. However, the crash following stimulant use typically involves intense depression, creating cycles of use to avoid low mood. Stimulants disrupt sleep, worsen anxiety, and can trigger or worsen psychotic symptoms. Regular stimulant use causes depletion of neurotransmitters, ultimately worsening the biological basis of depression. The short-term energy boost is far outweighed by long-term deterioration in mood and functioning.

Opioids, whether prescribed pain medications used beyond therapeutic purposes or illegal drugs such as heroin, create profound problems when combined with depression. Opioids provide powerful short-term relief from physical and emotional pain but cause physical dependence rapidly, creating additional problems of withdrawal and compulsive use. Opioid use severely impairs functioning, isolates people from support, creates legal and financial problems, and substantially increases overdose risk, particularly when combined with depression and suicidal thinking.

Addressing substance use alongside depression is essential. If substance use is minimal or experimental, cessation or reduction to low-risk levels might be achievable independently with support from self-help resources and your social network. If substance use is regular or problematic, specialist help from addiction services provides assessment, support for withdrawal if physical dependence exists, and treatment addressing both substance use and mental health. Attempting to treat depression whilst continuing significant substance use is unlikely to be effective, as substances continually undermine recovery efforts.

Some people worry that stopping substance use will worsen depression or anxiety symptoms, as substances have been used to cope with these symptoms. Whilst withdrawal might temporarily worsen symptoms, medium to long-term mood and anxiety improve with cessation. The key is to develop alternative coping strategies before or alongside stopping substance use, ensuring you have healthier ways to manage distress. CBT skills for depression, mindfulness practices, social support, and potentially medication for depression provide alternative resources for coping.

If alcohol or drug use has become entrenched, residential treatment programmes providing intensive support in a substance-free environment might be necessary. These programmes address both addiction and co-occurring mental health conditions simultaneously. Following residential treatment, ongoing support through mutual aid groups such as Alcoholics Anonymous or Narcotics Anonymous, continued mental health treatment, and development of substance-free social networks and leisure activities support sustained recovery from both conditions.

For people taking prescribed medications with addictive potential such as benzodiazepines for anxiety or opioids for pain, discussing your depression and any concerns about medication dependence with your prescriber allows appropriate management. Gradual reduction of these medications under medical supervision, substitution with non-addictive alternatives where possible, and intensive psychological treatment to develop alternative coping strategies addresses both medication dependence and underlying mental health conditions.

Technology, Social Media, and Screen Time: Managing Modern Challenges

Technology and social media present unique challenges for people with depression. Whilst technology offers benefits including access to information, connection with others, and therapeutic resources, excessive or inappropriate use can worsen depression through multiple mechanisms. Understanding these effects and managing technology use supports recovery.

Social media use is associated with increased depression, particularly excessive use or particular patterns of use. Social comparison is a powerful mechanism through which social media affects mood. Posts typically present idealised versions of people's lives, creating the impression that others are happier, more successful, and living better lives than you are. For people with depression already prone to negative comparisons with others, this social comparison is particularly damaging. Your depressed mind accepts these curated presentations as reality, confirming beliefs that your life is inadequate and that you are failing compared to others.

Passive scrolling through social media, consuming others' content without meaningful engagement, is associated with a worse mood compared to active use involving actual conversation and connection. Passive use provides an illusion of social connection whilst lacking the reciprocity and genuine interaction that a real connection requires. It fills time that could be spent in activities that actually improve mood. It can trigger rumination and negative thinking. Hours can be lost to mindless scrolling, creating guilt and sense of wasted time whilst providing little benefit.

The FOMO (fear of missing out) phenomenon, exacerbated by social media showing a constant stream of events and activities others are engaged in, creates anxiety and dissatisfaction. When you are depressed and isolated, seeing others appearing to have active social lives whilst you are withdrawn intensifies loneliness and beliefs that something is wrong with you. Managing this involves recognising that social media presents a biased sample of people's experiences, that many people feel similarly isolated even whilst appearing socially active online, and that comparing your internal experience with others' external presentations is an inherently unfair comparison.

Managing social media use involves several strategies. Monitoring and limiting time spent on social media using app timers or deliberate scheduling prevents excessive passive use. Curating your social media feeds by unfollowing or muting accounts that trigger negative comparisons or emotions creates a more supportive online environment. Engaging actively when you do use social media, by actually conversing with people and sharing genuinely, provides more benefit than passive consumption. Taking breaks from social media entirely, particularly during periods of low mood, allows space for other activities and reduces exposure to triggers. Using social media for specific purposes, such as maintaining genuine connections rather than an automatic habit, reduces problematic use.

Excessive general screen time, beyond social media specifically, affects depression through multiple pathways. Extended screen time is typically sedentary, reducing physical activity that supports mood. Screen time, particularly in the evening, disrupts sleep through blue light exposure, suppressing melatonin and stimulating content, interfering with wind-down. Screen time often replaces activities that would support a better mood, including face-to-face social interaction, outdoor time, hobbies, and exercise.

The passive consumption of content through television or videos rarely provides the meaningful engagement that supports well-being.

Setting boundaries around screen time supports recovery. This might include screen-free times such as the first hour after waking or the hour before bed, screen-free zones such as bedrooms or dining areas, one or two screen-free days per week, allowing focus on other activities, or limiting screen time to specific purposes rather than default time-filling. Using screen time intentionally for chosen entertainment, maintaining connections, or accessing resources feels different psychologically than mindless default use.

Technology can also support recovery when used intentionally. Mental health apps providing mood tracking, meditation guidance, CBT exercises, or sleep management can be valuable tools. Online therapy or support groups provide access to help that might not be locally available. Video calls maintain a connection with distant friends and family. Information resources about depression, accessed through reputable websites, support understanding and recovery. The key is intentional use aligned with recovery goals rather than default, mindless use.

Online support communities for people with depression can provide valuable connections with others who understand, reduce isolation, and offer practical tips and mutual support. However, quality varies enormously. Some online communities provide supportive, hopeful environments that encourage recovery efforts. Others might reinforce helplessness, facilitate excessive focus on symptoms without balanced attention to coping and recovery, or expose people to triggering content. Evaluating whether particular online spaces support or undermine your recovery and engaging selectively with those that help is important.

For people who choose to participate in online communities, setting boundaries protects well-being. This includes limiting time spent in these spaces, taking breaks if content becomes overwhelming, balancing time in online communities with real-world connection and activity, not allowing online communities to replace professional treatment when needed, and protecting anonymity and privacy by not sharing identifying information. Recognising when engagement with online spaces is becoming problematic, through signs such as spending excessive time online, feeling worse rather than better after engagement, comparing yourself negatively with others, or avoiding real-world activities in favour of online time, allows adjustment of use patterns.

Gaming, whilst potentially providing entertainment and distraction, can become problematic when used to avoid real-life difficulties, when it dominates time to the exclusion of other activities, or when it disrupts sleep schedules. The immersive, rewarding nature of games can provide temporary escape from depressive mood, but excessive gaming worsens depression through social isolation, physical inactivity, disrupted sleep, and neglect of responsibilities and self-care. If gaming has become excessive, gradually reducing gaming time whilst building in alternative activities, setting clear time limits on gaming sessions, avoiding gaming late at night to protect sleep, and seeking help if reducing gaming independently is unsuccessful, addresses problematic patterns.

For younger people, particularly adolescents and young adults, technology use presents particular challenges. This age group typically uses technology and social media more extensively than older adults, exposing them to a greater risk of negative effects. Academic pressure, complex social dynamics, identity formation, and developmental vulnerability to mental health problems combine with high technology use to create particular risks. Parents, educators, and young people themselves benefit from awareness of these risks and active management of technology use to protect mental health.

Technology also offers opportunities that previous generations lacked. Access to vast information resources, connection with like-minded individuals globally, creative outlets, learning opportunities, and mental health resources are all available through technology. The goal is not technology avoidance but rather intentional, balanced use that harnesses benefits whilst protecting against harms. This requires ongoing self-monitoring and adjustment of technology habits based on their impact on mood and functioning.

Self-Harm and Depression: Understanding and Addressing Deliberate Self-Injury

Self-harm, also referred to as deliberate self-injury or non-suicidal self-injury, commonly occurs alongside depression, particularly in young people. Self-harm typically involves deliberately injuring oneself, most commonly through cutting, burning, hitting, or scratching, without suicidal intent. Understanding why self-harm occurs, its relationship with depression, and how to address it is essential for people who self-harm and for those supporting them.

Self-harm serves various psychological functions that make it understandable, though harmful. The most commonly reported function is emotional regulation. Overwhelming emotional pain, which many people with depression experience, can feel unbearable. Physical pain from self-injury temporarily shifts focus from emotional pain to physical sensation, providing brief relief. The visible, concrete nature of physical injury feels more manageable than invisible emotional suffering. Some people report feeling emotionally numb during depression and use self-harm to 'feel something,' to confirm they are real and alive. Self-harm can provide a temporary sense of control when life feels chaotic and uncontrollable. For people who believe they deserve punishment, self-harm might represent self-directed anger and punishment for perceived inadequacies.

The temporary relief or other effects that self-harm provides create a reinforcing pattern where self-harm becomes a learned coping mechanism. When emotional distress builds, the person recalls that self-harm previously provided relief, making it tempting to repeat. This creates cycles where stress or emotional pain triggers self-harm urges, self-harm temporarily alleviates distress, the person experiences shame and guilt about self-harming, mood worsens, and vulnerability to future self-harm increases. Breaking this cycle requires understanding the functions self-harm serves and developing alternative, healthier ways to meet those needs.

Self-harm differs from suicidal behaviour in important ways, though they can coexist. Self-harm typically aims to cope with or express emotional pain without the intention to die, though injury occasionally has unintended serious medical consequences. Suicide attempts aim to end life due to unbearable suffering and the belief that death is the only solution. However, people who self-harm are at increased risk of eventual suicide compared to those who do not self-harm, particularly if self-harm is ongoing, if methods escalate in severity, or if depression worsens. The presence of self-harm should always be taken seriously and should prompt a thorough assessment of suicide risk as well as support to stop self-harming.

Medical attention following self-harm is important both to treat injuries and to access support. Even injuries that seem minor might require treatment to prevent infection or address more serious damage than initially apparent. Hospital emergency departments provide treatment for self-harm injuries. Staff in these settings are trained to respond supportively and without judgment. Medical assessment following self-harm typically includes a mental health assessment to determine risk, identify underlying difficulties, and arrange appropriate follow-up support. Whilst hospital attendance for self-harm can feel embarrassing or shameful, remember that healthcare professionals understand self-harm, want to help, and will not judge you.

Telling someone about self-harm, though frightening, is an important step towards recovery. This might be a trusted friend or family member, your GP, a therapist, a teacher, or a helpline. People often fear that disclosure will lead to forced hospitalisation, that people will react with anger or disgust, that they will be seen as attention-seeking, or that they will lose control over decisions about their care. In reality, most self-harm does not lead to hospitalisation and support is usually provided in community settings. Compassionate people respond with concern and a wish to help. Disclosure allows access to appropriate treatment and support.

Treatment for self-harm typically involves addressing underlying depression and other mental health difficulties, developing skills to manage emotions without self-injury, understanding the functions self-harm serves and finding alternative ways to meet those needs, and processing experiences or beliefs that contribute to self-harm. Cognitive behavioural therapy is effective for self-harm, as is dialectical behaviour therapy, which was specifically developed for people who self-harm. Therapy provides a safe space to explore the difficulties underlying self-harm, to develop new coping skills, and to gradually reduce and eventually stop self-harming behaviour.

Specific strategies help manage urges to self-harm. When an urge arises, using the 'urge surfing' technique recognises that the urges peak and then subside if you do not act on it. Observing the urge without judgment, noticing physical sensations and thoughts that accompany it, breathing slowly whilst reminding yourself the urge will pass, and occupying yourself with activities until the urge subsides, allows urges to reduce without self-harming. Urges typically last from minutes to an hour or so. Each time you successfully resist an urge, the pattern weakens slightly.

Distraction techniques that engage your mind fully can interrupt the progression from urge to action. Intensely physical activities such as vigorous exercise, squeezing ice cubes, having a cold shower, or snapping an elastic band on your wrist provide physical sensation without injury. Cognitive activities such as counting backwards, naming objects in the room, doing a puzzle, or calling someone absorb mental attention. Creative activities such as drawing, writing, or music channel emotional energy differently. Having a prepared list of distraction activities ensures you have options when urges arise rather than having to think of strategies when distressed.

Some people find that harm reduction approaches, where the goal is initially to reduce harm from self-injury rather than immediately stopping entirely, are helpful steps towards cessation. This might involve using less dangerous methods, ensuring wounds are cleaned and treated appropriately, reducing frequency gradually rather than attempting immediate cessation, or delaying self-harm for increasing periods when urges arise. Whilst complete cessation is the ultimate goal, harm reduction acknowledges that changing entrenched coping patterns takes time and that reducing harm whilst working towards stopping is valuable progress.

Understanding and addressing the emotions and situations that typically trigger self-harm helps reduce vulnerability to urges. Keeping a diary of self-harm incidents, noting what was happening beforehand, what you were thinking and feeling, and what happened afterwards, identifies patterns. Common triggers include interpersonal conflict or rejection, overwhelming stress, specific situations that recall past trauma or difficulties, physical discomfort or illness, or exposure to triggering content such as images or descriptions of self-harm. Once triggers are identified, you can develop plans for managing these situations differently, potentially avoiding some triggers entirely, and having prepared coping strategies ready for unavoidable triggers.

Grief, Loss, and Depression: Navigating the Intersection

Grief following bereavement or other significant losses commonly occurs alongside depression, creating complex emotional experiences that can be difficult to navigate. Understanding the relationship between grief and depression, recognising when grief becomes complicated or transforms into depression, and knowing how to support yourself through loss whilst managing depression is essential for recovery.

Normal grief, the natural response to loss, shares some features with depression, including sadness, loss of pleasure in usual activities, changes in sleep and appetite, difficulty concentrating, and withdrawal from others. However, grief and depression differ in important ways. Grief typically occurs in waves rather than being constant; moments of connection with good memories, laughter, and pleasure alternate with intense sadness. In depression, the low mood is more persistent and pervasive. Grief maintains focus on the person or thing that was lost; thoughts return repeatedly to memories, regrets, or yearning for the deceased. Depression focuses more on the self with thoughts of worthlessness and failure. Grief typically allows some comfort from others and from certain activities. Depression creates a more pervasive inability to experience pleasure or comfort.

The first weeks and months following a major loss typically involve intense grief that might resemble depression. This is normal. Crying, profound sadness, difficulty believing the loss is real, feeling the deceased person's presence, searching for them, experiencing anger about the loss, and social withdrawal all represent normal grief. Cultural expectations about grieving vary widely, but no single correct way to grieve exists. Your own pace and pattern of grieving is right for you as long as it gradually allows you to adapt to the loss.

Complicated grief, sometimes called prolonged grief disorder, occurs when intense grief symptoms persist beyond what is typical, usually beyond six to twelve months after the loss, without the gradual reduction in intensity and increase in functioning that normal grief involves. Signs of complicated grief include intense yearning for the deceased that dominates your thoughts and interferes with functioning, difficulty accepting the reality of the death, intense anger or bitterness about the loss, feeling that life is empty or meaningless without the deceased, avoiding reminders of the deceased to an extent that limits life, or feeling stuck in grief without movement towards acceptance and adaptation. Complicated grief requires professional treatment, typically involving specific complicated grief therapy that differs from standard grief support or depression treatment.

Depression can develop following bereavement, either concurrent with normal grief or after grief has resolved. The loss itself might trigger depression in people who are vulnerable due to biological factors, past depression history, or current life stress. The changes that follow loss, such as financial difficulties, role changes, loss of social connections that were shared with the deceased, or physical relocation, create ongoing stress that contributes to depression. Isolation following loss, if social withdrawal becomes entrenched, maintains depression. Whilst grief and depression can coexist, they are distinct experiences requiring different approaches.

Historical guidance that people should wait before treating depression that develops following bereavement, based on the belief that medication or therapy might interfere with natural grieving, is no longer considered appropriate. Depression following bereavement causes significant suffering and impairment and responds to treatment just as depression following other triggers does. Treating depression does not prevent healthy grieving; rather, treating depression enables you to grieve more effectively by reducing the additional burden of depressive symptoms such as hopelessness, guilt, and inability to recall positive memories. If depression symptoms persist beyond the first weeks after loss, or if symptoms are severe, seeking treatment is appropriate.

Losses beyond bereavement also trigger depression. Relationship breakdowns, job loss, loss of physical abilities through illness or injury, loss of independence, loss of home, loss of hopes or dreams, miscarriage or stillbirth, pet death, or any other significant loss can precipitate depression. These losses are often minimised by others or by yourself with thoughts such as 'it could be worse' or 'others have bigger problems,' but the impact of loss is real regardless of whether others validate it. Allowing yourself to grieve these losses without minimising your pain supports eventual adaptation.

Supporting yourself through loss whilst managing depression requires patience and self-compassion. Allowing yourself to feel grief without trying to suppress it or rush through it prevents complicated grief. Maintaining connections with supportive people, even when grief or depression makes you want to withdraw, provides essential support. Structure and routine protect against the complete collapse of functioning. A balance between activities that honour the loss and your grief with activities that maintain functioning and provide breaks from grief supports wellbeing. This is not avoiding grief but recognising that you cannot sustain intense grieving continuously.

Grief typically involves various emotional stages or tasks, though these do not unfold in neat, linear progression. You might experience denial or shock, where the loss does not feel real; anger at the deceased, at yourself, at circumstances, or at others; bargaining with thoughts of what you could have done differently; deep sadness and yearning for what is lost; and eventually acceptance where you adjust to life with the loss. Moving back and forth between these stages is normal. There is no correct timeline for this process. Some people reach acceptance relatively quickly; others take years. What matters is gradual movement towards acceptance rather than becoming stuck in earlier stages.

Practical aspects of grieving deserve attention alongside emotional processing. This includes dealing with the belongings of a deceased person, managing anniversary reactions when dates associated with the person arise, adjusting to life without the person in practical ways such as managing finances or household tasks previously done by them, and renegotiating your identity without the relationship that has ended. These practical adjustments are part of grief work, not separate from emotional processing.

Maintaining a connection with a deceased person whilst adapting to their absence represents healthy grieving. Continuing bonds with the deceased through maintaining selected possessions that hold meaning, creating memorial rituals that honour them, talking about them with others, engaging in activities they valued, or maintaining connection through spiritual or religious beliefs provides comfort for many people. This differs from complicated grief, where connection with the deceased prevents adaptation to life without them. The difference is whether remembering and honouring the deceased supports your life going forward or prevents your life from moving forward.

Anniversary reactions, where grief intensifies around dates associated with the person, such as birthdays, death anniversaries, or holidays, are normal and often persist for years or lifelong. Preparing for these times, planning how you will mark the day, arranging support, and allowing yourself to experience increased emotion without becoming alarmed helps manage anniversary reactions. Over time, anniversary reactions typically become less intense, though they might never disappear completely.

Children and adolescents grieve differently from adults due to developmental differences in understanding death, expressing emotion, and coping capacity. Young children might not understand the permanence of death and might repeatedly ask when the person will return. They might express grief through behaviour changes rather than words, through play themes involving death or loss, or through regression to earlier developmental stages. Adolescents might struggle particularly with grief as they are already navigating identity formation and might fear appearing different from peers. Providing developmentally appropriate information about death, maintaining routine and security whilst allowing expression of grief, answering questions honestly, and involving children in memorial activities appropriate for their age supports healthy grieving in young people.

Cultural and religious beliefs about death, the afterlife, and appropriate mourning practices significantly influence grieving. Some cultures encourage extended, publicly expressed mourning, whilst others favour more private grief. Some religious traditions provide specific rituals and practices that structure grieving. Understanding and respecting your own cultural and religious context, whilst recognising that individual grieving might not perfectly match cultural expectations, allows you to grieve in ways that feel authentic whilst maintaining important connections to your cultural or religious community.

Disenfranchised grief occurs when loss is not socially recognised or validated. Examples include grief following miscarriage or stillbirth where others might minimise the loss, grief following death of an ex-partner where the relationship ended but attachment remained, grief following death of a pet where others dismiss the significance, grief for estranged family members where complicated feelings of relief and sadness coexist, or grief following loss that others judge as resulting from your own choices. Lack of social recognition makes grieving more difficult and lonely. Seeking understanding people who validate your grief, allowing yourself to feel the full range of emotions even if others do not understand, and accessing professional support if needed helps navigate disenfranchised grief.

Cultural Factors in Depression: Understanding Diverse Experiences

Depression exists across all cultures, but cultural context significantly influences how depression is experienced, expressed, understood, and addressed. Cultural factors affect symptom presentation, help-seeking behaviours, stigma experiences, and treatment preferences. Understanding cultural dimensions of depression ensures appropriate, respectful, and effective support for people from diverse backgrounds.

Cultural variations in depression symptoms have been documented extensively. Whilst core symptoms such as low mood, loss of interest, and hopelessness appear across cultures, the prominence and expression of different symptoms vary. Some cultures emphasise somatic symptoms, including pain, fatigue, dizziness, or digestive problems, rather than psychological symptoms. This might reflect cultural beliefs about mind-body relationships, lesser stigma associated with physical illness compared to mental illness, or limited psychological vocabulary for describing emotional distress. Western clinical frameworks focusing heavily on psychological symptoms might miss depression presenting primarily with physical symptoms, potentially leading to underdiagnosis and inappropriate treatment focusing solely on physical causes.

Idioms of distress, culture-specific ways of expressing psychological suffering, provide culturally meaningful language for experiences that might not map neatly onto Western diagnostic categories. Examples include 'thinking too much' in African and Caribbean communities, describing rumination and worry; 'sinking heart' or 'heart distress' in Iranian culture describing depression and anxiety; 'nervios' in Latino cultures encompassing anxiety, depression, and stress; 'brain fag' in West African students describing cognitive and somatic symptoms associated with academic stress; or 'hwa-byung' in Korean culture, a syndrome of suppressed anger and resentment manifesting in physical and psychological symptoms. Mental health professionals' awareness of these idioms allows recognition and appropriate response to distress expressed in culturally specific ways.

Cultural beliefs about causes of mental health problems significantly affect help-seeking. Some cultures attribute mental illness to spiritual causes such as spirits, curses, or punishment for wrongdoing, leading people to seek help from religious or spiritual leaders rather than medical professionals. Some cultures emphasise physical or environmental causes rather than psychological explanations. Family or social factors might be emphasised over individual psychological factors. Genetic or hereditary explanations common in some cultures create fatalism about treatment possibilities. These differing causal attributions are not simply incorrect beliefs to be corrected but represent meaningful cultural frameworks for understanding distress. Effective treatment works with rather than against cultural understandings, bridging between cultural beliefs and evidence-based treatments.

Stigma associated with mental illness, whilst present across cultures, takes different forms and has varying intensity. Cultures emphasising family honour and collective identity might experience mental illness in a family member as bringing shame on the entire family, increasing pressure to hide difficulties. Mental illness might be seen as indicating moral weakness, lack of faith, or poor character rather than as medical condition. Concerns about marriage prospects for the person experiencing mental illness or their siblings might prevent families from acknowledging difficulties. Fear of being labelled 'mad' or 'crazy' with associated assumptions of dangerousness or permanence deters help-seeking. Normalising mental health discussions within communities, providing psychoeducation, and having visible role models from the community who speak openly about mental health experiences gradually reduces stigma.

Help-seeking patterns differ culturally. Some cultures emphasise handling problems within the family without outside involvement, viewing help-seeking as betrayal or failure. Some cultures trust traditional healers or religious leaders more than Western medical professionals, partly due to shared cultural understanding and partly due to negative experiences with or distrust of mainstream services. Language barriers, lack of culturally appropriate services, discrimination experiences, and immigration status fears deter some people from accessing services. Understanding and respect for these barriers from services, actively working to become more culturally accessible, and providing culturally adapted interventions improve access and outcomes.

Family involvement in mental healthcare varies culturally. Western mental healthcare typically emphasises individual autonomy and confidentiality. However, many cultures operate from more collectivist frameworks where families are expected to be involved in health decisions and where individual confidentiality might be seen as an inappropriate separation of person from family support. Balancing individual rights with culturally appropriate family involvement requires sensitive navigation. Excluding families entirely might conflict with cultural values and miss opportunities for family support. However, ensuring that the person experiencing depression retains agency and that confidentiality is maintained where the person requests it remains essential. This is particularly important in situations where family conflict or abuse might be present.

Migration, acculturation stress, and refugee experiences profoundly affect mental health. Refugees and asylum seekers experience depression at much higher rates than the general population due to pre-migration trauma, dangerous journeys, ongoing uncertainty about immigration status, family separation, poverty, and loss of home, identity, and all that was familiar. Acculturation stress affects all migrants to some degree as they navigate unfamiliar cultural norms, possible language barriers, discrimination, and changes in social status or professional identity. Supporting these populations requires trauma-informed approaches, practical support with basic needs and immigration processes, culturally appropriate mental health services, and community-based support that addresses isolation.

Religion and spirituality, important to many people's cultural identity, can influence depression in positive and negative ways. Religious involvement provides community support, meaning and purpose, coping rituals, and hope for many people. Faith can be a protective factor against depression or a source of strength during depression. However, religious frameworks might also contribute to shame or guilt, might delay appropriate mental health treatment if seen as lacking faith, or might involve religious leaders who lack understanding of mental health needs. Respectful integration of spiritual and religious perspectives into mental healthcare, collaboration with religious leaders where appropriate, and validation that faith and mental health treatment are compatible, not contradictory, support religiously oriented individuals.

Therapeutic approaches may require cultural adaptation to maximise relevance and effectiveness. This includes using culturally relevant examples and metaphors, addressing cultural values and beliefs explicitly, involving interpreters when needed whilst recognising interpretation challenges for psychological content, acknowledging and working with cultural norms around emotional expression and help-seeking, considering family and community context rather than only individual factors, and demonstrating cultural humility through acknowledging your own cultural lens and learning from clients about their cultural perspectives. Standardised Western psychological therapies, whilst evidence-based, can feel alien and irrelevant to people from different cultural backgrounds without thoughtful adaptation.

Racism and discrimination represent significant stressors affecting mental health for ethnic minority populations. Experiences of racism, whether overt discrimination or subtle microaggressions, are chronic stressors linked to depression and other mental health conditions. Historical and ongoing structural racism creates health inequalities including in mental health access and outcomes. Mental health services themselves might perpetuate discrimination through cultural insensitivity, stereotyping, or inadequate provision for diverse populations. Acknowledging the reality and impact of racism as a mental health risk factor, addressing structural barriers within services, and providing specific support for people dealing with racism-related distress are essential for equity.

For children and young people from ethnic minority backgrounds, navigating multiple cultural worlds – that of their family heritage and that of the wider society – creates particular pressures. Intergenerational conflicts between traditional expectations and contemporary cultural influences affect family relationships and identity formation. Experiences of racism or cultural marginalisation in schools or communities affect self-esteem and belonging. Mental health difficulties in young people from minority backgrounds might be particularly hidden due to cultural stigma or might be expressed through cultural idioms not recognised by school or health services. Culturally sensitive youth services, school support for diversity and inclusion, and support for parents navigating their children's bicultural experiences all contribute to mental health.

Long-term Management and Thriving Beyond Depression

Recovery from depression does not simply mean the absence of symptoms, but involves rebuilding your life, discovering or rediscovering meaning and purpose, developing resilience, and ultimately moving beyond merely surviving to genuinely thriving. This process takes time, unfolds gradually, and looks different for each person. Understanding what sustained recovery and flourishing involve supports this journey.

The concept of recovery has evolved beyond traditional medical focus on symptom remission to encompass broader ideas of personal recovery. Personal recovery involves developing a positive sense of self and identity beyond being 'a depressed person,' finding meaning and purpose through relationships, work, creativity, or service, experiencing hope and optimism about the future, empowerment and agency over your life, connection with others and community, managing symptoms that might persist whilst living a fulfilling life, and growth or positive change through the experience of having faced depression. This framework recognises that well-being involves much more than the absence of psychiatric symptoms.

Rebuilding your life following significant depression often requires attention to multiple life domains. Relationships might have been damaged or neglected during depression and require active repair and reinvestment. This involves reconnecting with people, apologising where appropriate for impacts of your depression on them, gradually rebuilding trust, and demonstrating through consistent action that you are engaged and reliable again. Some relationships might not survive the strain of depression, requiring acceptance and focusing energy on relationships that remain or developing new connections. Education or career might have been interrupted, requiring decisions about resuming previous paths or taking new directions. Practical matters including finances, living situation, or health might need addressing. This rebuilding is not returning to life exactly as it was before depression but creating life moving forward incorporating what you have learned.

Finding or rediscovering meaning and purpose represents essential aspects of thriving beyond depression. Depression strips away a sense of meaning, leaving existence feeling pointless. Intentionally cultivating meaning involves identifying your values – what matters most to you – and aligning life with these values through chosen activities and relationships. Meaning might come from work that feels purposeful, from contributing to others or causes you care about, from creative expression, from spiritual or religious involvement, from learning and growth, from relationships and family, or from connection with nature. What provides meaning is deeply personal; no universal source of meaning exists. Experimenting with different activities and reflecting on what feels meaningful to you guides this process.

Post-traumatic growth, positive psychological change resulting from struggling with challenging life circumstances, can follow depression. This is not suggesting depression is good or that people should be grateful for depression. Rather, having faced and overcome depression, some people report eventual recognition of personal strength they did not know they possessed, deeper relationships due to increased authenticity and vulnerability, increased appreciation for life and changed priorities, spiritual or philosophical development, and recognition of new possibilities. Not everyone experiences post-traumatic growth, and forcing this interpretation when it does not fit your experience is unhelpful. However, remaining open to potential growth whilst acknowledging the genuine difficulty of what you have been through represents a balanced perspective.

Developing resilience, the capacity to withstand and recover from adversity, protects against future depression whilst supporting thriving. Resilience is not a fixed trait you either have or lack, but rather involves skills and perspectives that can be developed. Components of resilience include realistic optimism that acknowledges difficulties whilst maintaining hope, strong connections with supportive people, a sense of agency and belief in your capacity to influence your circumstances, effective problem-solving skills, capacity to regulate emotions, physical health practices, sense of meaning and purpose, ability to learn from experience, and self-compassion. Depression initially depletes resilience, but recovery and deliberate cultivation of these factors gradually rebuild it.

Maintaining wellness requires ongoing attention and cannot be taken for granted after depression resolves. This involves continuing helpful practices developed during recovery, such as exercise, social connection, sleep hygiene, stress management, and balanced lifestyle. Monitoring your mood and recognising early warning signs of decline allows early intervention before significant relapse. Maintaining realistic expectations whilst holding high hopes represents important balance. Perfect happiness is not the goal; being human involves experiencing full range of emotions including difficult ones. What matters is overall trajectory towards wellbeing, capacity to enjoy life, engagement in valued activities, and ability to cope with difficulties when they arise.

Some people find that incorporating practices from positive psychology, which studies wellbeing and human flourishing rather than only treating problems, supports thriving. Gratitude practices involving regularly noting things you are grateful for, no matter how small, consistently demonstrate benefits for well-being. Acts of kindness, where you deliberately do things for others without expecting reward, boost mood. Savouring positive experiences, taking time to really notice and appreciate good moments rather than rushing past them, enhances positive emotion. Identifying and using your strengths, the qualities and abilities you possess, in new ways, provides satisfaction and confidence. Flow activities, where you are fully absorbed and time seems to pass without notice, provide particular satisfaction. These practices complement rather than replace depression treatment when needed.

Career development and work satisfaction significantly affect long-term well-being. If depression interrupts education or career, considering whether to return to the previous path or to make changes represents an important decision. Depression sometimes provides an enforced pause that allows reflection on whether the current direction is truly satisfying or whether changes are needed. Returning to unsatisfying work after recovery risks triggering relapse. However, making major career changes whilst still recovering requires caution as judgment might be impaired. Seeking guidance from careers advisors, trusted others, and therapists helps navigate these decisions. Many people find that depression and recovery change their priorities and values, leading to different career choices than they would have made before.

Financial recovery following depression, if depression caused financial difficulties through lost income, spending during episodes, or debt accumulation, requires patient attention. Seeking debt advice from specialist services, creating realistic budgets, rebuilding savings gradually, and addressing any ongoing financial stresses protect against depression recurrence. Financial stress is a potent depression trigger; addressing financial difficulties alongside other recovery efforts is essential.

Relationship satisfaction significantly predicts well-being. Investing in existing positive relationships, gradually withdrawing from toxic relationships, developing new relationships where the current social network is inadequate, and potentially seeking couples therapy if relationship difficulties exist, supports thriving. Depression often damages relationships; actively repairing and strengthening these connections, where relationships are salvageable and worth saving, represents important recovery work. Some people find that depression experience deepens relationships as people show up to support them, whilst other relationships fall away, providing clarity about who can be relied upon.

Creative expression, whether through art, writing, music, crafts, gardening, cooking, or any other creative pursuit, provides an outlet for emotion, a sense of accomplishment, absorption in enjoyable activity, and meaning. Many people discover creative interests during recovery that become ongoing sources of satisfaction. Depression robs creativity; reclaiming creative expression represents recovery of an important part of yourself.

Physical health maintenance supports ongoing mental health. Depression often leads to neglect of physical health; recovery involves reinstating health practices. Regular physical activity, balanced nutrition, adequate sleep, limiting alcohol, stopping smoking if applicable, regular health checks, and addressing any untreated physical health problems all contribute to sustained wellbeing. The connection between physical and mental health is bidirectional; attending to both creates a positive reinforcement cycle.

Contribution to others, whether through volunteering, mentoring, political or social activism, or simply being available to friends and family, provides purpose, connection, and evidence that your life makes a positive difference. Depression creates beliefs that you are a burden and have nothing to offer. Contribution directly contradicts these beliefs through concrete evidence of your value. This might initially feel uncomfortable if depression has left you feeling worthless, but gradually increasing contribution rebuilds a positive self-concept.

Spiritual or philosophical development, if this is meaningful to you, can be part of thriving. Depression raises existential questions about suffering, meaning, and life's purpose. Engaging with these questions through religious involvement, meditation practise, philosophical reading, or contemplation can deepen your understanding of yourself and life. For some people, depression becomes a catalyst for significant spiritual development that they ultimately value, despite the difficulty of the journey.

Accepting a changed relationship with depression, for people with recurrent depression, represents an important adjustment. Rather than viewing yourself as permanently damaged or as battling an enemy, viewing depression as chronic condition requiring ongoing management, similar to diabetes or asthma, reduces stigma and shame whilst maintaining vigilance. This acceptance does not mean resignation to being depressed; rather, it means realistic acknowledgment that you have vulnerability requiring attention whilst simultaneously believing you can live full, meaningful life.

Depression in Older Adults

Depression in older adults is common but often underdiagnosed and undertreated. Approximately fifteen to twenty percent of older adults experience significant depressive symptoms, though rates of major depression diagnosed clinically are somewhat lower. The tendency to view sadness and withdrawal as normal parts of ageing contributes to underrecognition. However, depression is never a normal part of ageing and always warrants attention and treatment.

Older adults face particular risk factors for depression. Multiple losses accumulate with age, including bereavement of spouse, siblings, and friends; loss of work role and associated identity through retirement; loss of independence through declining mobility or driving ability; loss of physical health and capabilities; and for some, loss of cognitive function. Social isolation increases with age as mobility declines, social networks shrink through deaths, and opportunities for social contact reduce. Chronic physical illness, extremely common in older age, increases depression risk substantially. Medications used to treat physical conditions might have depression as a side effect. Chronic pain, prevalent in older adults, contributes to depression. Financial constraints for some older adults create ongoing stress. For people in residential care, loss of autonomy, privacy, and familiar environment affects mood.

Depression presentation in older adults sometimes differs from younger adults. Somatic symptoms, including pain, fatigue, and gastrointestinal complaints, might be more prominent than mood symptoms. Some older adults deny feeling sad but experience anhedonia and loss of interest. Anxiety frequently accompanies late-life depression. Cognitive symptoms, including poor concentration, memory problems, and confusion, can be prominent, sometimes mimicking dementia. This 'pseudodementia' improves with depression treatment, distinguishing it from true neurocognitive disorder, though depression and dementia can coexist. Agitation and psychomotor changes might be particularly noticeable. Social withdrawal and self-neglect can be severe.

The relationship between depression and dementia is complex. Depression increases the risk of subsequently developing dementia, possibly through shared biological mechanisms or through depression's effects on brain health. Depression symptoms commonly occur in people with dementia, requiring treatment. Distinguishing depression from dementia, and recognising when both coexist, requires careful assessment. If memory problems improve significantly with depression treatment, this suggests depression rather than dementia was primary. However, if cognitive impairment persists despite depression improvement, dementia might be present. Comprehensive assessment, including cognitive testing, helps clarify the diagnosis.

Medical illness in older adults complicates depression diagnosis and treatment. Symptoms such as fatigue, sleep disturbance, and appetite changes might be attributed to physical illness when depression is actually present.

Conversely, attributing all symptoms to depression risks missing treatable physical illness. A thorough assessment considering both possibilities is essential. Many medications used to treat physical conditions common in older age can cause or worsen depression, including some blood pressure medications, corticosteroids, some Parkinson's disease medications, and some hormones. Reviewing medications with a doctor when depression develops helps identify whether medication changes might be beneficial.

Treatment for late-life depression is effective, though approaches require adaptation for older adults. Psychological therapy, particularly CBT, is effective for older adults and is often preferred first-line treatment. Therapy might require adaptations, including shorter, more frequent sessions if concentration is limited; use of written materials and memory aids; addressing age-specific concerns such as bereavement, loss of independence, and mortality; and involvement of family members where appropriate. Group therapy for older adults provides peer support and reduces isolation. Reminiscence therapy, focusing on positive memories from earlier life, can be valuable for older adults.

Antidepressant medication is effective in older adults but requires careful prescribing due to age-related changes in medication metabolism, increased sensitivity to side effects, and potential interactions with medications for physical conditions. Starting with lower doses and increasing gradually ('start low, go slow') reduces side effects whilst achieving therapeutic effect. SSRIs are generally well-tolerated in older adults, though monitoring for hyponatraemia (low sodium) is important as older adults are at higher risk. Tricyclic antidepressants, whilst effective, have more side effects in older adults, including falls risk and cognitive effects, making them less preferred. Monitoring during antidepressant treatment in older adults includes regular review of side effects, physical health parameters, and medication interactions.

Electroconvulsive therapy (ECT), whilst often viewed with concern, can be particularly appropriate for severe late-life depression, especially when psychotic symptoms are present, when suicide risk is high, when the person is not eating or drinking, or when medication is ineffective or causes unacceptable side effects. ECT in older adults requires careful medical assessment due to anaesthetic risks, but is often very effective and can be life-saving. Modern ECT techniques with brief pulse stimulation and unilateral electrode placement minimise cognitive side effects.

Addressing social isolation in older adults requires creative approaches. Befriending schemes where volunteers provide regular social contact reduce isolation.. Community centres and day programmes provide structured activities and social opportunities. Technology, including video calls, allows connection with distant family. For people with mobility limitations, arranging transport to activities or bringing activities to them addresses practical barriers. Addressing hearing or vision loss that might contribute to social withdrawal improves capacity for connection. Encouraging maintained involvement in previous interests and roles to the extent possible preserves identity and meaning.

Physical activity programmes tailored for older adults, including gentle exercise classes, walking groups, or seated exercise, provide physical health benefits, social contact, and mood improvement. Exercise programmes designed for older adults with various physical capabilities allow participation regardless of fitness level. Activities such as tai chi provide gentle exercise whilst supporting balance and reducing fall risk.

Bereavement support specifically for older adults recognises that losing a spouse after decades of marriage represents the loss of a partner, best friend, daily companion, and shared life. The practical challenges of learning to manage tasks previously done by a spouse, combined with intense grief and often a reduced social network, create particular vulnerability. Bereavement groups for widowed older adults provide peer support and understanding. Practical support with tasks such as managing finances, home maintenance, or cooking that might have been the spouse's responsibility supports adjustment.

For older adults in residential care, ensuring appropriate assessment and treatment for depression is essential. Staff training in recognising depression helps identify residents who need support. Mental health services providing outreach to care homes improve access. Activities programmes in care homes that provide meaningful engagement, choice, and social contact support mood. Maintaining links with family and friends through visits and calls provides connection. For people with dementia in care homes, person-centred care approaches that understand behaviour as communication of unmet needs support wellbeing.

Suicide risk in older men is particularly high. Older men complete suicide at higher rates than any other demographic group, though rates vary by country. Risk factors include recent bereavement, physical illness, social isolation, and access to lethal means. Older adults who attempt suicide typically use more lethal methods and are more likely to complete suicide than younger people. Assessment of suicide risk in older adults requires direct, compassionate questioning about suicidal thoughts. Protective factors, including strong family connections, religious faith, ongoing meaningful roles, and effective treatment for depression, reduce risk.

Loneliness, distinct from social isolation (objective lack of social contact), is a subjective feeling of being alone or disconnected even when others are present. Loneliness is associated with depression, physical health problems, and mortality risk. Addressing loneliness requires attention to the quality rather than only the quantity of social contact. Meaningful relationships where the person feels understood and valued matter more than numerous superficial contacts. Interventions addressing loneliness include group activities bringing together people with shared interests, one-to-one befriending, reducing barriers to social participation, and therapy addressing negative beliefs about self or others that might maintain loneliness.

Palliative care services, providing support for people with serious progressive illnesses, increasingly recognise the importance of addressing psychological and emotional needs alongside physical symptom management. Depression in the context of serious illness requires treatment, not dismissal as 'understandable.' Supporting quality of life, meaning, dignity, and connection in the final stages of life represents essential care regardless of prognosis. Advance care planning, allowing people to express preferences about future care, provides a sense of control and can reduce distress.

Depression in Men: Understanding Gender Differences

Men experience depression at approximately half the rate of women based on diagnosed cases, though actual rates might be closer than this gap suggests due to underdiagnosis in men. Men are substantially more likely to complete suicide than women, despite lower depression diagnosis rates. Understanding how depression manifests in men, barriers to help-seeking, and effective approaches for engaging men in treatment is essential for reducing the burden of male depression.

Depression in men sometimes presents differently than in women. Whilst sadness and tearfulness are recognised depression symptoms, men might more commonly present with irritability, anger, and aggressive behaviour rather than sadness. Emotional numbness or emptiness might be more acceptable to acknowledge than sadness for some men. Physical symptoms, including pain, digestive problems, and fatigue, might be emphasised over psychological symptoms. Risk-taking behaviour, reckless driving, or increased substance use might represent attempts to cope with underlying depression. Overworking and excessive focus on achievement might mask depression. Some men continue to function at work or in other roles whilst deteriorating internally, making depression less visible to others.

Traditional masculine norms emphasising strength, stoicism, self-reliance, and emotional control contribute to underrecognition and undertreatment of depression in men. These norms create beliefs that experiencing depression indicates weakness or failure, that men should cope with problems independently without help, that emotional expression is unmanly, and that seeking help is an admission of inability to cope. These beliefs deter help-seeking and lead some men to minimise or deny symptoms even to themselves. Cultural variation exists in masculine norms, with some cultures having more flexible gender expectations, but restrictive masculine norms are widespread and harm men's mental health.

Barriers to help-seeking in men include stigma and fear of judgment, difficulty recognising and labelling emotional experiences due to limited emotional vocabulary in some men, belief that mental health problems are not 'real' health problems, previous negative experiences with healthcare, concerns about treatment including medication side effects or therapy, lack of male-specific mental health services, and practical barriers such as work commitments and difficulty getting appointments. Some men only seek help when a crisis occurs or when their partner insists, having struggled alone for extended periods.

Engaging men in treatment requires approaches that address these barriers. Mental health campaigns targeting men use messaging emphasising that seeking help is not weak, that depression is common and treatable, and that maintaining mental health is similar to maintaining physical health. Using language and framing that resonates with men, such as focusing on problem-solving, skills development, and specific goals rather than open-ended emotional exploration, might feel more acceptable. Offering practical, action-focused therapy rather than only talk therapy appeals to some men. Men's groups providing peer support in less formal settings than traditional therapy might be a more acceptable entry point.

Anger and Rage as Masks for Depression

Whilst sadness and tearfulness are commonly recognised symptoms of depression, many men experience and express their depression through anger, irritability, and even rage. This manifestation can make depression in men particularly difficult to identify, as both the individual and those around him may not recognise these symptoms as indicators of depression. Research consistently demonstrates that men are significantly more likely than women to express depressive symptoms through externalised behaviours such as anger outbursts, aggressive responses, and irritability, rather than through internalised symptoms such as crying or expressing sadness.

This pattern has important implications for recognition and treatment. Men experiencing depression may find themselves 'snapping' at family members over minor issues, experiencing disproportionate road rage, or feeling a persistent undercurrent of frustration that seems to have no clear cause. These anger responses often feel out of character and may be accompanied by guilt or remorse afterwards, yet the pattern persists.

Workplace mental health initiatives are important for reaching men, as many men identify strongly with their work role and spend significant time at work. Workplace programmes offering mental health screening, manager training in recognising and responding to mental health difficulties, Employee Assistance Programme counselling, and workplace culture change, reducing stigma can improve outcomes. Occupational health services accessible through work provide an alternative pathway to mental health support that might feel more acceptable than traditional mental health services.

Physical activity interventions appeal to many men and provide evidence-based depression treatment whilst avoiding explicit mental health framing that might deter engagement. Men's exercise groups, sports participation, or outdoor activities provide mood benefits, social connection with other men, and a sense of achievement. For men who are uncomfortable discussing emotions directly, side-by-side activities where conversation occurs naturally during shared activity, rather than face-to-face emotional discussion, might feel more comfortable.

Partners of depressed men often recognise changes before the man acknowledges difficulties. Partners might notice increased irritability or withdrawal, reduced interest in sex, increased drinking, or personality changes. Supporting partners of depressed men through providing information about male depression, suggesting how to raise concerns supportively, and encouraging professional help whilst recognising that ultimately the man must engage voluntarily, helps partners support effectively whilst managing their own distress.

Online mental health resources and applications might appeal to men who prefer anonymous help or who find face-to-face services difficult. Self-help CBT programmes, mental health websites targeting men, and anonymous online peer support provide accessible options. Whilst not suitable for everyone or for severe depression, these resources might be valuable first steps or supplements to face-to-face treatment.

The high male suicide rate requires urgent attention. Men are more likely to use lethal means in suicide attempts and are less likely to have had recent mental health service contact before suicide. Improving detection of depression in men, reducing stigma, enabling help-seeking, ensuring mental health services are accessible and acceptable to men, training people who interact with men in recognising distress and encouraging help-seeking, and reducing access to lethal means, particularly in men identified as at-risk, all contribute to suicide prevention.

Relationship breakdown, job loss, financial difficulties, and legal problems are particularly strong triggers for depression and suicide in men. These losses threaten identity and masculine ideals of being a provider and protector. Support during these life events, acknowledging the real difficulties whilst encouraging help-seeking and emphasising that struggling does not indicate personal failure, might reduce risk.

Fatherhood represents an important context for male mental health. Whilst postnatal depression receives attention in mothers, paternal postnatal depression affects approximately ten percent of new fathers, typically developing later than maternal postnatal depression. Risk factors include the partner's depression, relationship difficulties, financial stress, unplanned pregnancy, and previous mental health problems. Symptoms include irritability, withdrawal, anxiety, and overwork. Recognition and treatment are important for the father's well-being, relationship quality, and child development.

Depression in Women: Understanding Specific Vulnerabilities

Women experience depression at approximately twice the rate of men, a difference emerging in adolescence and persisting through much of adulthood. Multiple biological, psychological, and social factors contribute to this gender difference. Understanding women-specific aspects of depression ensures appropriate recognition and treatment.

Hormonal factors contribute to women's increased depression vulnerability. Puberty, when hormonal changes begin, coincides with the emergence of higher depression rates in girls compared to boys. The menstrual cycle influences mood in some women, with premenstrual syndrome affecting mood in the week before menstruation and, in severe form, premenstrual dysphoric disorder causing significant mood symptoms. Pregnancy and the postpartum period represent times of hormonal fluctuation and increased depression risk. Perimenopause and menopause involve hormonal changes that increase depression risk for some women. However, hormones do not solely explain women's higher depression rates; psychological and social factors significantly contribute.

Perinatal depression, encompassing depression during pregnancy and the year following childbirth, affects approximately ten to fifteen percent of women. Antenatal depression during pregnancy sometimes goes unrecognised, as symptoms might be attributed to normal pregnancy experiences. Postnatal depression typically develops within weeks of birth but can develop at any time in the first year. Risk factors include previous depression or anxiety, depression or anxiety during pregnancy, difficult pregnancy or birth, a baby with health problems or difficulties such as colic or sleep problems, lack of practical and emotional support, relationship difficulties, previous pregnancy loss, young maternal age, and social isolation or disadvantage.

Postnatal depression differs from 'baby blues,' a very common experience of mood swings, tearfulness, and anxiety in the first week or two after birth, affecting fifty to eighty percent of women. Baby blues resolve without treatment and do not significantly impair functioning. Postnatal depression involves more persistent and severe symptoms that interfere with functioning and bonding with the baby. Symptoms include persistent sadness or emptiness, overwhelming anxiety particularly about baby's health, difficulty bonding with baby or feeling disconnected, thoughts of being inadequate mother or that baby would be better off without you, irritability or anger, significant sleep disturbance beyond what is normal with newborn, loss of interest and pleasure, difficulty concentrating or making decisions, and in severe cases, thoughts of harming self or baby.

Postnatal depression requires treatment, not dismissal as a normal adjustment to motherhood. Untreated postnatal depression affects a mother's well-being, mother-infant bonding, relationship with partner, and child development. Treatment includes psychological therapy tailored for perinatal depression, addressing adjustment to motherhood, relationship with infant, and depression symptoms; antidepressant medication when appropriate, carefully selected for safety during breastfeeding if applicable; practical support with baby care and household tasks allowing mother time for self-care and rest; partner involvement in treatment and support; and mother-baby groups providing peer support and reducing isolation. Health visitors play important roles in identifying and supporting women with postnatal depression.

Postpartum psychosis, whilst rare, affects approximately one in one thousand women, is a psychiatric emergency requiring immediate treatment. Symptoms develop rapidly, usually within two weeks of birth, and include confusion, disorientation, disturbed or delusional beliefs, particularly about the baby, hallucinations, extreme mood changes, unusual behaviour, and severely disturbed sleep. Postpartum psychosis requires specialist psychiatric treatment, usually involving brief admission to a mother-baby unit where mother and infant can stay together whilst mother receives treatment. With appropriate treatment, recovery is usually complete, though the risk of recurrence in future pregnancies exists.

Premenstrual dysphoric disorder (PMDD) represents a severe form of premenstrual syndrome where mood symptoms cause significant distress and impairment. Symptoms occur in the week or two before menstruation and resolve around when menstruation begins. Symptoms include marked mood swings, irritability or anger, depressed mood or hopelessness, anxiety, decreased interest in activities, difficulty concentrating, fatigue, appetite changes, sleep disturbance, and physical symptoms. PMDD differs from premenstrual syndrome by greater severity and functional impairment. Treatment includes lifestyle interventions such as regular exercise, stress management, adequate sleep, and reduced caffeine and alcohol; psychological therapy, particularly CBT; SSRIs, which are effective for PMDD and can be taken only during the symptomatic period; hormonal treatments in some cases; and tracking symptoms across multiple cycles to confirm diagnosis and identify patterns.

Menopause and perimenopause represent times of increased depression vulnerability for some women. The fluctuating and eventually declining hormone levels during perimenopause can affect mood. Perimenopause symptoms, including hot flushes and night sweats, disrupt sleep, potentially contributing to depression. This midlife period often involves other stressors, including caring for ageing parents whilst supporting adolescent children, relationship changes, and changes in physical appearance and health. Some women with no previous depression develop depression during perimenopause. Women with a history of depression or previous sensitivity to hormonal changes (such as postnatal depression or PMDD) are at higher risk. Treatment options include hormone replacement therapy, which might improve mood as well as other menopausal symptoms; antidepressant medication, with some antidepressants also helping hot flushes; psychological therapy addressing adjustment to life stage; and lifestyle approaches including exercise, stress management, and social support.

Sexual violence and domestic abuse disproportionately affect women and substantially increase depression risk. The trauma of sexual assault, domestic violence, stalking, or other abuse causes depression, PTSD, anxiety, and other mental health difficulties. Victims often experience shame, guilt, and self-blame despite abuse being the perpetrator's responsibility. Fear of not being believed or being blamed deters help-seeking. Services supporting survivors of sexual violence and domestic abuse provide specialist support addressing both practical safety issues and mental health impacts. Trauma-focused psychological therapy helps process traumatic experiences and address resulting mental health difficulties. Recognising the link between abuse and depression, routinely enquiring about abuse experiences in sensitive ways, and providing appropriate trauma-informed care improve outcomes.

Body image concerns and eating disorders are more common in women than men and increase depression risk. Societal pressures regarding appearance, weight, and ageing disproportionately affect women. Body dissatisfaction is extremely common in women and is linked to depression. Eating disorders, including anorexia nervosa, bulimia nervosa, and binge eating disorder, commonly co-occur with depression. Treatment addressing both depression and an eating disorder simultaneously is essential. Body image work within therapy, challenging societal messages about women's bodies, and developing self-worth not based on appearance, supports recovery.

Multiple roles and expectations create stress for many women. Balancing work and family responsibilities, societal expectations of being a primary caregiver, whilst also having a career, and insufficient support structures create chronic stress. The 'mental load' of managing family logistics, appointments, activities, and emotional needs of family members, typically falling disproportionately to women, creates cognitive and emotional burden. Addressing these stressors requires individual coping strategies, but also requires societal changes creating better support for working parents, a more equal division of household and caring responsibilities, and recognition of unpaid caring work predominantly done by women.

Infertility affects approximately one in seven couples and can trigger depression, particularly in women who might experience repeated disappointment with failed conception attempts, grief for imagined children and future, stress of fertility treatments, relationship strain, and social isolation if friends are having children. The intensity of grief can surprise people who have not experienced infertility. Support groups for people experiencing infertility, counselling addressing grief and decision-making about treatment, and validation that infertility represents real loss all support emotional wellbeing during this difficult experience.

Pregnancy loss through miscarriage, stillbirth, or termination for medical reasons causes grief that sometimes goes unrecognised or minimised by others. Even early pregnancy loss represents a real loss of the imagined future and attachment to pregnancy. Later pregnancy loss or stillbirth involves all the grief of losing a child. Support includes validation that grief is real and appropriate regardless of gestation, specific bereavement support for pregnancy loss, memorial rituals for some people, and screening for depression following pregnancy loss, as risk is elevated.

Depression in LGBTQ+ Individuals

Lesbian, gay, bisexual, transgender, queer, and other sexual and gender minority individuals experience depression at substantially higher rates than heterosexual and cisgender populations. This increased prevalence results from minority stress, including discrimination, stigma, family rejection, victimisation, and internalised negative beliefs about sexual orientation or gender identity. Understanding these specific challenges ensures appropriate, affirming support.

Minority stress theory explains elevated mental health difficulties in LGBTQ+ populations through cumulative effects of discrimination, expectations of rejection, concealment of identity, and internalised stigma. These stressors are chronic and socially-based rather than inherent to LGBTQ+ identity itself. In supportive, accepting environments, mental health disparities reduce significantly, demonstrating that societal factors, rather than sexual orientation or gender identity per se, drive increased depression rates.

Coming out, the process of disclosing sexual orientation or gender identity to others, represents a significant life event with potential for both positive outcomes, including living authentically and negative outcomes, including rejection and discrimination. Coming out is not a single event but an ongoing process occurring with different people across time. Some LGBTQ+ individuals are out in all contexts; others are out selectively; still others are not out to anyone. The stress of concealing an important identity, whilst protecting against discrimination, can contribute to depression. However, coming out in unsupportive environments carries real risks. Decisions about coming out require careful consideration of safety, support, and personal readiness.

Family rejection of LGBTQ+ identity significantly increases depression and suicide risk, particularly in young people. Conversely, family acceptance powerfully protects mental health. Some LGBTQ+ young people experience rejection, including being forced to leave home, religious-based attempts to change sexual orientation or gender identity, or emotional rejection and lack of support. Others experience full acceptance. Many families struggle initially but gradually move towards acceptance. Supporting families to understand and accept LGBTQ+ family members improves outcomes. Resources for families, including PFLAG and similar organisations, provide education and support for parents and families.

School and workplace discrimination, bullying, and harassment create hostile environments affecting mental health. LGBTQ+ young people experience bullying at substantially higher rates than their peers, contributing to depression, anxiety, and suicidality. Workplace discrimination, including overt discrimination such as harassment or termination, microaggressions, and exclusion from social networks, affects well-being. Legal protections against discrimination exist in some but not all jurisdictions. Even where protections exist, discrimination persists. Inclusive schools and workplaces with non-discrimination policies, visible support, and inclusive practices protect mental health.

Religious and cultural conflicts arise for LGBTQ+ individuals from religious or cultural backgrounds with traditional views on sexuality and gender. Reconciling LGBTQ+ identity with faith or cultural identity can be deeply challenging. Some individuals resolve conflicts by leaving their religious community; others find affirming religious communities that embrace LGBTQ+ individuals; still others hold both identities whilst experiencing ongoing tension. Counselling addressing religious or cultural conflicts, connecting with affirming religious communities where desired, and processing grief over lost religious community or family relationships supports emotional wellbeing.

Healthcare experiences of discrimination or insensitivity deter some LGBTQ+ individuals from seeking mental health care. Assumptions of heterosexuality, questions about sexual history that assume opposite-sex partners, a lack of understanding about specific LGBTQ+ health needs, or overt discrimination all occur. Seeking LGBTQ+-affirmative therapists who understand minority stress and LGBTQ+ experiences, asking about therapists' experience and approach regarding LGBTQ+ clients, and connecting with LGBTQ+-specific mental health services where available improves access to appropriate care.

Transgender and gender diverse individuals experience particularly high rates of depression, anxiety, and suicidality. Gender dysphoria, distress resulting from incongruence between gender identity and assigned sex, contributes to depression. However, societal factors, including discrimination, family rejection, barriers to gender-affirming healthcare, violence risk, and lack of legal recognition, significantly contribute to mental health difficulties. Access to gender-affirming care, including hormone therapy and surgeries when desired, substantially improves mental health outcomes. Social support, legal recognition of gender identity, and reduction in discrimination all support wellbeing.

Intersectionality recognises that individuals hold multiple identities that interact to shape experiences. LGBTQ+ individuals of colour face both homophobia or transphobia and racism. LGBTQ+ individuals with disabilities navigate multiple minority identities. LGBTQ+ immigrants might come from contexts where LGBTQ+ identities face greater legal or social consequences. These intersecting identities create unique stressors requiring an understanding of multiple systems of oppression and their interactions.

Connection with the LGBTQ+ community provides crucial support, reducing isolation and providing a sense of belonging. LGBTQ+ social groups, community centres, support groups, and pride events offer opportunities for connection. Online communities provide access for people in areas with limited LGBTQ+ communities or for those not yet comfortable accessing in-person LGBTQ+ spaces. Positive LGBTQ+ role models and seeing others living authentic lives provide hope and normalisation.

Suicide prevention in LGBTQ+ populations requires specific attention, given substantially elevated suicide rates, particularly in young people and transgender individuals. Risk factors include family rejection, bullying, discrimination, lack of support, and internalised stigma. Protective factors include family acceptance, school and community support, connection with the LGBTQ+ community, and access to affirming mental health care. Crisis resources specifically for LGBTQ+ individuals, including The Trevor Project, provide specialised support.

Substance use is elevated in LGBTQ+ populations partly as coping mechanism for minority stress and partly through cultural factors, including historical connections between the LGBTQ+ community and bar culture. Addressing substance use alongside depression, understanding minority stress contributing to substance use, and connecting with LGBTQ+-affirming addiction services support recovery.

Depression in Children and Adolescents

Depression in children and adolescents is increasingly recognised as common and serious. Approximately two to three percent of children and five to eight percent of adolescents experience depression. Recognition is essential as childhood and adolescent depression, if untreated, predicts ongoing mental health difficulties, affects education and development, and increases suicide risk.

Depression presentation differs across developmental stages. Young children might not articulate sadness but show irritability, clinginess, somatic complaints, regression in development, reduced play, or behaviour problems. School-age children might express sadness more directly but also show irritability, academic difficulties, social withdrawal, and somatic complaints. Adolescents might experience typical depression symptoms but with particular prominence of irritability, risk-taking behaviour, academic decline, social withdrawal or peer conflict, and changes in appearance or self-care.

Risk factors for youth depression include genetic vulnerability with family history of depression, early adversity including abuse, neglect, or household dysfunction, bullying or peer victimisation, academic stress or learning difficulties, chronic physical illness, family conflict, parental mental illness particularly maternal depression, poverty and disadvantage, LGBTQ+ identity with lack of acceptance, trauma exposure, and neurodevelopmental conditions including ADHD or autism spectrum disorder. However, some young people develop depression without obvious risk factors, and many young people with risk factors do not develop depression.

Academic pressure and performance expectations contribute to adolescent depression. The increasing academic demands, examination pressure, university entrance competition, and early specialisation create chronic stress. Social media allows constant comparison with peers' apparent achievements. For some young people, academic difficulties related to undiagnosed learning disabilities or ADHD create ongoing frustration and damaged self-esteem. Balanced approach to achievement, emphasis on effort and progress over grades, diverse routes to success, and validation of non-academic strengths protect mental health.

Social relationships hold enormous importance for adolescent wellbeing. Peer acceptance, friendships, and romantic relationships are central to adolescent identity and happiness. Bullying, social exclusion, friendship breakdowns, or romantic relationship difficulties hit hard. Social media creates additional complexity, with social comparison, cyberbullying, and fear of missing out contributing to depression. Supporting healthy relationships, addressing bullying, teaching social skills, and managing social media use support emotional wellbeing.

Family factors significantly influence youth depression. Parental warmth and support protect against depression. Family conflict, harsh or inconsistent parenting, lack of supervision, and poor parent-child communication increase risk. Parental mental illness, particularly maternal depression, increases risk through genetic factors and through effects on parenting and family environment. Family-based interventions addressing communication, problem-solving, and conflict management improve outcomes for depressed young people.

Assessment of depression in young people involves multiple informants including the young person, parents, and teachers. Young people and parents often report different symptoms, with parents noticing behavioural changes whilst young people report internal experiences. Comprehensive assessment considers information from multiple sources, developmental context, and potential contributing factors. Distinguishing normal developmental mood fluctuations from clinical depression requires consideration of severity, duration, and functional impairment.

Treatment for youth depression adapts evidence-based approaches for developmental level. Psychological therapy is first-line treatment for mild to moderate depression. Cognitive behavioural therapy adapted for young people helps identify and challenge negative thoughts, increase pleasant activities, improve problem-solving, and build coping skills. Interpersonal therapy for adolescents addresses relationship difficulties and life transitions contributing to depression. Family therapy involves family in treatment, addressing family communication and dynamics. Therapy adaptations for young people include shorter sessions, use of activities and creative methods, involvement of parents in age-appropriate ways, and addressing developmentally relevant concerns.

Antidepressant medication for children and adolescents requires careful consideration due to concerns about efficacy and safety. Fluoxetine is licensed for depression in children and adolescents in the UK and has the best evidence base. Other SSRIs are sometimes used. Medication is typically reserved for moderate to severe depression or when psychological therapy is ineffective or unavailable. Close monitoring, particularly in early treatment stages, is essential due to a slight increase in suicidal thinking reported in some young people starting antidepressants. Regular follow-up allows assessment of benefits and side effects and adjustment of treatment. Psychological therapy should accompany medication treatment.

School-based interventions address youth depression through multiple pathways. Universal mental health education teaches all students about mental health, reduces stigma, and promotes help-seeking. Screening programmes identify students with depression symptoms, allowing early intervention. School counsellors provide accessible support. Teacher training in recognising mental health difficulties and responding supportively creates a supportive school environment. Anti-bullying programmes reduce a significant risk factor. Schools partnering with mental health services improve access to specialist support.

Suicide in young people is devastating and, whilst relatively rare, is increasing in some countries. Suicide is the second or third leading cause of death in adolescents and young adults in many developed countries. Risk factors include depression and other mental illnesses, previous suicide attempts, substance use, impulsivity, access to lethal means, family history of suicide, recent stressful events, including relationship breakdowns or bullying, and LGBTQ+ identity with a lack of support. Warning signs include talking about suicide, giving away possessions, withdrawing from friends and activities, increased substance use, reckless behaviour, and sudden calmness after a period of distress. Taking suicide talk seriously, restricting access to means, involving mental health services, and creating safety plans reduces risk.

Prevention of youth depression involves multiple levels of intervention. Universal promotion of emotional well-being through teaching emotional regulation, social skills, and coping strategies provides a foundation. Targeted interventions for at-risk young people, including those with a family history, experiencing adversity, or showing early symptoms, prevent progression to depression. Early identification and treatment of depression prevent chronic difficulties. Addressing societal factors, including poverty, educational pressure, bullying, and discrimination, creates environments supporting mental health.

Transition from child and adolescent mental health services (CAMHS) to adult mental health services represents a vulnerable period. Services are structured differently, approaches differ, and therapeutic relationships end. Poor transition planning risks disengagement from services. Good transition involves preparation, joint meetings between CAMHS and adult services, gradual transition, and attention to the young person's concerns. Some areas have youth services for ages 16-25, providing continuity during transition years.

Depression in University and College Students

University students experience high rates of depression, with approximately fifteen to twenty percent experiencing clinically significant symptoms. The transition to university, academic pressures, financial stress, and developmental tasks of late adolescence and emerging adulthood create vulnerability. Understanding student-specific risk factors and providing accessible support is essential.

Academic stress in higher education differs from school. Increased workload and expectations, independent study requiring self-motivation, high-stakes examinations, dissertation or thesis projects, competitive grading in some fields, and uncertainty about career prospects create ongoing pressure. For students who previously excelled academically, a sudden struggle in a more challenging environment damages self-esteem. Perfectionism drives some students to unsustainable work patterns, risking burnout.

Transition to university involves multiple simultaneous changes. Leaving home and family support, establishing new social networks, managing independent living, including cooking, cleaning, and budgeting, navigating a new academic environment, and possibly moving to a new city or country create adjustment demands. First-generation university students face additional challenges navigating unfamiliar systems without family experience to draw on. Mature students balance study with family and work responsibilities.

Financial stress significantly affects student mental health. Student debt, inadequate maintenance support, cost of accommodation, and difficulty finding part-time work create pressure. Students from disadvantaged backgrounds face particular financial stress. Financial concerns distract from studies, force students into excessive part-time work, compromising academic performance, and contribute to depression and anxiety. Student financial support services, emergency funds, and advice about benefits and grants provide essential support.

Social isolation affects some students despite living in student accommodation. Difficulty making friends, feeling different from other students, living off-campus, commuting from family home, or mature student, separating from traditional-age students, creates isolation. International students navigate cultural adjustment alongside other stressors.

Students from minority backgrounds might feel isolated in predominantly white institutions. University societies and clubs, student support services, and peer support programmes address isolation.

Substance use is common in university culture and can trigger or worsen depression. Drinking culture on many campuses, recreational drug use, and using substances to cope with stress or anxiety create risks. Excessive alcohol use worsens depression. Cannabis use, particularly heavy use, increases depression risk. Stimulant use for academic performance enhancement creates cycles of use and crash. University drug and alcohol services, student health services, and national addiction services provide support.

Academic failure or withdrawing from courses due to depression represents a significant loss of identity, investment of time and money, and an imagined future. Students who withdraw often struggle with shame and a sense of failure. Some students take a temporary leave of absence, allowing treatment and recovery before returning. Others change course or leave permanently. Processing grief about changed plans, addressing depression that led to withdrawal, and developing new plans gradually support adjustment.

University counselling services provide accessible mental health support. Most universities offer short-term counselling, often time-limited but valuable for addressing specific difficulties. Demand typically exceeds capacity, creating waiting lists, particularly during examination periods. Some students access counselling through their GP, though capacity varies. Online counselling and mental health apps supplement face-to-face services. University wellbeing services provide broader support, including peer support, workshops, and crisis support.

Academic adjustments for students with depression, provided through disability services in UK universities, support equal access to education. Adjustments might include extensions for coursework, arrangements for missed lectures such as recorded lectures, alternative examination arrangements such as extra time or a separate room, reduced or flexible timetable, an intermission from studies with guaranteed return, note-taking support, or modified placement requirements. Accessing adjustments requires disclosure to disability services and typically medical evidence.

Many students benefit significantly from adjustments that allow them to complete their studies.

Postgraduate students face particular pressures. PhD students navigate independent research, supervisory relationships, isolation, thesis writing, and career uncertainty. Imposter syndrome, feeling inadequate despite achievements, is common. Perfectionism and high standards drive some postgraduate students to unhealthy work patterns. Long hours, uncertain employment prospects, and comparison with peers achieving career milestones create stress. Postgraduate-specific support through graduate schools, peer support groups, and supervisory training improves outcomes.

Building and Maintaining a Support Network

Social support represents one of the most powerful protective factors against depression and facilitates recovery when depression occurs. However, depression often damages social relationships and makes reaching out difficult. Understanding different types of support, how to build and maintain supportive relationships, and how to navigate social difficulties created by depression supports recovery.

Types of Social Support and Their Importance

Social support encompasses multiple distinct types, each serving different functions. Emotional support involves empathy, caring, reassurance, and a sense of being understood and valued. This might include having people you can talk to about feelings, who listen without judgment, who express care and concern, and who validate your experiences. Practical support involves tangible help with tasks and problems. This might include help with childcare, transport to appointments, assistance with household tasks when you are unwell, financial help in crisis, or help navigating systems and paperwork. Informational support involves advice, guidance, and information. This might include medical information about depression and treatment, advice about navigating services, suggestions for coping strategies, or shared experiences of what helped others. Social companionship involves spending enjoyable time with others in shared activities. This includes having people to do activities with, casual social interaction, and a sense of belonging to groups or communities.

Different people provide different types of support, and different situations require different support types. Close family and friends typically provide primarily emotional support, practical help, and companionship. Healthcare professionals provide informational support and treatment. Peer support groups provide shared understanding and practical suggestions from lived experience. Casual acquaintances and colleagues provide companionship and a sense of connection. A well-functioning support network includes a variety of relationships serving different support functions.

The quality of relationships matters more than quantity. A few close, supportive relationships protect mental health more effectively than many superficial relationships. However, different relationships serve different purposes. Close relationships provide intimacy and deep support. Broader social networks provide a sense of community, diverse perspectives, and opportunities for varied interactions. Both contribute to well-being.

Identifying Your Current Support Network

Mapping your current support network helps identify existing sources of support and gaps to address. Consider who provides emotional support – who can you talk to about feelings and difficulties? Who provides practical help when you need it? Who provides useful information and advice? Who do you spend enjoyable time with? Some people appear in multiple categories; others provide only certain types of support. All are valuable.

Recognising people who provide support, even if in small ways, counters depression's tendency to overlook positive aspects of your social world. You might have more support than depression allows you to recognise. Perhaps a neighbour who checks in occasionally, a colleague who asks how you are, a relative you rarely see but who has expressed concern, or an online acquaintance who shares interests. Whilst none alone constitutes strong support, together these connections provide a network.

Identifying gaps in your support network allows purposeful action to address deficiencies. Perhaps you have practical support but lack emotional support. Perhaps you have nobody to do enjoyable activities with. Perhaps you need more information about depression and treatment options. Identifying specific gaps guides efforts to build support in needed areas.

Building New Supportive Relationships

Building new relationships whilst depressed presents challenges, as depression reduces motivation for social interaction, impairs social skills through flattened affect and reduced responsiveness, creates negative thinking about self and others, and drains energy. However, gradually increasing social contact, even when difficult, supports recovery. Small, manageable steps build momentum.

Joining groups based on shared interests provides structured social contact with built-in conversation topics. This might include exercise classes, hobby groups, book clubs, volunteer organisations, religious or spiritual communities, art or music groups, walking groups, or online communities around shared interests. Showing up regularly allows familiarity and relationships to develop gradually without pressure for immediate intimacy. Shared activity provides natural conversation material and reduces the awkwardness of purely social interaction.

Reconnecting with old friends or acquaintances who have drifted away sometimes provides an easier path to support than building entirely new relationships. People often respond positively to contact after gaps, particularly if you explain you have been going through a difficult time. Even if relationships cannot be fully restored, some connection might be reestablished. Be prepared that some people will not respond or will not be supportive, and try not to interpret this as a reflection on your worth.

Developing relationships takes time and cannot be rushed. Initial contact might involve only brief, superficial interaction. Gradually, as comfort develops, interactions can deepen. Inviting someone for coffee, suggesting a meeting for a walk, offering help with something, or simply chatting more extensively next time you encounter them moves relationships forward incrementally. Not every interaction will progress to a close friendship, and that is normal. Persistence and patience are required.

Reciprocity in relationships involves both giving and receiving support. Depression makes receiving support necessary, but can leave you feeling you have nothing to offer. However, reciprocity does not mean equal exchange at every moment. During depression, you might primarily receive support. As you recover, opportunities arise to reciprocate through returning support to those who helped you, offering support to others experiencing difficulties, contributing to group activities or organisations, or using your experience to help others through peer support or volunteering. Reciprocity across time rather than immediate exchange characterises good relationships.

Maintaining Existing Relationships During Depression

Depression strains relationships through withdrawal, irritability, reduced reciprocity, and emotional distance. Maintaining relationships during depression, even in minimal ways, prevents complete isolation and preserves relationships important for long-term wellbeing. This requires balance between meeting some social obligations and not overwhelming yourself.

Being honest with close friends and family about struggling, to the extent you feel comfortable, allows them to understand changes in your behaviour and adjust expectations. People cannot support you if they do not know you need support. Brief explanation such as 'I am going through difficult time with my mental health and cannot be as sociable as usual' provides information without requiring detailed disclosure. This prevents people interpreting withdrawal as disinterest in them.

Maintaining minimal contact, even when you cannot manage usual interaction level, keeps relationships alive. Brief text messages, occasional phone calls even if only checking in briefly, or attending some social events even if leaving early maintains connection. Explaining that you are struggling and that brief contact is all you can manage currently preserves goodwill whilst acknowledging limitations.

Accepting that some relationships might not survive depression, painful though this is, represents a realistic adjustment. Some people lack the capacity to support someone with mental health difficulties, whether due to their own struggles, limited understanding, or discomfort with mental illness. Others might not be willing to adjust expectations or accept changed circumstances. Whilst sad, relationships ending reveal people who cannot be relied upon, potentially freeing energy for relationships that do withstand difficulty. Not everyone needs to remain in your life.

Apologising and making amends after recovery for the impacts of depression on relationships helps repair damage. This might include acknowledging missing important events, explaining behaviour that was hurtful or confusing, expressing appreciation for support provided, and demonstrating through action that you are engaged again. Most people who care about you will understand and forgive the impacts of illness, particularly if you take responsibility for making amends.

Navigating Unsupportive or Difficult Relationships

Not all relationships are supportive or healthy. Some relationships actively contribute to depression through criticism, invalidation, excessive demands, or abuse. Recognising unhealthy relationships and setting boundaries or ending relationships protects mental health.

Signs of unsupportive relationships include dismissing or minimising your difficulties, blaming you for depression, suggesting depression is not real or is your fault, using your depression against you in arguments, refusing to accommodate reasonable needs during illness, placing excessive demands on you despite your illness, or becoming angry about impacts of depression on them without empathy for your struggle. These responses, whilst sometimes stemming from misunderstanding or their own distress, are harmful.

Setting boundaries in difficult relationships protects your well-being. This might involve limiting contact frequency or duration, refusing to discuss certain topics that result in criticism or invalidation, ending conversations that become destructive, or requiring respectful treatment as a condition of continued relationship. Some people will respect boundaries once clearly communicated. Others will resist or violate boundaries, indicating deeper relationship problems.

Ending consistently harmful relationships, even with family members, sometimes becomes necessary for recovery. The cultural expectation of maintaining family relationships regardless of behaviour can make this feel impossible or wrong. However, toxic relationships damage mental health, and distancing yourself from harmful people, even family, is appropriate self-protection. This might mean infrequent contact, surface-level only contact, or complete ending of contact. Grief about lost relationships or family you wish you had requires processing, sometimes with therapeutic support.

Professional boundaries protect therapist-client relationships. Whilst therapeutic relationships provide important support, they differ from friendships. Therapists provide boundaried, professional support during sessions but are not available outside sessions in ways friends are. Understanding this boundary prevents disappointment and ensures the therapeutic relationship remains effective. Seeking multiple sources of support rather than relying solely on the therapist meets broader support needs.

Online Support Communities: Benefits and Risks

Online communities for people with depression provide accessible support, particularly for people with limited local support or for whom online interaction feels more comfortable than face-to-face. However, online communities vary enormously in quality, and thoughtful participation protects well-being.

Benefits of online depression support include accessibility from home without travel or scheduling constraints, anonymity allowing discussion of sensitive topics, finding others with similar specific experiences, immediate availability when support is needed, less pressure than face-to-face interaction, and exposure to diverse perspectives and coping strategies. For people in rural areas, with disabilities limiting mobility, or with social anxiety, online support might provide the only accessible option.

Risks include exposure to triggering content, including descriptions of severe symptoms or suicidal ideation, reinforcement of hopelessness if community focuses only on suffering without recovery, comparison with others who seem worse off, creating guilt or others who seem to cope better creating inadequacy, receiving inaccurate information presented as fact, becoming substitute for face-to-face relationships and professional treatment, and spending excessive time online. Additionally, the lack of non-verbal communication online creates misunderstanding risk.

Evaluating online communities before extensive engagement protects well-being. Look for communities that balance acknowledging difficulty with hope and recovery focus, encourage professional treatment rather than suggesting online community alone is sufficient, moderate content to prevent harmful posts, provide accurate information supported by evidence, and demonstrate respectful, supportive culture. Communities dominated by extreme despair, glorification of suffering, anti-treatment attitudes, or toxic dynamics should be avoided.

Using online communities constructively involves setting time limits to prevent excessive use, balancing online interaction with offline activities and relationships, taking breaks if content becomes overwhelming, avoiding comparison with others, fact-checking information, maintaining anonymity for privacy, and supplementing with professional treatment when needed. Online support as a component of a broader support network provides value. As the sole or dominant source of support, it is insufficient.

Hope, Recovery, and Life After Depression

Whilst this book has addressed depression's difficulties, challenges, and suffering in detail, it is essential to emphasise that recovery is possible, common, and achievable. The vast majority of people who experience depression recover, even from severe episodes. Many people eventually experience not just absence of depression but genuine flourishing. Maintaining hope during depression is difficult but essential. Understanding that depression is temporary, that effective treatments exist, and that your future can be bright despite current darkness supports perseverance through the recovery journey.

The Nature of Recovery: What to Expect

Recovery from depression is rarely linear. Rather than steady daily improvement, recovery typically involves gradual overall improvement with fluctuations, including good days and difficult days. Early in recovery, difficult days might outnumber good days. Gradually, the ratio shifts with more good days than bad. Eventually, bad days become occasional rather than frequent. Understanding this pattern prevents discouragement when difficult days occur after improvement has begun.

The timeline for recovery varies widely depending on depression severity, treatment approach, individual factors, and life circumstances. Some people experience significant improvement within weeks of starting effective treatment. Others require months. For people with severe or treatment-resistant depression, recovery might take longer and might involve trying multiple treatments. However, even people with severe depression typically experience improvement eventually with appropriate, persistent treatment.

Recovery milestones provide encouragement and mark progress. Early milestones might include completing self-care tasks most days, attending work or social activities even if difficult, experiencing moments of pleasure or interest, sleeping more consistently, or noticing reduced suicidal thoughts. Middle recovery milestones might include completing full workdays or social activities without overwhelming exhaustion, genuinely enjoying some activities, initiating activities rather than only responding to requirements, improved concentration, and reconnecting with people. Later milestones might include sustained periods of good mood, looking forward to future, pursuing new goals and activities, resilience when difficulties occur, and helping others.

Recognising progress can be difficult during recovery as depression creates negative bias making you discount improvements. Keeping a diary tracking mood, activities, and achievements provides concrete evidence of progress over time. People around you might notice improvements before you do. Deliberately noting positive changes and successes, no matter how small, counters depression's tendency to minimise progress.

Recovery is not perfection. Experiencing occasional low mood, stress, or sadness is normal human experience distinct from depression. Aiming for constant happiness is unrealistic and sets you up for disappointment. Rather, recovery involves capacity to experience full range of emotions including difficult ones, overall trajectory of wellbeing, engagement in valued activities and relationships, ability to cope with life's inevitable difficulties, and quality of life that feels satisfying.

Common Concerns About Recovery

Many people with depression hold concerns about recovery that, whilst understandable, can become barriers. Addressing these concerns directly supports hope and engagement with recovery efforts.

'What if treatment doesn't work for me?' represents a common fear. Whilst not every treatment works for every person, and finding effective treatment might require trying multiple approaches, the vast majority of people eventually find a treatment that helps significantly. Persistence, open communication with healthcare providers about what is and is not helping, and willingness to try different approaches usually lead to effective treatment. Even people initially labelled as having treatment-resistant depression often eventually respond to combination approaches, novel treatments, or comprehensive interventions.

'What if I relapse after recovery?' is a realistic concern as depression recurrence risk exists, particularly for people with previous episodes. However, recurrence is not inevitable. Many people never experience another episode. For those who do, knowing that you recovered before provides evidence that you can recover again. Additionally, learning from your first experience about warning signs, helpful coping strategies, and when to seek help allows earlier intervention if symptoms return, potentially preventing full relapse. Ongoing management strategies, including maintaining helpful practices developed during recovery, monitoring mood, and accessing support early if symptoms emerge, reduce recurrence risk.

'What if I can't return to normal?' raises questions about whether life can ever feel normal again after depression. This concern reflects depression's impact on identity and sense of self. Many people do return fully to their previous life and functioning. Others find that depression changes them permanently, sometimes in negative ways, such as increased vulnerability to stress, but often also in positive ways, such as increased empathy, changed priorities, or deeper appreciation for good times. 'Normal' might be different from before, but this does not mean worse. Many people find a new normal after depression feels more authentic and meaningful than their previous life.

'I'm afraid of losing the identity of being depressed' might sound counterintuitive, but it reflects that chronic depression can become central to identity. When you have been depressed for an extended period, depression shapes how you see yourself and how others see you. Recovery requires developing a new identity not centred on illness. This transition, whilst ultimately positive, involves grief for a familiar if unwanted identity and navigation of who you are beyond depression. Therapy often helps with this identity work.

'I don't deserve to recover' reflects the guilt and low self-worth characteristic of depression. You might believe your depression is a punishment you deserve, that recovery is only for others more worthy, or that you do not deserve happiness. These beliefs are depression speaking, not the truth. Everyone deserves recovery, relief from suffering, and an opportunity for a good life, including you. Working in therapy to challenge beliefs about not deserving recovery is often necessary.

Recovery Stories and Messages of Hope

Whilst every person's experience of depression and recovery is unique, common themes emerge from recovery stories that provide hope and inspiration. These are not to minimise individual suffering or suggest recovery is easy, but to emphasise that recovery truly is possible.

Many people report that what felt like permanent darkness during depression eventually lifted, often without them noticing the exact moment things began improving. Looking back, they can identify when life started feeling livable again, but during recovery, the changes felt so gradual they were imperceptible day-to-day. This speaks to the importance of persistence even when improvement feels imperceptible.

People who recover frequently describe reaching a point where they actively engaged with treatment and recovery work rather than passively receiving treatment. This shift from passive recipient to active participant in recovery represents an important turning point. It might involve committing fully to therapy homework, making lifestyle changes recommended, reaching out for support, or deciding that they want recovery enough to do the difficult work required. This is not blaming people for not recovering if they have not reached this point, but recognising that active engagement, when you can muster it, powerfully facilitates recovery.

Relationships often emerge in recovery stories as a crucial element. Someone believing in you when you cannot believe in yourself, someone refusing to give up on you, or someone providing practical help that kept you going during the worst times frequently appears in recovery narratives. This emphasises the importance of maintaining at least some connections during depression and accepting help when offered.

Small moments of pleasure or interest during depression, even when overall mood remains low, often represent early signs of recovery. Noticing birdsong, enjoying a meal, laughing at something funny, or feeling momentary contentment provides evidence that the capacity for positive emotion remains even if dormant. These moments gradually increase in frequency and duration until eventually positive experiences become common again.

Many people describe their experience of depression as a journey that, whilst extremely difficult, ultimately taught them important lessons, increased their empathy and compassion, showed them their own strength, clarified their values and priorities, or deepened their relationships. This is not suggesting depression is good or that people should be grateful for depression. Depression is a devastating illness causing immense suffering. However, finding meaning in the experience afterwards, recognising growth that occurred, and using the experience to help others can transform what felt like meaningless suffering into an experience that contributed something valuable. This post-traumatic growth does not occur for everyone, and forcing this interpretation is unhelpful. However, remaining open to potential positive changes that might emerge supports holistic healing.

The message that recovery is possible even from very severe depression, even after multiple failed treatments, even when you have given up hope, even when nobody believes in you, even when you feel hopeless – this message is crucial. Countless people who felt certain they would never recover, who were told they would always be ill, who attempted suicide believing death was only escape, are now living full, meaningful, happy lives. You can be one of them.

Crisis Management and Emergency Situations

Whilst much of recovery involves gradual progress through consistent application of treatment and self-management strategies, crises occasionally arise requiring immediate intervention. Understanding how to recognise a crisis, access emergency support, manage acute suicidal thinking, and support someone else in crisis can be life-saving.

Recognising When Crisis Intervention Is Needed

Crisis represents a state where an immediate safety risk exists or where usual coping mechanisms have completely broken down, leaving the person unable to function or make decisions. Not every difficult period constitutes a crisis requiring emergency intervention, but certain situations absolutely do require immediate professional help.

Active suicidal intent with a specific plan and means available represents a clear emergency. If you are experiencing strong urges to end your life, have developed a specific plan for how you would do this, and have access to the means to carry out the plan, you need immediate help. This is particularly urgent if you feel you cannot keep yourself safe, if you are actively making preparations such as writing goodbye notes or giving away possessions, or if you feel calm and resolved about ending your life after a period of distress. Call emergency services (999 in the UK), go to the accident and emergency department, call the crisis team if you are known to mental health services, or call Samaritans on 116 123.

Psychotic symptoms, including hallucinations, delusions, severe confusion, or loss of contact with reality, constitute emergencies, particularly if accompanied by risk to self or others. Psychotic depression, whilst relatively uncommon, is extremely serious. If you are experiencing voices telling you to harm yourself, beliefs that you or others are in danger, severe paranoia, or cannot distinguish reality from false perceptions, immediate psychiatric assessment is needed.

Complete inability to care for yourself, including not eating or drinking for an extended period, severe self-neglect, inability to get out of bed or perform basic self-care, or catatonic states, represents a medical emergency. Severe depression can be physically dangerous through dehydration, malnutrition, and medical complications of immobility. Hospital admission might be necessary to ensure physical safety whilst intensive treatment begins.

Risk to others, whilst less common in depression than some other conditions, occasionally occurs, particularly in psychotic depression or when severe depression combines with substance intoxication or withdrawal. If you are experiencing thoughts of harming others, particularly if these are specific and you feel unable to control them, an urgent psychiatric assessment protects both you and others.

Accessing Emergency Mental Health Support

Multiple pathways exist for accessing urgent mental health support, each appropriate in different circumstances. Understanding options allows you to access appropriate help level quickly.

Emergency services via 999 should be called if immediate risk to life exists, if you have taken overdose or injured yourself severely, if you are unable to keep yourself safe from suicide, or if severe psychiatric emergency such as psychotic episode is occurring. Ambulance services and police respond to mental health emergencies and will arrange transport to accident and emergency department or, where available, specialist psychiatric liaison services. Calling 999 is appropriate and important when a crisis is severe; do not worry about wasting emergency services' time when a genuine emergency exists.

Accident and Emergency departments at hospitals provide assessment and initial management of mental health crises. Psychiatric liaison services, increasingly available in A&E departments, include mental health professionals who can assess and provide immediate intervention. A&E can arrange admission to a psychiatric ward if needed, can provide medical treatment for overdose or self-harm injuries, can administer emergency medication to manage acute distress, and can arrange follow-up with crisis teams or other community services. Attending A&E for a mental health crisis is entirely appropriate; psychiatric emergencies are as legitimate as physical emergencies.

Crisis Resolution and Home Treatment teams, available in many areas of the UK, provide intensive home-based support for people in mental health crisis. These teams can visit multiple times daily, provide support and treatment at home, avoiding hospital admission when possible, monitor risk, administer medication if needed, and provide rapid response when contacted. If you are known to mental health services, you should have a contact number for the local crisis team. If not, your GP or A&E can arrange a referral. Crisis teams operate 24 hours a day and provide a vital alternative to hospital admission for many people.

Your GP, whilst primarily office-based, can provide urgent appointments for mental health crises during working hours. GPs can assess risk, arrange immediate referral to mental health services, prescribe medication, arrange admission if necessary, and provide medical treatment for self-harm. If you are registered with a GP surgery, calling first thing in the morning, explaining it is an urgent mental health situation, usually secures a same-day appointment. Out of hours, NHS 111 can arrange an urgent GP assessment.

Mental health crisis lines provide immediate telephone support when you need to talk to someone, but the situation may not require an ambulance or hospital. Samaritans (116 123) operate 24 hours daily providing non-judgemental emotional support for people in distress. Other helplines, including Mind's Infoline, CALM (Campaign Against Living Miserably), and Papyrus for young people, provide specialist support. These services cannot provide medical treatment but offer crucial support, can help you safety plan, can help decide what professional support to access, and can simply provide a human connection when you feel alone.

Managing Acute Suicidal Thoughts

Experiencing suicidal thoughts, even intense ones, does not inevitably lead to a suicide attempt. Thoughts are not actions. Many people experience suicidal thoughts during severe depression, but do not act on them. Learning to manage these thoughts when they arise reduces risk and helps you remain safe whilst accessing appropriate treatment.

Safety planning involves creating a detailed plan while you are relatively calm, outlining specific steps to take when a crisis occurs. The plan should be written down and kept accessible. It should be shared with a trusted person who can support you in following it. A comprehensive safety plan includes identifying your personal warning signs that crisis is developing such as increased hopelessness, specific thoughts or urges, withdrawal from others, or increased substance use; listing coping strategies you can use independently such as safe places to go, distracting activities, grounding techniques, or exercise; identifying people and social settings that provide distraction including specific friends or family members with contact details, public places you could go, or activities you could engage in; listing people you can ask for help including specific names and phone numbers of friends, family, therapist, GP, or crisis team; listing professionals and agencies to contact in crisis including crisis team number, Samaritans, GP out-of-hours number, or 999; and identifying means restriction steps such as removing or securing potentially harmful items, giving medication to trusted person to dispense daily, or avoiding locations associated with suicidal thinking.

Means restriction, limiting access to means of suicide, is one of most effective suicide prevention strategies. Research consistently demonstrates that restricting access to lethal means reduces suicide rates. If you are experiencing suicidal thoughts, take active steps to restrict access to means. This includes giving excess medication to trusted person who can dispense only daily amounts, securing or disposing of sharp objects, avoiding locations from which you might jump, not keeping excessive alcohol at home, and ensuring others know to restrict access to means if you appear at increased risk. This is not suggesting removing all potential means is possible or that you would necessarily use any specific means, but reducing immediate access creates time for crisis to pass and for intervention to occur.

Distraction and delay techniques recognise that suicidal urges, like other urges, peak and then subside. If you can delay acting on urge for even short period, the intensity might reduce sufficiently for you to access help or for urge to pass. Promise yourself to wait specific period such as one hour, one day, or one week before acting on thoughts. During this time, use intense distraction including calling someone, going to public place where you will not be alone, engaging in absorbing activity, or going to hospital. Each time you successfully delay, you demonstrate to yourself that urges can be survived.

Grounding techniques help during acute suicidal crisis by connecting you to present moment and physical reality. Simple techniques include holding ice cubes in hands focusing on physical sensation, stamping feet or moving body vigorously, naming objects in the environment describing them in detail, splashing cold water on face, eating something with strong flavour, or using strong scent. These techniques interrupt spiral of distressing thoughts by shifting attention to physical sensations.

Challenging thoughts about suicide involves recognising that suicidal thinking during depression reflects illness not reality. Common thoughts include 'others would be better off without me' (untrue – suicide devastates those left behind), 'nothing will ever get better' (untrue – depression is treatable and temporary), 'I cannot bear this pain' (you are bearing it, moment by moment, and with support and treatment it will lessen), and 'suicide is the only solution' (untrue – it is permanent solution to temporary problem, and other solutions exist even if invisible right now). Writing down these thoughts and evidence against them when calmer provides resource to refer to during crisis.

Committing to staying safe, either to yourself or to trusted person, creates external motivation when internal motivation falters. Making explicit commitment such as 'I will not harm myself before my appointment on Thursday' or 'I will call someone before acting on thoughts' provides structure. Renewing commitment daily or weekly, particularly during high-risk periods, maintains focus on staying alive long enough for treatment to work.

Understanding that suicidal thoughts are symptom of depression, not accurate assessment of your situation, provides perspective. Depression creates cognitive distortions making situation appear hopeless, making negative outcomes seem inevitable, and making suicide seem reasonable solution. These perceptions are illness-generated, not reality-based. Reminding yourself 'this is depression talking' creates distance from thoughts without requiring you to believe positive things you cannot believe whilst depressed.

Supporting Someone Else in Crisis

Supporting someone experiencing mental health crisis can be frightening and challenging. You might fear saying wrong thing, feel uncertain about how serious situation is, worry about breaching confidentiality, or feel overwhelmed by responsibility. Understanding basic principles of crisis support allows you to help effectively whilst protecting your own wellbeing.

Taking suicidal talk seriously represents most important principle. Never dismiss, minimise, or challenge someone expressing suicidal thoughts with responses like 'you don't really mean that' or 'you have too much to live for.' These responses, though often well-intentioned, invalidate the person's experience and reduce likelihood they will seek help. Instead, listen without judgment, take thoughts seriously, ask directly about plans and access to means, and help the person access appropriate support. Research clearly demonstrates that asking about suicide does not plant ideas or increase risk;

rather, it shows you take their distress seriously and opens conversation about getting help.

Asking directly about suicidal thoughts and plans, if someone seems very distressed or you have concerns, is appropriate and important. You might say 'are you having thoughts of ending your life?' or 'do you have a plan for how you would do this?' These direct questions feel uncomfortable but provide essential information about risk level. If the person has specific plan and access to means, situation is more urgent than vague thoughts without plan. Direct questioning demonstrates your willingness to discuss difficult topic and provides opportunity for person to voice thoughts they might have been hiding.

Staying with the person if they are in immediate danger prevents isolation and provides supervision. Do not leave someone alone if suicide risk is acute. If you cannot stay, arrange for someone else to stay, or help the person get to A&E or call emergency services. Your physical presence, even without extensive conversation, provides safety and reminds person they are not alone.

Removing or securing means of suicide, if possible, reduces immediate risk. This might include taking excess medication, removing sharp objects, or simply ensuring person is in safe environment without easy access to means. Do this collaboratively where possible, explaining you are doing this to keep them safe because you care about them. If person is unwilling to give up means or if you cannot secure means, this elevates urgency of getting professional support.

Helping access professional support rather than trying to manage crisis alone protects both the person in crisis and yourself. You are not trained clinician and should not attempt to be. Your role is to provide immediate support, take concerns seriously, and facilitate connection with appropriate services. This might mean calling GP together, going to A&E together, calling crisis team if they are known to services, or calling 999 if immediate danger exists. Offering to make calls, provide transport, or accompany them provides practical support whilst ensuring professional assessment occurs.

Following up after immediate crisis passes demonstrates ongoing support. People often feel embarrassed or ashamed after crisis, worry they have burdened others, or fear judgment. Checking in the next day, expressing care and concern, and offering continued support helps person feel less alone. Continuing to monitor situation in following days and weeks, encouraging engagement with treatment, and maintaining connection provides ongoing protective factor.

Setting boundaries protects your own wellbeing. Supporting someone in crisis can be emotionally exhausting and stressful. You cannot be available 24 hours daily. You cannot take responsibility for someone else's safety indefinitely. Setting boundaries about when you are available, encouraging professional support, and ensuring you have your own support are essential. It is appropriate and necessary to say 'I care about you and want to help, but I am not able to be your only support. We need to involve professionals who can provide the help you need.'

Looking after yourself after supporting someone in crisis is important. Vicarious trauma affects people who support others through crisis. You might experience disturbed sleep, intrusive thoughts about the crisis, anxiety, or your own low mood. Talking to someone about your experience, accessing support for yourself if needed, and engaging in self-care activities helps process the experience. Supporting someone in crisis is significant emotional labour; acknowledging this and caring for yourself afterwards is not selfish but necessary.

Preventing Depression: Building Resilience and Protective Factors

Whilst not all depression is preventable, given biological vulnerability and unpredictable life circumstances, substantial evidence indicates that protective factors and resilience-building reduce depression risk and can prevent recurrence. Understanding prevention across different levels – individual actions, community interventions, and societal changes – provides comprehensive approach to reducing depression's impact.

Primary Prevention: Reducing Risk Before Depression Develops

Primary prevention aims to reduce depression incidence in people who have never experienced depression. Whilst universal prevention is not realistic or necessary, targeted prevention for at-risk groups and general promotion of mental health protective factors benefit population health.

Building emotional resilience in children and young people represents a crucial early prevention strategy. Resilience involves the capacity to adapt to adversity, regulate emotions, maintain connections with others, and maintain hope. Schools can promote resilience through social and emotional learning programmes, teaching emotional awareness, regulation strategies, problem-solving skills, and healthy relationship skills. Parenting programmes teaching responsive, warm parenting and appropriate discipline support healthy child development. Early intervention services for children experiencing adversity prevent the entrenchment of difficulties.

Promoting help-seeking and reducing stigma increases the likelihood that people experiencing early symptoms access treatment before depression becomes severe. Public education campaigns about depression symptoms, treatability, and the importance of early help-seeking gradually change attitudes. Visible role models speaking about mental health experiences normalise help-seeking. Training for teachers, workplace managers, and community leaders in recognising mental health difficulties and encouraging support reduces barriers to accessing help.

Addressing social determinants of health including poverty, inequality, discrimination, and lack of opportunity represents fundamental prevention strategy. Depression rates are substantially higher in disadvantaged populations. Policies reducing poverty through adequate welfare systems, good quality employment, affordable housing, and accessible education indirectly prevent depression. Whilst individual therapeutic approaches are essential for people with depression, population-level reduction in depression requires addressing structural factors creating vulnerability.

Supporting parents and families, particularly during perinatal period, prevents depression in parents and promotes healthy child development reducing children's future depression risk. Home visiting programmes for new parents, accessible perinatal mental health services, high-quality childcare, parental leave allowing time with infants, and support for families experiencing difficulties all contribute to prevention.

Promoting physical health through encouraging physical activity, healthy eating, good sleep, and limiting substance use prevents depression whilst supporting general health. Public health campaigns, school physical education, urban planning creating walkable communities with green spaces, and policies limiting alcohol and tobacco access contribute to prevention. Physical and mental health are inseparable; promoting physical health promotes mental health.

Creating connected communities where people know neighbours, have spaces to gather, and experience sense of belonging protects against depression. Community development initiatives, volunteering infrastructure, community centres and libraries, and urban design promoting interaction all build social capital, protecting mental health. Loneliness and isolation increase depression risk; connected communities reduce isolation.

Secondary Prevention: Early Intervention to Prevent Progression

Secondary prevention involves identifying and treating depression early, preventing mild symptoms from progressing to severe depression and preventing a chronic course. Early intervention reduces suffering, prevents complications, and improves outcomes.

Screening for depression in high-risk populations or in routine healthcare identifies cases that might otherwise go unrecognised. Some GP surgeries routinely screen for depression, particularly for people with chronic physical illness or pregnant women. Screening alone is insufficient; positive screens must lead to assessment and treatment. However, systematic screening identifies people who might not spontaneously report psychological symptoms.

Improving access to early intervention, particularly psychological therapy, allows people with emerging symptoms to access help before depression becomes severe. Traditional mental health services often have long waiting lists, meaning mild symptoms have progressed to moderate or severe by the time treatment begins. Rapid access to brief psychological interventions, computerised CBT, peer support, or counselling for mild to moderate symptoms prevents escalation. In the UK, Improving Access to Psychological Therapies services provide relatively rapid access to evidence-based psychological therapy.

Indicated prevention programmes target individuals showing early symptoms but not meeting full diagnostic criteria. Cognitive behavioural approaches delivered in group format or through self-help resources, problem-solving therapy, or interpersonal counselling provided at the early symptom stage prevent progression to clinical depression in a substantial proportion of recipients. Schools might offer such programmes to students showing early signs. Primary care might offer brief interventions.

Self-monitoring and early intervention for people with previous depression prevent relapse. People with depression history are at elevated risk of recurrence. Learning to recognise personal early warning signs, such as sleep disturbance, increased irritability, social withdrawal, or negative thinking, allows early action. Developing a relapse prevention plan specifying actions to take when warning signs occur, such as increasing social contact, reinstating helpful activities, contacting a therapist or GP, or increasing medication if previously reduced, allows a rapid response, preventing a full episode.

Tertiary Prevention: Preventing Chronic Course and Complications

Tertiary prevention aims to reduce disability, complications, and recurrence in people who have experienced depression. This includes effective treatment reducing duration of episodes, relapse prevention strategies, and rehabilitation addressing functional impairment.

Ensuring adequate treatment duration prevents premature discontinuation leading to relapse. Antidepressants should typically continue for at least six months after symptom remission. Psychological therapy should continue until stable recovery achieved. Many people discontinue treatment prematurely when symptoms improve, leading to rapid relapse. Education about importance of completing treatment course improves adherence.

Maintenance treatment for recurrent depression prevents or reduces the frequency of episodes. People with three or more episodes of depression, or with severe episodes, often benefit from continuing antidepressant medication long-term. Long-term psychological therapy, such as monthly maintenance sessions after acute treatment, prevents recurrence. Balancing the benefits of prevention against the burden of ongoing treatment requires individualised decision-making considering recurrence risk, treatment preferences, and individual circumstances.

Preventing suicide in people with depression through comprehensive risk assessment, safety planning, restricted means access, intensive support during high-risk periods, and involving families represents crucial tertiary prevention. Suicide is not an inevitable outcome of depression; most people with depression never attempt suicide. Systematic attention to suicide risk and evidence-based prevention strategies reduces suicide rates.

Rehabilitation approaches address functional impairment persisting after symptom remission. Supported employment helps people return to work after depression. Cognitive remediation addresses cognitive impairment. Social skills training and supported socialisation help rebuild social networks. Occupational therapy addresses practical living skills. Whilst symptom-focused treatment is the primary intervention, functional recovery requires additional attention.

Lifestyle Factors in Depression Prevention

Certain lifestyle factors consistently emerge in research as protective against depression. Whilst lifestyle changes alone do not treat clinical depression and should not replace professional treatment, these factors reduce risk and support recovery and prevention.

Regular physical activity represents one of the most robust protective factors. Exercise has direct biological effects on mood through endorphins, neuroplasticity, and inflammation reduction. Exercise also provides structure, achievement, and often social contact. Guidelines recommend 150 minutes of moderate-intensity aerobic activity weekly plus strength training twice weekly. Even smaller amounts provide benefit. Finding activities you enjoy increases the likelihood of sustaining exercise. Building activity into daily routine through active transport, taking stairs, or walking meetings makes activity sustainable.

Adequate sleep protects mental health. Chronic sleep deprivation increases depression risk. Prioritising sleep through consistent bedtime routines, limiting screen time before bed, creating a comfortable sleep environment, and addressing sleep disorders such as sleep apnoea prevents sleep-related depression risk. Seven to nine hours nightly suits most adults. Individual sleep needs vary; prioritising adequate sleep for your needs protects health.

A healthy diet, particularly a Mediterranean-style diet rich in vegetables, fruits, whole grains, fish, nuts, and olive oil, is associated with reduced depression risk. Ultra-processed foods, excessive sugar, and poor nutritional quality increase risk. Whilst diet does not cause or cure depression, nutritional status affects brain function. Eating regular meals, limiting alcohol, staying hydrated, and consuming varied, nutrient-dense foods support mental health.

Limiting alcohol consumption protects against depression. Whilst moderate drinking might not harm most people, regular heavy drinking substantially increases depression risk. UK guidelines recommend not exceeding 14 units weekly, spread across at least three days with several alcohol-free days. People with depression history might benefit from avoiding alcohol entirely, given its depressogenic effects. Reducing alcohol consumption if it exceeds guidelines benefits both physical and mental health.

Not smoking or stopping smoking benefits mental health. Smokers have higher depression rates than non-smokers. Whilst many smokers believe smoking reduces stress, it actually increases anxiety and stress between cigarettes. Stopping smoking, though initially difficult, improves mental health medium to long term. NHS stop smoking services provide effective support.

Spending time in natural environments, sometimes called green time or nature exposure, protects mental health. Time in parks, the countryside, near water, or other natural settings reduces stress and improves mood. Even urban green spaces provide benefits. Building regular nature exposure into routine, whether through walks, gardening, or simply sitting outside, provides a simple, accessible protective factor.

Maintaining social connections throughout life protects against depression. Investing in relationships, making time for friends and family, joining groups, volunteering, and generally maintaining social engagement provides protection. Whilst depression makes social engagement difficult, making social connections a priority during well periods builds a protective network available during vulnerable periods.

Engaging in meaningful activities that align with values and provide purpose protects mental health. This might be work, volunteering, creative pursuits, spiritual involvement, or any activity that feels meaningful to you. Passive leisure, such as television watching, provides less protection than active engagement in valued activities. Identifying what matters to you and building life around these values creates a resilient foundation.

Managing stress through regular relaxation, mindfulness practise, time management, saying no to excessive demands, and work-life balance reduces risk. Chronic stress depletes resources and increases depression vulnerability. Whilst some stress is unavoidable, managing controllable stress and developing stress resilience through coping skills provides protection.

Self-Help Resources and Tools for Managing Depression

Whilst professional treatment is important for depression, self-help strategies and resources play an essential complementary role in recovery. Understanding available self-help options, how to use them effectively, and when self-help alone is insufficient ensures you can access appropriate level of support for your circumstances.

Books and Written Self-Help Resources

Self-help books based on cognitive behavioural therapy and other evidence-based approaches can provide valuable support, particularly for mild to moderate depression. These books typically guide you through structured programmes teaching skills for managing symptoms. They work best when you work through them systematically, completing exercises rather than simply reading, and when you apply skills learned to your daily life.

The effectiveness of self-help books varies considerably. Books based on evidence-based therapies such as CBT, behavioural activation, or mindfulness have the strongest research support. Books should provide clear, practical strategies rather than only theoretical information. Interactive workbooks requiring active participation typically prove more effective than passive reading. Choosing books recommended by mental health professionals or based on treatment manuals ensures quality.

Using self-help books effectively requires commitment and structure. Set aside regular time for working through the book rather than attempting to read it all at once. Complete all exercises, even when they feel difficult or pointless; consistent practise builds skills. Apply strategies learned to real situations in your life. Track your progress using mood diaries or exercise completion records provided. Consider working through a book with a friend or in a self-help group for mutual support and accountability.

Limitations of self-help books include that they provide a generic approach which might not address your specific circumstances, they lack personalisation that a therapist provides, they cannot assess your progress or adjust approach, and they require significant self-motivation which depression depletes. Self-help books work best for motivated individuals with mild to moderate symptoms who prefer independent work. They can supplement professional therapy but rarely substitute entirely for moderate to severe depression.

Online Resources and Digital Interventions

Computerised CBT programmes deliver structured CBT through interactive websites or applications. Programmes such as MoodGYM, Beating the Blues, or commercially available applications provide guided self-help with progress tracking. Some programmes are available free through NHS or other health services; others require purchase. These programmes typically include psychoeducation about depression, interactive exercises teaching CBT skills, homework assignments, and mood monitoring.

Advantages of computerised interventions include accessibility from home at convenient times, anonymity, which some people prefer, a structured progressive approach, and lower cost than face-to-face therapy. Research demonstrates effectiveness for mild to moderate depression. However, engagement and completion rates are often low; many people start but do not complete programmes. Lack of human contact and personalisation limits appeal for some. Computerised interventions work best when supported by brief therapist contact, even if only through email or phone.

Mental health applications for smartphones provide mood tracking, meditation guidance, CBT exercises, crisis management resources, and peer support. Quality varies enormously. Apps should be evidence-based rather than simply commercial products with no research backing. NHS Apps Library and similar resources provide evaluated, quality-assured applications. Using apps effectively involves selecting a specific app for a specific purpose rather than downloading many apps then using none, enabling notifications for reminders if helpful, using app features regularly rather than one-off, and reviewing whether app is actually helping or is simply another unused item on your phone.

Online therapy platforms connecting people with therapists for video, phone, or text-based therapy increase accessibility, particularly for people with mobility limitations, rural residents, or those preferring remote therapy. Effectiveness appears broadly similar to face-to-face therapy for mild to moderate depression. However, ensure the therapist is properly qualified and registered. Some online platforms employ counsellors without appropriate training. Talking Therapies UK (www.talkingtherapies.co.uk) can provide appropriately qualified professional support.

Websites providing information about depression, treatment options, and self-help strategies support informed decision-making. Reliable websites include NHS website, Mind, Rethink Mental Illness, the Royal College of Psychiatrists, and Talking Therapies UK. Be cautious of websites providing misleading or dangerous advice, particularly those promoting unproven alternative treatments, discouraging professional treatment, or providing overly simplistic solutions. Any website providing health information should cite evidence sources and clearly identify who is responsible for the content.

Mindfulness and Meditation Resources

Mindfulness involves paying attention to the present moment with acceptance rather than judgment. Regular mindfulness practise reduces depression symptoms, prevents relapse, and supports wellbeing. Mindfulness can be learned through classes, books, applications, or online resources. Many people begin with guided meditations before progressing to independent practise.

Mindfulness-Based Cognitive Therapy (MBCT), an eight-week group programme combining mindfulness meditation with CBT elements, was specifically developed to prevent depression relapse. MBCT is available through some NHS services and private providers. Research demonstrates a substantial reduction in relapse risk for people with recurrent depression. MBCT teaches formal meditation practices, mindfulness in daily activities, and CBT skills for relating differently to negative thoughts.

Informal mindfulness practise integrated into daily life makes mindfulness accessible without requiring extensive meditation sessions. Mindful eating involves paying full attention to the eating experience, noticing taste, texture, and sensations. Mindful walking involves noticing sensations of walking, your feet contacting the ground, and your surroundings. Mindful breathing involves periodically pausing to notice breathing for a few breaths. These brief practices, repeated throughout the day, cultivate mindfulness without requiring major time commitment.

Meditation applications such as Headspace, Calm, or Insight Timer provide guided meditations, meditation timers, and structured courses. Free versions typically provide basic content; paid subscriptions provide full libraries. Starting with short guided meditations, perhaps five to ten minutes, allows habit formation without overwhelming commitment. Consistency matters more than duration; daily brief practise benefits more than occasional longer sessions.

Yoga, tai chi, and qigong combine movement with mindfulness and breath awareness. These practices provide physical activity benefits alongside mindfulness and relaxation. Classes are widely available. Online videos allow home practise. These movement-based practices suit people who find sitting meditation difficult or who respond well to physical activity.

Acceptance and Commitment Therapy (ACT) self-help resources teach psychological flexibility, values clarification, and committed action alongside mindfulness. ACT workbooks, online resources, and applications help people develop acceptance of difficult internal experiences whilst taking action aligned with values. ACT provides an alternative approach to CBT's focus on changing thoughts, instead emphasising changing the relationship with thoughts.

Support Groups and Peer Support

Peer support involves people with lived experience of mental health difficulties supporting each other. Peer support provides unique benefits, including shared understanding from lived experience, hope through connecting with people further in recovery, practical tips learned from experience, reduced isolation through connection with others who understand, and validation that experiences and feelings are normal responses to depression.

Depression support groups operate in many areas, provided by mental health charities, NHS services, or grassroots organisations. Groups might be time-limited with a structured programme or ongoing with rolling membership. Some groups are facilitated by professionals; others are peer-led. Group formats vary from structured topic-based discussions to unstructured sharing. Finding a group that suits your preferences requires trying different options.

Peer support services employ people with lived experience of mental health difficulties to provide one-to-one support, run groups, or work within mental health teams. Peer support workers bring a valuable perspective, can model recovery, and often connect particularly well with service users. NHS mental health services increasingly employ peer support workers. Independent peer support organisations also exist.

Online support communities provide accessible peer support, particularly for people unable to attend face-to-face groups. Forums, social media groups, and dedicated platforms connect people with depression globally. However, quality varies. Helpful online communities balance acknowledging difficulty with hope and recovery focus, provide accurate information, maintain a supportive culture, and encourage professional treatment. Less helpful communities focus only on suffering, reinforce hopelessness, or provide misinformation.

Mutual aid groups for addiction, such as Alcoholics Anonymous or Narcotics Anonymous, benefit people with depression and co-occurring substance use. The community support, structured programme, and emphasis on peer accountability support recovery from both conditions. Whilst spiritual elements do not suit everyone, many people find profound value in mutual aid programmes.

Creating Personal Wellness Plan

Wellness plans, also called recovery plans or wellness recovery action plans, provide personalised documents outlining what keeps you well, warning signs of decline, and actions to take when symptoms develop. Creating comprehensive wellness plan whilst feeling relatively well ensures you have guidance available during difficult periods when decision-making is impaired.

Components of comprehensive wellness plan include listing what you are like when you are well, describing mood, energy, interests, sleep, and social engagement at baseline. This provides reference point for recognising when things are declining. List daily maintenance activities that keep you well such as exercise, sleep schedule, healthy eating, social contact, and enjoyable activities. Listing triggers and early warning signs helps recognise when intervention is needed. These might include sleep disturbance, increased irritability, withdrawal from others, or specific life circumstances that historically trigger difficulties.

Action plans specify what to do when warning signs appear. This might include increasing social contact, resuming activities you have let slip, contacting therapist, reviewing coping strategies, or involving trusted friends. Plans should be specific and practical rather than vague. Instead of 'look after myself better,' specify 'return to gym three times weekly, ensure eating three meals daily, and call Sarah for coffee this week.' Crisis plans outline what to do if symptoms become severe, including who to contact, how to access crisis services, and advance decisions about treatment if you become too unwell to make decisions.

Supporters' roles specify how others can help during different stages. When you are well, supporters might simply maintain normal contact and encourage wellness activities. When warning signs appear, supporters might remind you of your action plan, provide practical help, or encourage professional contact. In crisis, supporters might need to contact services on your behalf or provide intensive support. Discussing these roles with supporters whilst well ensures everyone understands expectations.

Reviewing and updating wellness plans regularly ensures they remain relevant. Every few months, review whether listed warning signs remain accurate, whether planned actions are realistic and helpful, and whether contact information is current. Revise based on experience of what works. After episodes of illness, update plan incorporating lessons learned about triggers, effective strategies, and unhelpful responses.

Navigating the Healthcare System and Treatment Services

Successfully accessing and navigating mental health services requires understanding how systems work, advocating for your needs, and persisting when difficulties arise. The healthcare system can feel bureaucratic, confusing, and impersonal. However, understanding how to navigate it effectively improves access to appropriate treatment.

General practise: Your Gateway to Mental Health Services

General Practitioners represent the usual first point of contact for mental health difficulties in the UK NHS. GPs can assess depression, provide initial treatment, prescribe medication, refer to specialist services, provide sick notes for employment, and coordinate care across services. Building effective working relationship with your GP facilitates good care.

Preparing for GP appointments about mental health maximises limited appointment time. Write down key points you want to communicate including main symptoms, how long they have lasted, how they affect your daily functioning, previous mental health history, current life circumstances contributing to difficulties, medications or therapies tried previously, and specific requests such as referral, medication, or sick note. Bringing written notes prevents forgetting important information when anxious.

Describing symptoms accurately helps GPs understand severity. Be specific about how depression affects sleep, appetite, energy, concentration, relationships, and work. Mention any suicidal thoughts, even if you feel uncomfortable doing so. GPs cannot assess risk without knowing suicidal ideation exists. Explain functional impairment such as 'I have missed two weeks of work' or 'I cannot leave the house' rather than only emotional symptoms. Functional impairment demonstrates severity more clearly than subjective distress alone.

Continuity of care, seeing same GP when possible, improves outcomes. Your GP gets to know you, understands your history, and builds therapeutic relationship. If seeing regular GP is difficult due to appointment availability, consider booking advance appointments or double appointments for complex discussions. Some surgeries offer extended appointments specifically for mental health.

If you feel your GP is not taking your concerns seriously or is not providing appropriate help, you have several options. Request second opinion from different GP in the practise. Some GP practices have GP with special interest in mental health who might provide more specialist input. Make formal complaint to practise manager if you believe care is inadequate. Register with different practise if relationship with current practise is irretrievably damaged. Advocate persistently for yourself; do not assume rejection of your request for help means you are not unwell enough.

NHS Talking Therapies (Previously NHS Talking Therapies)

NHS Talking Therapies services provide rapid access to psychological therapies for mild to moderate depression and anxiety. Services offer telephone assessment, guided self-help with supporter contact, structured group programmes, and individual therapy. Self-referral is available in most areas through online forms or by telephone, without requiring GP referral.

Assessment appointments, typically conducted by telephone or video, involve a detailed discussion of difficulties, completion of outcome measures, and recommendation of appropriate intervention level. Be honest during assessment; understating difficulties results in inadequate treatment, whilst exaggerating may result in inappropriate referral. The assessment is not trying to catch you out but to determine how best to help.

Treatment options vary by individual need and service availability. Low-intensity interventions, including guided self-help, computerised CBT, or psychoeducational groups, suit mild difficulties. High-intensity interventions, including individual CBT, counselling, or interpersonal therapy for six to twenty sessions, suit moderate difficulties. Some services offer long-term therapy for complex presentations. If initial treatment is ineffective, step-up to more intensive intervention should be offered.

Waiting times for NHS Talking Therapies should typically be under six weeks for the first appointment, with treatment beginning soon after. However, demand frequently exceeds capacity, creating longer waits. If waiting becomes unacceptably long, contact the service to enquire about your referral status. Consider private therapy if finances allow, and waiting is affecting your functioning. Some charities provide low-cost counselling during waiting periods.

Engaging actively with therapy maximises benefit. Attend appointments even when difficult, complete between-session tasks, be honest about what is and is not helping, and raise concerns promptly rather than disengaging. If a personality clash with the therapist affects engagement, requesting a different therapist is appropriate. Not every therapeutic relationship works; finding a good fit improves outcomes.

Community Mental Health Teams and Specialist Services

Community Mental Health Teams (CMHTs) provide specialist assessment and treatment for moderate to severe mental health difficulties. Access usually requires GP referral. CMHTs include psychiatrists, community psychiatric nurses, psychologists, occupational therapists, and social workers. They provide medication management, psychological therapy, care coordination, and support for people with complex or severe difficulties.

Assessment by CMHT involves detailed psychiatric evaluation, risk assessment, and formulation of problems. This typically takes one or more lengthy appointments. The team then decides whether to accept you for treatment, what treatment to offer, and which team member will be your care coordinator. If CMHT does not accept your referral, they should provide a clear explanation and advise on appropriate alternative services.

Care coordinators, your main point of contact within CMHT, coordinate your care across services, monitor your progress, provide support, and arrange reviews. Building a relationship with your care coordinator facilitates good care. Communicate openly about difficulties, attend appointments reliably, and contact them if circumstances change or a crisis develops. Care coordinators cannot provide 24-hour availability but should provide clear information about accessing help out of hours.

Care plans developed collaboratively outline problems, goals, interventions, responsibilities, and review dates. Care plans should reflect your priorities and preferences, not solely professional opinion. You have the right to a copy of your care plan. Review and update care plans regularly as circumstances change. If disagreements arise about the care plan, these should be documented, and you can request a second opinion or advocacy support.

Private Mental Health Services

Private therapy is available from www.Talkingtherapies.co.uk[1]. Private psychiatry, or other mental health services, provide alternatives to the NHS with advantages including rapid access, longer appointment times, greater choice of therapist, and sometimes access to treatments not routinely available through the NHS. However, cost restricts access for many people. Private fees vary widely but typically range from fifty to two hundred pounds per therapy session and two hundred to four hundred pounds for psychiatric consultation.

Finding reputable private practitioners requires checking professional registration. Psychologists should be registered with the Health and Care Professions Council. Psychiatrists should be registered with the General Medical Council. Psychotherapists should be registered with the United Kingdom Council for Psychotherapy or the British Association for Counselling and Psychotherapy. Registration ensures the practitioner is qualified and accountable to the professional body. Recommendations from GP, friends, or reliable sources help identify suitable practitioners.

Clarifying costs, appointment frequency, and expected treatment duration before starting prevents financial difficulties. Discuss fees openly, ask about sliding scale fees or whether payment plans are available, and understand cancellation policies. Some practitioners offer reduced rates for students or people on low incomes. Private medical insurance might cover some mental health treatment; check policy details.

Transitioning between NHS and private services requires coordination. Inform your GP if receiving private treatment, as they need a complete picture of your care. Ask the private practitioner to send letters to your GP updating them. If private treatment proves unaffordable to continue, discuss with your practitioner and GP about transitioning care back to NHS services.

Voluntary Sector Services and Charities

Mental health charities and voluntary organisations provide valuable services, often more accessible than NHS services. Mind, Rethink Mental Illness, Samaritans, and numerous local organisations offer helplines, peer

1. http://www.Talkingtherapies.co.uk

support, drop-in centres, employment support, housing support, and advocacy. Some charities provide counselling services, often on sliding scale fees more affordable than private therapy.

Drop-in centres and community centres run by mental health charities provide welcoming spaces for social contact, activities, and peer support without referral or diagnosis requirements. These services reduce isolation and provide a sense of community. Many have a recovery focus, helping people rebuild lives beyond simply managing symptoms. Looking for services in your local area through online searches, asking a GP, or contacting national charities for local branch information identifies available options.

Advocacy services support you in navigating services, understanding your rights, making complaints, attending meetings, or expressing your views when you feel unable to do so alone. Independent Mental Health Advocates have a specific legal role supporting people detained under the Mental Health Act, but advocacy is also available more broadly. Advocacy proves particularly valuable when you disagree with professionals, when you feel your voice is not heard, or when navigating complex systems feels overwhelming.

Employment support services, including job clubs, supported employment schemes, and back-to-work support specifically for people with mental health conditions, help with CV writing, application preparation, interview skills, workplace adjustments, and ongoing support when employed. These services understand mental health challenges and provide tailored support that generic employment services might not offer.

Your Rights and Legal Protections

Understanding your legal rights regarding mental health treatment, employment, benefits, and protections against discrimination empowers you to advocate for appropriate care and fair treatment. Whilst navigating legal frameworks can feel daunting, knowing your rights ensures you receive the treatment you are entitled to and protects against discrimination.

The Mental Health Act and Your Rights

The Mental Health Act 1983 (amended 2007) governs compulsory detention and treatment for mental disorder in England and Wales. Most people with depression receive treatment entirely voluntarily in community settings. However, in rare circumstances where depression is extremely severe with a high risk to oneself, compulsory admission might occur. Understanding the Act ensures you know your rights if this affects you.

Detention under the Mental Health Act, called sectioning, can only occur if specific criteria are met: you have a mental disorder, detention is necessary for your health or safety or for the protection of others, and appropriate treatment is available. The least restrictive option should always be used. Different sections of the Act allow detention for assessment (Section 2, up to 28 days) or treatment (Section 3, initially up to six months, renewable). Police can also take someone to a place of safety for assessment (Section 136) if they appear to have a mental disorder and are at immediate risk.

Rights while detained include being informed why you are detained, what section you are detained under, and what this means; receiving written information about your rights; having access to Independent Mental Health Advocate who can support you; requesting Mental Health Tribunal to review your detention; appealing to hospital managers about your detention; contacting a solicitor; having mail and telephone contact; receiving visitors; and refusing certain treatments unless specific criteria are met.

Consent to treatment while detained varies by treatment type. Medication can be given without consent for the first three months of detention, after which either your consent or a second opinion is required. Electroconvulsive therapy requires either your consent or, if you lack the capacity to consent or refuse, a second opinion stating treatment is appropriate. Some treatments, including psychosurgery, require both your consent and an independent second opinion regardless of capacity.

Mental Health Tribunals provide an independent review of detention. You can apply to the tribunal to appeal detention. Tribunal hears evidence from you, your representative, hospital staff, and an independent psychiatrist. The tribunal can discharge you from the section if it finds criteria for detention are not met. You have the right to legal representation at a tribunal, available free through legal aid.

Community Treatment Orders allow supervised treatment in the community after discharge from hospital detention. These remain controversial but aim to prevent the 'revolving door' of repeated admissions.

Conditions might include living in a specific place, attending appointments, and accepting treatment. Breach of conditions can result in a recall to the hospital. You have rights, including tribunal appeals for Community Treatment Orders.

The Mental Capacity Act and Decision-Making

The Mental Capacity Act 2005 protects people who lack capacity to make specific decisions and supports planning for situations where you might lack capacity. Having depression does not mean you automatically lack capacity. Capacity is decision-specific and time-specific; you might have capacity to make some decisions but not others, or might lack capacity when very unwell but regain it with treatment.

Capacity assessment involves determining whether you can understand information relevant to a decision, retain that information long enough to make a decision, use and weigh information as part of the decision-making process, and communicate your decision. Lack of capacity must not be assumed based on age, appearance, condition, or behaviour. Capacity assessment should assume capacity unless proved otherwise, and should support you to make a decision wherever possible.

Advance decisions to refuse treatment, previously called living wills, allow you to specify treatments you would refuse if you lost capacity. This must be made when you have capacity, must be specific about treatments refused and circumstances in which refusal applies, and must be written and witnessed if refusing life-sustaining treatment. Advance decisions allow you to maintain some control over treatment even if you become too unwell to make decisions.

Lasting Power of Attorney allows you to appoint someone to make decisions on your behalf if you lose capacity. Health and welfare Lasting Power of Attorney covers medical treatment decisions. Property and financial affairs Lasting Power of Attorney covers financial matters. These documents must be made while you have capacity and are registered with the Office of the Public Guardian. They provide a safeguard ensuring someone you trust makes decisions aligned with your values if you cannot.

Deprivation of Liberty Safeguards apply when someone lacks capacity and arrangements made for their care amount to deprivation of liberty. This might occur in hospitals or care homes. Safeguards ensure that deprivation of liberty is necessary and proportionate, regularly reviewed, and that the person has representation and the right to challenge. These protections prevent inappropriate restrictions on people's freedom.

Employment Rights and the Equality Act

The Equality Act 2010 protects people with disabilities, including mental health conditions, from discrimination in employment, education, and the provision of services. Depression that is long-term (lasting or likely to last 12 months or more) and has a substantial adverse effect on the ability to carry out normal day-to-day activities qualifies as disability under the Act. This entitles you to protection from discrimination and the right to reasonable adjustments.

Direct discrimination occurs when someone treats you less favourably because of your disability than they would treat someone without disability. This might include refusing to employ you, denying promotion, or dismissing you because of your depression. Direct discrimination is unlawful except in very limited circumstances where being non-disabled is a genuine occupational requirement.

Indirect discrimination occurs when a policy or practise applies to everyone but particularly disadvantages people with your disability without justification. This might include requiring perfect attendance when your depression necessitates occasional absences for treatment, or requiring shift patterns incompatible with medication side effects. Employers must justify such requirements as a proportionate means of achieving a legitimate aim.

Reasonable adjustments require employers to take positive steps to remove disadvantages faced by disabled employees. Adjustments might include flexible working hours, reduced hours during difficult periods, amended duties, extra time for tasks, a quiet workspace, regular supervision meetings providing support, or phased return after absence. What is 'reasonable' depends on the effectiveness of the adjustment, practicality, cost, and the employer's resources. Large employers are expected to make more extensive adjustments than small employers.

Disclosure of depression to employers is your choice. However, protection under Equality Act and access to reasonable adjustments typically require disclosure. Consider timing disclosure carefully, balance privacy concerns against practical benefits of adjustments, disclose to the appropriate person, such as occupational health or HR, rather than colleagues, and confirm adjustments in writing. You control how much detail to disclose; a general statement that you have a health condition requiring adjustments is sufficient.

If you experience discrimination, initially raise concerns informally with your employer, explaining what has occurred and why you believe it is discriminatory. If informal resolution fails, follow formal grievance procedures outlined in your employment contract or staff handbook. Contact ACAS (Advisory, Conciliation and Arbitration Service) for free advice about your rights and options. Consider an Employment Tribunal claim if discrimination continues. Tribunal claims must usually be brought within three months of the discriminatory act. Seek legal advice or support from disability discrimination specialists.

Benefits and Financial Support

Several benefits might be available if depression affects your ability to work or increases living costs. The benefits system is complex and changes frequently. Seeking advice from Citizens Advice, welfare rights services, or mental health charities ensures you access the benefits you are entitled to.

Universal Credit replaces several previous benefits for people of working age. If depression affects your ability to work, you might qualify for Universal Credit with additional elements for limited capability for work. Assessment involves a work capability assessment determining whether your condition prevents work or limits what work you can do. Medical evidence from your GP or psychiatrist supporting your claim is essential.

Personal Independence Payment (PIP) provides financial support for people with long-term health conditions or disabilities affecting daily living or mobility. Depression might entitle you to PIP if it substantially affects activities including preparing food, managing medication, washing and bathing, managing toilet needs, communicating, reading, making money decisions, engaging with others, or planning journeys. Assessment considers what you can do safely, reliably, and repeatedly. Bad days count; do not minimise difficulties during assessment.

Employment and Support Allowance might be available if your National Insurance contributions history qualifies you or if you have a low income. Work capability assessment determines eligibility. ESA provides income replacement when depression prevents work. Contributory ESA is time-limited for those placed in a work-related activity group but unlimited for those in a support group with the most severe limitations.

Other benefits might include Council Tax Reduction, Housing Benefit (being replaced by Universal Credit housing element), Carer's Allowance if you care for someone else, or various disability benefits for children. Each benefit has specific eligibility criteria. Claiming some benefits might affect others. Seek advice about how different benefits interact and which you should claim.

Appealing benefit decisions when you disagree with the assessment or award is your right. Mandatory reconsideration is the first stage, where the Department for Work and Pensions reviews its decision. If still dissatisfied, you can appeal to an independent tribunal. Tribunals frequently overturn DWP decisions. Prepare thoroughly for appeal, including obtaining supporting evidence from medical professionals, making a clear written statement explaining how your condition affects you, and obtaining representation from Citizens Advice or a solicitor. Success rates for represented appellants are substantially higher than unrepresented.

Conclusion: Your Journey Forward

If you have read this far, you have journeyed through a comprehensive exploration of depression – its nature, its impact, its treatment, and paths to recovery. The information provided might feel overwhelming in its comprehensiveness. You do not need to remember everything, implement every strategy, or master every technique. What matters is taking away understanding that depression is treatable, that you are not alone, and that recovery is possible for you.

Key Messages to Remember

Depression is an illness, not weakness or failure. You did not choose depression, and you are not responsible for having depression. However, you can take an active role in recovery. This paradox – depression is not your fault, but recovery is your responsibility – represents a crucial understanding.

Self-blame is unhelpful. Self-compassion combined with committed action facilitates recovery.

Depression is treatable. The vast majority of people with depression recover, even from severe episodes. Treatment works. Psychological therapy, medication, lifestyle changes, social support, and self-help strategies all contribute to recovery. Not every treatment works for every person, but finding effective treatment through persistence and appropriate professional support typically leads to significant improvement.

Recovery takes time and rarely follows a linear path. Expecting rapid, uninterrupted improvement sets one up for disappointment. Recovery typically involves gradual overall improvement with fluctuations, setbacks, and plateaus. These fluctuations are normal, not evidence of failure. Patience and persistence are essential. Continue treatment and self-help efforts even when progress feels imperceptible. Small improvements accumulate over time into a substantial recovery.

You are not alone in experiencing depression. Millions of people globally experience depression. Services, support groups, online communities, and friends or family members who have experienced depression provide connection and understanding. Depression creates profound loneliness and isolation. Reaching out, even when every instinct tells you to withdraw, connects you with support that facilitates recovery.

Professional help is available and appropriate. Depression exceeds what you should manage alone. Healthcare professionals, including GPs, therapists, psychiatrists, and mental health nurses have expertise in treating depression. Accessing professional help is not a weakness but a wise decision to access appropriate treatment. If first contact with services is not helpful, persist in seeking appropriate support.

Self-help and self-management complement professional treatment. The strategies, techniques, and information in this book provide tools you can implement alongside professional treatment. Taking an active role in recovery through applying CBT techniques, increasing activities, maintaining social connections, managing sleep and nutrition, and using crisis resources when needed supports recovery beyond what treatment alone provides.

Hope is justified and important. When depressed, hopelessness feels like an accurate assessment of reality. It is not. It is a symptom of illness that will resolve with treatment and time. Maintaining hope, even when difficult, sustains you through the recovery journey. If you cannot feel hope, borrow hope from others who believe in your recovery until you can believe it yourself.

Your Path Forward

Standing at the beginning, middle, or end of recovery from depression, your path forward involves choices and commitment. You have choices about treatment approaches to try, professionals to work with, lifestyle changes to implement, and the pace of recovery to accept. You commit to make to yourself – a commitment to keep trying even when discouraged, to seek help when needed, to treat yourself with compassion, and to believe that a better future is possible.

Start where you are. If you are in crisis, immediate priority is safety. Use crisis resources, access emergency services, and tell someone trusted how you are feeling. If you are severely depressed but not in crisis, the priority is accessing professional assessment and treatment. Contact your GP, refer yourself to Talking Therapies, or contact crisis services if struggling. If you are moderately depressed, a combination of professional treatment and self-help strategies provides a comprehensive approach. If you are experiencing mild symptoms or early warning signs of relapse, self-help strategies and rapid access to therapy might be sufficient. If you are recovering or have recovered, focus shifts to maintaining wellness, preventing relapse, and living life aligned with your values.

Choose one or two strategies to begin with rather than attempting to implement everything simultaneously. Perhaps start with monitoring mood and identifying patterns. Or implement activity scheduling, ensuring regular pleasant activities. Or practise one CBT technique like thought records. Or focus on improving sleep. Or reach out to one person for support. Small changes implemented consistently have a greater impact than ambitious plans that feel overwhelming and are quickly abandoned.

Be patient with yourself. Recovery does not happen quickly or easily. Some days you will feel motivated and hopeful. Other days, you will feel despair and want to give up. This is normal. The difficult days do not mean you have failed or that recovery is impossible. They mean you are human and experiencing an illness that affects your mood. Keep going. Tomorrow might be a better day. If not tomorrow, then the day after. Eventually, good days outnumber bad days, and bad days become occasional rather than constant.

Track your progress to remind yourself that you are moving forward even when it feels like nothing is changing. Keep a diary, mark a calendar, take photos, write letters to yourself, or use any method that creates a record of your journey. Months from now, looking back at where you started will demonstrate progress invisible day-to-day.

Seek help when you need it. Recovery is not a solitary journey you must navigate alone. Professional help, support from friends and family, peer support, and community services all provide valuable assistance. Asking for help is not an admission of failure but recognition that connection and support facilitate healing. Nobody recovers from depression entirely alone.

Remember that setbacks and relapses, if they occur, do not erase the progress you have made. You cannot return to the person you were before developing the skills, understanding, and resilience you have built through recovery. If depression returns, you face it with more resources, more self-awareness, and evidence that recovery is possible because you have achieved it before.

Final Words

Depression is one of the most common and most painful of all human experiences. The suffering it causes is real, profound, and touches every aspect of life. If you are experiencing this suffering now, please know that countless others have stood where you stand, have felt the hopelessness you feel, have struggled as you struggle, and have recovered to live full, meaningful, happy lives.

The darkness of depression is temporary even when it feels permanent. Light exists even when you cannot see it. Help is available even when you feel beyond help. Recovery is possible even when you cannot imagine it. These statements might feel like empty platitudes when depression has you in its grip. They are not. They are truth spoken by countless people who have walked through depression and emerged on the other side.

You deserve compassion, support, and effective treatment. You deserve recovery and good life. Depression might tell you otherwise. Depression might tell you that you deserve to suffer, that you are beyond help, that giving up makes sense. These are lies depression tells. The truth is that you are worth helping, you are worth fighting for, and your life has value even when you cannot see it.

This book has provided information, techniques, and resources to support your recovery. The knowledge in these pages matters less than what you do with it. Reading about depression does not treat depression. Implementing strategies, accessing treatment, reaching out for support, and persisting through difficulties create change. You must take action. But you do not have to take perfect action or immediate action or confident action. You simply have to take the next small step, and then the next, and then the next. Small steps, repeated consistently, carry you from darkness into light.

We at Talking Therapies UK (www.talkingtherapies.co.uk) are committed to supporting people experiencing depression and other mental health difficulties. Professional, evidence-based therapy provides crucial support for recovery. If you need professional help, we encourage you to reach out. This self-help resource does not replace the need to seek appropriate medical, professional advice.

Your story does not end with depression. Depression might be part of your story, perhaps a significant chapter, but it is not the final chapter, and it does not define you. You are not 'a depressed person.' You are a person who is experiencing depression. This distinction matters. Depression is something happening to you, not who you are. As you recover, you reclaim identity beyond illness, rediscover interests and passions, rebuild relationships, and create a life that extends far beyond surviving depression to genuinely thriving.

Please take care of yourself. Be patient with yourself. Reach out for help. Keep going even when difficult. Your life matters. Your well-being matters. Your recovery is possible and worth fighting for. Better days are ahead.

Appendices: Tools and Resources for Your Recovery Journey

The following appendices provide practical worksheets, forms, and detailed guidance for techniques discussed throughout this book. You can photocopy these pages or recreate the formats in notebooks for repeated use. Alternatively, many of these tools are available as downloadable forms through Talking Therapies UK at www.talkingtherapies.co.uk.

Working with Automatic Thoughts: Detailed Examples

Understanding automatic thoughts conceptually is important, but developing skill in identifying and restructuring your own thoughts requires practise with numerous examples. This section provides detailed worked examples of common automatic thoughts in depression, demonstrating the complete process of identification, evaluation, and restructuring.

Example One: Social Situation. Sarah notices her mood drop significantly after a conversation with colleagues at work. When she examines what went through her mind, she identifies the automatic thought: 'They think I am boring and do not want to talk to me.' Examining evidence for this thought, Sarah notes that the conversation was brief and that colleagues seemed distracted. However, examining evidence against the thought, she recognises that colleagues were busy preparing for a meeting, the brief conversation was typical for that time of day, one colleague did smile at her and comment on a shared project, and in the past these same colleagues have initiated longer conversations with her and invited her to lunch. The thinking errors present include mind-reading (assuming she knows what colleagues think without evidence), personalising (assuming their distraction relates to her specifically rather than their workload), and mental filtering (focusing on the brief conversation whilst ignoring previous positive interactions).

Sarah develops an alternative thought: 'The conversation was brief because colleagues were busy preparing for their meeting, not because they find me boring. They have shown interest in talking with me on other occasions, and I have no actual evidence they think negatively of me.' Her belief in the original automatic thought decreases from 80 per cent to 30 per cent, and her sadness intensity reduces from 70 per cent to 40 per cent. Whilst she still feels some discomfort, the intensity has reduced significantly through examining her thinking.

Example Two: Task Performance. Michael starts a work project and almost immediately has the thought: 'I cannot do this, I am going to fail.' This thought generates intense anxiety (85 per cent) and makes him want to avoid the project entirely. Evidence for the thought includes that the project is complex, he feels overwhelmed looking at all the components, and his concentration has been poor recently. Evidence against includes that he has completed similar projects in the past, his manager assigned this project to him, indicating confidence in his ability, he has relevant skills and experience, and feeling overwhelmed at the start of complex projects is normal and does not predict failure.

Michael identifies all-or-nothing thinking (viewing success or failure as the only outcomes with no middle ground), fortune-telling (predicting failure without evidence), and emotional reasoning (interpreting his feeling of being overwhelmed as evidence that the task is impossible). His alternative thought is: 'This project is complex, and feeling overwhelmed initially is understandable, but I have the skills and experience to complete it. I have done similar work successfully before. If I break it into manageable steps and work systematically, I can accomplish this.' Belief in the original thought decreases from 90 per cent to 35 per cent, and anxiety reduces from 85 per cent to 50 per cent. He decides to spend ten minutes outlining an approach to the project rather than avoiding it entirely.

Example Three: Physical Appearance. Jennifer looks in the mirror and thinks, 'I look terrible, no wonder no one finds me attractive.' This triggers shame (75 per cent) and sadness (65 per cent). Evidence for might include that she is not wearing makeup, her hair needs washing, and she is wearing old clothes. Evidence against includes that she is tired and dishevelled because she has not been taking care of herself due to depression (not because of inherent unattractiveness), her partner has expressed attraction to her on numerous occasions, friends have complimented her appearance, and she is judging herself far more harshly than she would judge anyone else in similar circumstances.

Thinking errors include magnification (exaggerating the importance of current appearance), labelling (defining herself globally based on one aspect), and should statements (holding herself to unrealistic standards about always looking a certain way). Alternative thought: 'I look tired and dishevelled today because I have not been taking care of myself, which is understandable given that I am depressed. This does not mean I am fundamentally unattractive. People who care about me are concerned about my well-being, not judging my appearance harshly. When I am feeling better and taking care of myself again, I will look more like myself.' Belief in original thought reduces from 75 per cent to 40 per cent, and shame reduces from 75 per cent to 45 per cent.

Example Four: Making Mistakes. David makes a small error in an email to a client and immediately thinks, 'I am completely incompetent, I cannot do anything right.' This generates intense anxiety (80 per cent) and guilt (70 per cent). Evidence for the thought includes that he did make an error and that he has made some other mistakes recently. Evidence against includes that the error was small and easily correctable, the client responded understanding the minor typo without concern, he has sent hundreds of successful emails and managed many successful client relationships, recent mistakes relate to concentration difficulties from depression rather than incompetence, and he is holding himself to a standard of perfection that is unrealistic.

Thinking errors include all-or-nothing thinking (one mistake means complete incompetence), overgeneralisation (one error becomes 'cannot do anything right'), labelling (defining himself as incompetent based on specific behaviours), and magnification (exaggerating the significance of the small error). Alternative thought: 'I made a small, understandable error that had no serious consequences. Everyone makes occasional mistakes, and this does not mean I am incompetent. I have successfully managed numerous client relationships and completed countless tasks correctly. My recent mistakes relate to depression affecting my concentration, not to fundamental incompetence.' Belief in original thought decreases from 85 per cent to 25 per cent, anxiety reduces from 80 per cent to 35 per cent, and guilt reduces from 70 per cent to 30 per cent.

These examples demonstrate several important principles. First, automatic thoughts often involve multiple thinking errors simultaneously, and identifying these errors helps evaluate the thought's accuracy. Second, alternative thoughts should be balanced and believable rather than opposite extremes; simply replacing 'I am incompetent' with 'I am completely competent' would not be credible. Third, examining thoughts typically reduces belief in them and emotional intensity, though rarely to zero, which is entirely appropriate. The goal is reduction in distress and more balanced thinking, not elimination of all negative thoughts or feelings. Fourth, the process becomes more natural with practise, eventually becoming an integrated skill that happens more automatically.

My Depression First-Aid Kit (Quick Reference)

This quick reference guide provides immediate strategies to use when experiencing a dip in mood or feeling overwhelmed by depressive symptoms. These techniques are drawn from the comprehensive strategies detailed throughout this book.

Feeling Stuck in Bed?

Apply the Five-Minute Rule. Commit to just five minutes of movement. Action creates motivation.

Mind Racing at Night?

Get up. Move to another room. Do not watch the clock. Return to bed only when genuinely drowsy.

Overwhelmed by Tasks?

Break it down. 'Clean the kitchen' becomes 'wash one cup.' Focus on the smallest possible step.

Spiral of Negative Thoughts?

Ask: 'What would I say to a friend who thought this?' Apply compassion to your own situation.

Feeling Isolated?

Send one text message. A simple 'thinking of you' keeps the connection alive.

Hopelessness About Recovery?

Remember: depression distorts perception. Have you had moments of feeling slightly better? That proves change is possible.

Appendix A: Detailed Thought Record Worksheet

The thought record is a central tool in cognitive behavioural therapy for identifying and challenging negative automatic thoughts. This appendix provides detailed guidance on completing each column of a thought record, common pitfalls to avoid, and examples to illustrate the process.

Thought Record Template Structure

A comprehensive thought record contains seven columns, each serving a specific purpose in the cognitive restructuring process. Column one records the situation triggering the emotional response. Be specific about when, where, and what happened. Rather than 'bad day at work,' write 'presentation to managers at 2pm, they asked challenging questions, felt my face flush.' Specific details help you identify patterns and make the situation concrete rather than vague.

Situation:

Emotions:

Automatic Thoughts:

Evidence For:

Evidence Against:

Alternative Thought:

Re-rate Emotions:

Action Plan:

Column two identifies the emotions experienced in that situation. Name the specific emotions rather than general 'bad feelings.' Emotions might include sad, anxious, angry, guilty, ashamed, frustrated, or hopeless. You can experience multiple emotions simultaneously. Rate each emotion's intensity from zero (not present) to one hundred (most intense imaginable). This rating allows you to track whether emotions change after cognitive work.

Column three captures automatic thoughts – the thoughts, images, or memories that went through your mind in that situation. These are often rapid and might seem to appear automatically without deliberate thinking. You might need to reconstruct them by asking yourself 'what was going through my mind just then?' or 'what does this situation mean about me?' Automatic thoughts often take characteristic forms such as predictions ('I will fail'), mind-reading ('they think I am incompetent'), labelling ('I am a failure'), or should statements ('I should have done better').

Column four examines evidence supporting the automatic thought. What facts support this thought being accurate? Be strict about distinguishing facts from interpretations. 'My manager frowned' is fact; 'my manager disapproves of me' is interpretation. Only include genuine evidence, not feelings ('I feel like a failure' is not evidence that you are a failure). This column is often quite short because negative thoughts usually have limited factual support.

Column five examines evidence against the automatic thought. What facts contradict this thought? What would you tell a friend having this thought? Have there been times when this thought was not true? What strengths or past successes contradict this thought? This column is typically longer than column four because our negative thoughts often ignore substantial contradictory evidence. Take time to consider all possible evidence against the thought.

Column six develops an alternative, more balanced thought considering all evidence from columns four and five. This is not positive thinking or self-reassurance but realistic thinking. The alternative thought acknowledges difficulties whilst incorporating overlooked evidence. It should feel more believable than both the extremely negative automatic thought and any implausibly positive thought. The alternative thought might include words like 'sometimes,' 'although,' 'some evidence suggests,' or other qualifiers acknowledging complexity.

Column seven re-rates emotion intensity after developing the alternative thought. Has the intensity decreased? Often emotions reduce significantly though rarely disappear completely. If emotions remain unchanged, consider whether you truly believe the alternative thought, whether you have identified the most distressing thought, or whether additional automatic thoughts need addressing. Sometimes multiple thought records are needed to address a single situation fully.

Common Challenges in Using Thought Records

Many people initially struggle with thought records for predictable reasons. Identifying automatic thoughts proves difficult when you are new to noticing your thinking. Thoughts occur so rapidly and automatically that they feel like facts rather than thoughts. Practising throughout the day by periodically pausing and asking 'what am I thinking right now?' builds awareness. When emotions intensify, immediately pause and ask 'what just went through my mind?'

Distinguishing thoughts from emotions confuses many people initially. 'I felt like a failure' expresses a thought ('I am a failure'), not an emotion. The emotion might be sadness, shame, or guilt. Ask yourself 'what emotion word describes this feeling?' to identify the actual emotion. Emotions are typically one-word labels; thoughts are sentences or phrases containing meaning.

Finding evidence against negative thoughts feels impossible when depression has convinced you the negative thought is absolutely true. If you genuinely cannot identify any contradictory evidence, you might not have identified the core automatic thought yet. Alternatively, try asking yourself what friend would say, what you would have said before depression, or what you might say when recovered. Sometimes examining evidence with a therapist helps you see contradictory evidence your depression blinds you to.

Creating alternative thoughts that feel convincing rather than like empty platitudes requires practise. If alternative thought feels false, it is probably too positive or does not acknowledge real difficulties. Balance is key. Include acknowledgment of genuine challenges whilst incorporating overlooked evidence. 'Nothing ever goes right for me' might become 'this situation did not go as hoped, which is disappointing, but I have succeeded in other situations and will have future opportunities.'

Using thought records becomes easier with practise. Initially each record might take twenty to thirty minutes. With experience, the process becomes quicker and eventually becomes automatic. You begin challenging thoughts as they occur without needing to write them down. However, continuing to write thought records for particularly distressing situations ensures thorough processing rather than superficial reassurance.

Worked Examples of Thought Records

Example one illustrates a common social situation. Situation: sent text message to friend three hours ago, no response yet. Emotions: anxious (70), sad (60). Automatic thought: she is ignoring me, I have upset her, she does not want to be friends anymore. Evidence for: message has not been answered for three hours, usually she responds quickly. Evidence against: she mentioned yesterday she had busy day at work today, she has been reliable friend for five years, last week she initiated plans for us to meet, when I was late responding to her message last month she did not assume I was ignoring her, there are many reasons for not responding immediately including being in meetings, phone battery died, or being busy. Alternative thought: she is probably busy with work as she mentioned, she will reply when she has time, one delayed response does not mean the friendship is ending, I am catastrophising because my anxiety makes me fear rejection. Re-rated emotions: anxious (30), sad (20).

Example two illustrates a work situation. Situation: made mistake in report sent to supervisor. Emotions: ashamed (80), anxious (70), sad (60). Automatic thought: I am incompetent, I will be fired, I can never do anything right. Evidence for: the mistake was my responsibility, supervisor will see it, I feel terrible about it. Evidence against: everyone makes occasional mistakes, I have produced good quality work previously, supervisor has given positive feedback on most of my work, the mistake can be corrected, this is first significant error in six months of work, supervisor knows I generally work carefully, feeling terrible does not mean I am incompetent. Alternative thought: I made a mistake which I regret, but one error does not make me incompetent, I can correct it and learn from it, my supervisor will understand that humans make mistakes occasionally, most of my work is accurate. Re-rated emotions: ashamed (40), anxious (35), sad (25).

Example three illustrates depression-related thoughts. Situation: woke up feeling low, thinking about the day ahead. Emotions: hopeless (85), sad (80). Automatic thought: I will feel this way forever, nothing helps, I cannot cope with another day feeling like this. Evidence for: I have felt depressed for three months, treatment has not worked immediately, I am tired of feeling this way. Evidence against: I have had previous episodes of depression and recovered, I started medication only three weeks ago and it takes four to six weeks to work, my therapist said recovery takes time, I have had some slightly better days recently, many people recover from depression, feeling hopeless is symptom of depression not accurate prediction of future, yesterday I managed to go for walk which I could not do two weeks ago. Alternative thought: I am experiencing a difficult morning, which is common in depression, I will not feel this way forever even though depression makes me feel hopeless, treatment takes time to work and I am in early stages, small improvements are occurring even if hard to see, I can get through today one hour at a time. Re-rated emotions: hopeless (50), sad (60).

These examples demonstrate that alternative thoughts are realistic, balanced, acknowledge real difficulties whilst incorporating overlooked evidence, and result in genuine though not complete emotion reduction. Perfect emotion elimination is not the goal; the goal is reduced intensity allowing you to function and take helpful action.

Appendix B: Activity Monitoring and Scheduling Forms

Activity monitoring and scheduling forms help you track current activities, identify patterns, and plan increases in helpful activities. This appendix provides detailed templates and guidance for effective use of activity scheduling.

Weekly Activity Monitor Template

The weekly activity monitor provides hour-by-hour record of activities throughout the week. Creating a blank seven-day schedule with hours from waking to sleep allows you to record what you actually do. Each hour slot should have space to write the activity and rate it for pleasure (P, from zero to ten) and achievement (A, from zero to ten). Pleasure ratings indicate how much you enjoyed the activity; achievement ratings indicate how much sense of accomplishment the activity provided.

Time / Activity Mood (0-10) Energy (0-10)

6-9am

9-12pm

12-3pm

3-6pm

6-9pm

9-12am

12-3am

3-6am

Completing the activity monitor involves recording every activity throughout the week. Be honest; the monitor is for your use only. Record even activities that seem unimportant like lying in bed, watching television, or scrolling on phone. These activities are relevant data. Rate each activity immediately or at end of day whilst you still remember. Over the week, patterns emerge regarding which activities improve mood, which times of day are most difficult, and how much time is spent in different activity types.

Analysing the completed monitor helps plan changes. Calculate total time in different activity categories such as work, self-care, household tasks, leisure, social contact, exercise, and rest. Note which activities received highest pleasure and achievement ratings. Identify periods of day that are particularly empty or difficult. Consider balance across activity types; excessive time in necessary activities without pleasure or social contact contributes to low mood, whilst excessive rest without productive activity also worsens mood.

Planning the next week involves selecting specific activities to add, increase, or modify based on the analysis. If pleasant activities are minimal, schedule at least one daily pleasant activity, starting with brief activities if longer ones feel overwhelming. If achievement activities are absent, schedule small tasks that provide accomplishment such as completing household chore, working on hobby project, or tackling neglected task. If social contact is minimal, schedule specific social interaction even if brief phone call or text exchange. If entire days lack structure, add structure through scheduled meals, wake time, and key activities.

Activity Scheduling Principles and Guidelines

Effective activity scheduling follows several evidence-based principles. Schedule should be realistic for your current functioning level. Overly ambitious schedules set you up for failure. If currently spending most of day in bed, scheduling full day of activities is unrealistic. Schedule two or three activities initially, gradually increasing as functioning improves. Remember that small steps consistently implemented are more effective than large steps quickly abandoned.

Balance different activity types across the week. Necessary activities maintain functioning but do not improve mood significantly. Pleasant activities improve mood through enjoyment. Achievement activities improve mood through accomplishment. Social activities provide connection and reduce isolation. Physical activities provide biological mood benefits. A well-balanced schedule includes all types rather than focusing exclusively on one category.

Schedule activities at specific times rather than vague intentions. 'Go for a walk' as a general plan rarely happens. 'Go for a twenty-minute walk at 10 am' is specific and more likely to occur. Treating scheduled activities as appointments you must keep, setting reminders on your phone, and preparing necessary items in advance all increase follow-through.

Grade activities from easier to more difficult, starting with easier activities to build momentum and confidence. If leaving the house feels overwhelming, start with activities at home. Progress to brief trips outside, then longer outings, then more socially complex activities. Success with easier activities builds self-efficacy, supporting attempts at more difficult activities.

Review and adjust the schedule weekly based on experience. Note which scheduled activities were completed and which were not. Understand barriers to non-completion; were activities too difficult, scheduled at the wrong times, or did unexpected circumstances interfere? Adjust next week's schedule, addressing identified barriers. Celebrate completed activities rather than criticising yourself for incomplete ones. Completing even fifty percent of planned activities represents substantial achievement when depressed.

Sample Activity Schedule Progression

The following example illustrates a realistic progression over weeks for someone with moderate depression. Week one baseline shows most time in bed or on the sofa watching television, minimal self-care with showering every few days, irregular meals often missed, no social contact except brief texts, and no activities outside the home. Total pleasure activities per week: one or two brief periods, average rating three. Total achievement activities per week: none. Total social contact: minimal.

Week two intervention adds small changes: set wake time of 9am daily regardless of sleep quality, shower three times this week, eat one proper meal daily at table not in bed, send meaningful text to one friend, and take five-minute walk around block twice this week. These minimal changes provide structure and small increases in activity without overwhelming. Success with these creates foundation for further increases.

Week three builds on success from week two: maintain 9 am wake time, shower four times this week, eat two meals daily at the table, make one phone call to a friend or family member, extend walks to ten minutes three times weekly, and complete one small household task such as washing dishes or one load of laundry. Activities remain manageable whilst gradually increasing.

Week four continues progression: maintain 9 am wake time, shower daily, eat three meals daily at the table, arrange one face-to-face social activity even if a brief coffee meeting, walk fifteen minutes four times weekly, complete two household tasks weekly, and engage in one leisure activity such as reading, creative pursuit, or watching a film you have wanted to see. Activity levels continue increasing whilst maintaining realistic expectations.

By week eight, schedule might include: 8 am wake time, daily shower, regular meals, two social activities weekly including at least one outside home, exercise five times weekly at least twenty minutes, regular household tasks maintaining home, two to three leisure activities weekly, consideration of resuming work or voluntary work even if part-time initially, and maintained daily structure with planned activities. This represents significant progress from baseline whilst remaining realistic and graduated.

This progression illustrates that recovery involves many small steps over weeks and months, not a rapid transformation. Your own progression will be individual, possibly faster or slower depending on depression severity, life circumstances, and other treatments you are receiving. The principle remains: start small, build gradually, celebrate progress, and maintain patience.

Appendix C: Comprehensive Safety Plan Template

A safety plan is a personalised, practical plan that outlines steps to take when experiencing a suicidal crisis. Unlike suicide prevention contracts, which are ineffective, safety plans provide concrete actions improving safety. This appendix provides a detailed template and guidance for creating individualised safety plan.

Components of a Comprehensive Safety Plan

Part one identifies personal warning signs indicating crisis may be developing. These are specific thoughts, images, feelings, behaviours, or situations that typically precede suicidal crisis for you. Examples might include specific thoughts such as 'everyone would be better off without me,' physical feelings such as intense agitation or numbness, behaviours such as giving away possessions or withdrawing completely, or situations such as relationship conflict or work stress. List all warning signs you have noticed in past crises. Awareness of warning signs allows earlier intervention.

Warning Signs:

Internal Coping:

People for Support:

Professionals to Contact:

Make Environment Safer:

Reasons for Living:

Part two lists coping strategies you can use independently without contacting others. These are activities that have helped in past when distressed or that research suggests are helpful. Examples include using cold water on the face, vigorous exercise, watching a favourite comedy show, listening to calming music, engaging in creative activity, going to a place you feel safe, using grounding techniques, reading inspirational texts, or looking at photos of loved ones. List at least five coping strategies. Include strategies that have worked previously, even if they seem simple.

Part three identifies people and social settings that provide distraction. These are individuals you can contact for support and distraction, and places you can go where you will not be alone. List specific names with current phone numbers. Include friends, family members, acquaintances, or anyone you feel comfortable contacting. Note any special considerations such as

'Sarah available weekday evenings' or 'Uncle John, good listener but lives far away so phone only.' List public places you can go such as a library, café, park, shopping centre, or community centre. Being around others, even without direct interaction, can reduce immediate risk.

Part four lists people you can ask for help. These are individuals you trust to help during crisis, who understand you experience depression, and who you can speak honestly with about suicidal thoughts. List names and contact details. Note what specific help each person can provide. 'Mum can provide emotional support and practical help,' 'therapist can help me work through thoughts,' 'friend Alex will come and stay with me.' Some people from part three might also appear here if they can provide deeper support.

Part five lists professional agencies and crisis lines to contact. Include your GP surgery with out-of-hours number, local crisis team number if you are known to mental health services, Samaritans (116 123), emergency services (999), and local A&E department with address. Having this information written prevents having to search for contacts during a crisis when thinking is impaired. Include any other relevant local crisis services.

Part six addresses means restriction – steps to make your environment safer by limiting access to lethal means. This might include giving excess medication to a trusted person to dispense daily doses only, securing or disposing of sharp objects, avoiding certain locations associated with suicidal thoughts, such as bridges or high buildings, limiting alcohol access, and informing a trusted person about means restriction so they can help maintain it. While comprehensive means restriction is impossible, limiting most accessible means creates obstacles, buying time for the crisis to pass.

Part seven identifies reasons for living. When suicidal, accessing reasons for living feels impossible. Writing them when calmer creates a resource to refer to during a crisis. Reasons might include people you care about and who care about you, future goals or hopes, even if they feel unattainable currently, responsibilities such as caring for pets or children, values you hold such as religious beliefs or commitment to giving treatment fair chance, or anything else that gives you reason to continue. Even small reasons count. Your cat needs you. You want to see how your favourite show ends. Your niece would miss you. These are legitimate reasons.

Completing Your Personal Safety Plan

Complete safety plan when you are relatively calm, not during active crisis. If you have therapist, complete plan together in session. If completing independently, ensure at least one trusted person knows about your plan and has copy. Review and update plan every few months or after any crisis, incorporating lessons learned about what helped and what did not.

Keep safety plan accessible. Store copies in multiple locations: on your phone as photo or note, in your wallet, by your bed, and in car if you drive. Give copy to trusted person who can refer to it if you are unable to during crisis. Having plan immediately available when needed increases likelihood you will use it.

practise using elements of safety plan before crisis occurs. Try coping strategies when experiencing mild distress to discover which are most helpful. Ensure phone numbers are current and that you know how to access services. Familiarity with plan increases likelihood you will follow it during crisis when thinking is impaired and motivation is low.

Commit to following safety plan when warning signs appear. Tell yourself 'if I notice warning signs, I will go to my safety plan and follow the steps.' Share this commitment with trusted others who can remind you to use plan if they notice warning signs. The plan only works if you use it; making commitment in advance increases follow-through.

Sample Safety Plan

The following sample safety plan illustrates what a completed plan might look like. Remember that your plan will be individualised to your specific situation, supports, and preferences. This example is for illustration only.

Warning signs: thoughts that others would be better off without me, images of harming myself, feeling completely numb and disconnected, not answering messages from friends, sleep worse than usual, increased drinking, giving away possessions, feeling that nothing will ever improve.

Coping strategies I can use alone: take hot bath focusing on physical sensations, go for long walk, hold ice cubes until urge reduces, call and leave myself voicemail listing reasons to live, watch comedy show that usually makes me laugh, work on jigsaw puzzle, write in journal, cuddle my dog.

People and places for distraction: Sophie (friend, phone number), John (brother, phone number), local library open daily 9am-6pm, coffee shop on High Street, park near my house, gym especially Saturday morning when it is busy with familiar people.

People I can ask for help: Mum (phone number, can talk honestly with her and she will come over), therapist (phone number, appointments Wednesday afternoons but can call in crisis), Sophie (phone number, has talked me through difficult times before), Sarah (crisis team nurse, phone number, knows my history).

Professional contacts: GP surgery (phone number), out-of-hours GP (phone number), Crisis Team (phone number, operates 24 hours), Samaritans 116 123, Emergency Services 999, St Mary's Hospital A&E (address).

Making environment safer: give week's worth of medication at a time to Mum who dispenses daily, locked away sharp knives at Mum's house, avoid bridge on riverside path when feeling low, limit alcohol by not keeping any at home.

Reasons for living: my family especially Mum and brother would be devastated, my dog Murphy needs me, I want to see my niece grow up, my therapist believes I can recover, part of me still hopes things can get better, my best friend Sophie would miss me, I have not yet tried all available treatments.

This sample demonstrates a realistic, personalised safety plan. Creating your own plan involves honest reflection about your specific warning signs, available supports, and what has helped previously. The act of creating the plan itself can provide hope by demonstrating you have resources and supports you can draw upon during crisis.

Appendix D: Values Assessment and Goal-Setting Worksheets

Understanding your values and setting meaningful goals aligned with those values provides direction and motivation for recovery. This appendix provides structured exercises for clarifying values and translating them into actionable goals.

Life Domains Values Assessment

Values clarification involves reflecting systematically across major life domains. For each domain described below, identify the values that matter most to you and rate how much your current life reflects those values. This assessment reveals discrepancies between what matters to you and how you are currently living, highlighting areas where changes might restore meaning and improve wellbeing.

Family and intimate relationships domain encompasses your role as partner, spouse, parent, child, sibling, or other family member. Consider what kind of relationship partner you want to be. Values might include being loving, supportive, honest, present, affectionate, or committed. Consider what kind of parent you want to be if you have children. Values might include being nurturing, patient, playful, providing stability, teaching important lessons, or being available. Consider your role in your family of origin. Values might include staying connected, providing support, maintaining traditions, or creating healthy boundaries. For each identified value, rate from zero to ten how much your current life reflects this value. Significant gaps between importance and current living indicate areas requiring attention.

Friendships and social relationships domain encompasses the kinds of friend you want to be and the social connections you want to maintain. Values might include being loyal, supportive, fun, trustworthy, available, a good listener, or adventurous. Consider the breadth and depth of social connections you want. Do you value many acquaintances or few close friends? Do you value social involvement in community or preference for intimate small groups? Rate how much your current social life reflects your values.

Work, career, and education domain encompasses your relationship with work and learning. Consider what values guide your work life. Values might include helping others, creativity, financial security, learning, achievement, leadership, collaboration, craftsmanship, service, or work-life balance. If currently unemployed due to depression, consider what values you want work to reflect when you return. Rate how aligned your current work situation is with your values, or if unable to work currently, rate zero reflecting this discrepancy.

Personal growth and health domain encompasses how you care for yourself physically, mentally, emotionally, and spiritually. Values might include prioritising health, continuous learning, self-compassion, emotional awareness, physical fitness, healthy boundaries, or spiritual development. Depression typically creates large gap in this domain as self-care deteriorates. Rate how much your current self-care reflects your values.

Leisure and recreation domain encompasses how you spend free time and what activities bring joy and relaxation. Values might include creativity, adventure, relaxation, learning, nature connection, cultural engagement, play, or balance. Depression often eliminates leisure activities entirely. Consider what matters to you about leisure time when well. Rate current alignment.

Community and citizenship domain encompasses your role in community and contributions to society. Values might include environmental responsibility, political engagement, social justice, volunteering, supporting causes you believe in, or being good neighbour. Rate how much your current life reflects these values.

Spirituality and meaning domain encompasses religious or spiritual beliefs and practices if relevant to you. Values might include faith, connection with something larger than self, prayer or meditation practise, religious community involvement, or finding transcendent meaning. Not everyone has spiritual values, which is entirely valid. If spirituality matters to you, rate alignment with your values.

After completing values ratings across all domains, identify the domains with largest gaps between what matters and current living. These domains represent opportunities for changes that might restore meaning. Small actions moving towards values, even when depression persists, provide purpose and counteract depression's meaninglessness.

SMART Goal-Setting Framework

Translating values into achievable goals requires specificity. The SMART framework provides structure for creating goals that are Specific, Measurable, Achievable, Relevant, and Time-bound. Each component increases likelihood of goal attainment.

Specific goals clearly define what you will do. Vague goals like 'be healthier' or 'improve relationships' lack direction. Specific goals might be 'exercise three times weekly for thirty minutes' or 'call my mother once weekly for conversation.' Specificity eliminates ambiguity about whether goal has been pursued. Ask yourself exactly what action you will take, when you will take it, where it will occur, and who is involved if relevant.

Measurable goals allow you to track progress and know when goal is achieved. If goal cannot be measured, you cannot determine success. 'Feel better' is not measurable; 'reduce depression symptoms as measured by questionnaire from score of 20 to score below 10' is measurable. 'Spend more time with friends' is not measurable; 'meet friend for activity once weekly' is measurable. Include specific metrics or frequencies making progress trackable.

Achievable goals are realistic given your current circumstances, resources, and functioning level. Overly ambitious goals set you up for failure and discouragement. If currently spending most days in bed, goal of running marathon in three months is not achievable. Goal of walking around block three times this week is achievable. As you accomplish smaller goals, you can increase challenge. Achievability depends on honest assessment of current functioning.

Relevant goals connect to your values and to recovery from depression. Goals should matter to you, not be what others think you should do. A goal is relevant if accomplishing it moves you towards valued living or directly addresses depression. 'Learn to juggle' might be achievable but is not relevant unless juggling connects to important value. 'Attend therapy sessions weekly' is highly relevant to depression recovery.

Time-bound goals include specific timeframe for completion or regular review. Open-ended goals lack urgency and are easily postponed indefinitely. 'Eventually exercise more' provides no timeline. 'Begin walking programme this week, walking ten minutes three times weekly for next month, then review and adjust' provides clear timeframe. Include start date, target completion date, or regular review schedule.

Example values-to-goals progression: Value in family relationships domain: 'being present and engaged parent to my children.' Current rating: 3 out of 10 due to depression making me withdrawn. Goal: 'spend thirty minutes daily engaged in activity with children where I am fully present without phone, five days this week.' This goal is specific (thirty minutes, engaged activity, no phone), measurable (can count days achieved), achievable (thirty minutes is manageable even when depressed), relevant (directly addresses valued parenting), and time-bound (five days this week with review at week end).

Example values-to-goals progression: Value in personal health domain: 'taking care of my physical health.' Current rating: 2 out of 10 due to neglecting exercise, eating poorly, and irregular sleep. Goal: 'establish consistent bedtime of 11pm and wake time of 7am, five nights this week.' This initial goal addresses one aspect of health domain with realistic expectations. After establishing sleep routine, subsequent goals might address exercise and nutrition. Breaking large values gaps into multiple sequential goals prevents overwhelm.

Breaking Goals into Action Steps

Even SMART goals sometimes feel overwhelming. Breaking goals into smaller action steps makes them manageable. For each goal, identify every action required for completion. Then sequence these actions. Then commit to completing first action step.

Example goal breakdown: Goal: 'Join and attend exercise class once weekly starting this month.' Action steps: research available local exercise classes online or through council leisure guide, identify three classes that match my fitness level and schedule, visit leisure centre to observe one class and collect timetable, register for class and pay for month, add class to calendar with reminder, prepare bag with necessary items night before first class, attend first class, evaluate experience and decide whether to continue or try different class, attend regularly if suitable.

This goal breaks into eight action steps. Completing first step – research classes – feels manageable even when depressed and unmotivated. Completing this step builds momentum for next step. Approaching goals through small action steps reduces procrastination and overwhelm.

Tracking Progress Towards Goals

Regular progress review maintains focus and allows adjustment. Weekly reviews work well for most goals. During review, note which action steps were completed, obstacles encountered, what helped progress, and adjustments needed. Celebrate completed action steps rather than criticising yourself for incomplete steps. If consistently failing to progress towards goal, reassess whether goal is achievable currently or whether it needs modification.

Progress tracking form includes: goal statement, action steps for this week, completion status for each action step, obstacles encountered, supports that helped, adjustments for next week, and reflection on progress. Maintaining written record demonstrates progress over time even when subjectively feels like nothing is changing.

Some goals will be achieved quickly, providing sense of accomplishment. Other goals are ongoing without clear endpoint, such as 'maintain regular exercise routine' or 'stay connected with friends.' These ongoing goals require regular review to ensure continued alignment with values and adjustment to maintain motivation.

Appendix E: Comprehensive Sleep Hygiene Guidelines and Sleep Diary

Sleep disturbance is both symptom and maintaining factor in depression. Improving sleep through sleep hygiene techniques and consistent routine significantly supports mood improvement. This appendix provides detailed, evidence-based sleep hygiene guidelines and sleep diary template for tracking patterns.

Evidence-Based Sleep Hygiene Recommendations

Consistent sleep-wake schedule represents the most important sleep hygiene principle. Your body has circadian rhythm regulating sleepiness and wakefulness. Irregular sleep schedule disrupts this rhythm, making good sleep difficult. Go to bed at approximately same time every night and wake at same time every morning, including weekends. Yes, weekends. Sleeping late on weekends creates 'social jet lag' that disrupts your rhythm. Choose wake time you can maintain seven days weekly. Choose bedtime allowing seven to nine hours sleep opportunity. Maintain this schedule even when sleep was poor previous night; this consolidates your sleep schedule over time.

Bed is for sleep and sex only. Using bed for other activities including eating, working, watching television, or using phone trains your brain to associate bed with wakefulness. Reserve bed exclusively for sleep and intimate activity. When you get into bed, your brain should receive signal 'time to sleep' not 'time to watch videos' or 'time to worry.' If you cannot sleep after twenty minutes in bed, get up and go to different room for calm activity such as reading. Return to bed only when sleepy. This stimulus control strengthens association between bed and sleep.

Bedroom environment should promote sleep. Room should be cool, dark, and quiet. Temperature of 16-18 degrees Celsius is optimal for most people. Use blackout curtains or eye mask to eliminate light. Use earplugs or white noise machine if environment is noisy. Ensure mattress and pillows are comfortable. Remove or cover electronics with lights. Some people find weighted blankets improve sleep. Invest in bedroom environment; you spend approximately one-third of life there.

Light exposure affects sleep through effects on melatonin production. Bright light exposure during day, particularly morning sunlight, strengthens circadian rhythm and improves nighttime sleep. Spend time outdoors daily, sit near windows, or use bright artificial light in morning. Conversely, reduce light exposure in evening. Dim lights in your home two hours before bed. Avoid bright overhead lights, using lamps instead. Blue light from screens suppresses melatonin more than other light wavelengths. Stop using screens one hour before bed, or use blue light filters and keep screens dimmed if you must use them.

Regular physical activity improves sleep, but timing matters. Exercise promotes deeper, more restorative sleep. However, vigorous exercise within three hours of bedtime can be alerting. Schedule exercise earlier in day. If evening exercise is your only option, choose gentler activities like yoga or walking. Consistency of exercise matters more than intensity for sleep benefits. Even daily walks improve sleep.

Diet and substance use significantly affect sleep. Avoid caffeine at least six hours before bedtime; caffeine's half-life means it remains in your system for hours. This includes coffee, tea, energy drinks, cola, and chocolate. Avoid heavy meals within two hours of bedtime, though light snack may help some people. Avoid spicy or acidic foods that might cause heartburn disrupting sleep. Limit fluid intake in evening to reduce nighttime waking for bathroom. Alcohol might make you fall asleep faster but severely disrupts sleep architecture, reducing sleep quality. Avoid alcohol within three hours of bedtime.

Establish relaxing pre-sleep routine signalling your body that sleep time approaches. Begin routine at same time nightly, one hour before target bedtime. Your routine is individual but might include taking warm bath, gentle stretching or yoga, reading relaxing book, listening to calming music, using relaxation exercises, writing in gratitude journal, or preparing things for next morning. Avoid stimulating activities including work, difficult conversations, intense television or books, social media, or anything that activates you mentally or emotionally.

Manage worries and racing thoughts that interfere with sleep. If worry keeps you awake, set aside 'worry time' earlier in evening where you write concerns and potential solutions. Tell yourself 'I have already addressed worries; sleep time is not problem-solving time.' Keep notepad by bed for jotting down any urgent thoughts so you can release them knowing they are captured for tomorrow. Use mental techniques like counting backwards from one hundred, visualising peaceful scenes, or repeating calming phrase. If anxiety about not sleeping develops, remind yourself 'being awake is not catastrophe; I can function tomorrow even if sleep is poor.'

Avoid clock-watching which creates anxiety about sleep. Turn clock face away from view. Checking time when unable to sleep increases frustration and anxiety, making sleep more elusive. If you find yourself mentally calculating hours of sleep remaining, this is clock-watching even without physically looking. Redirect attention to relaxation rather than sleep monitoring.

Sleep Diary Template and analysis

Keeping sleep diary for two weeks identifies patterns and provides baseline for evaluating sleep hygiene improvements. Daily entries should record: time you got into bed, approximate time you fell asleep, number and duration of nighttime awakenings, final wake time, time you got out of bed, naps during previous day (times and duration), ratings of sleep quality from one to ten, and daytime functioning rating from one to ten.

Calculate sleep efficiency from diary data. Sleep efficiency equals total sleep time divided by time in bed, multiplied by one hundred. For example, if you were in bed from 11pm to 7am (eight hours) but estimate you actually slept six hours with two hours spent awake, sleep efficiency is 75 percent. Healthy sleep efficiency is 85 percent or higher. Low sleep efficiency suggests you are spending too much time in bed awake, which is counterproductive. Sleep restriction therapy, conducted under professional guidance, deliberately reduces time in bed to match actual sleep time, consolidating sleep and improving efficiency.

Analyse completed two-week diary for patterns. Is your sleep schedule consistent or highly variable? Do you sleep better on certain nights? What factors correlate with better or worse sleep – activity levels, stress, substance use, screen time? What is your sleep efficiency? What symptoms are most problematic – difficulty falling asleep, frequent waking, early morning waking, unrefreshing sleep? Identifying patterns guides targeted interventions.

Common sleep diary revelations include discovering you sleep better than you thought – perception of sleep is often worse than reality – discovering highly variable schedule creating sleep problems, realising caffeine or alcohol use is consistently followed by poor sleep, or noticing weekends disrupt weekday sleep patterns. These insights guide specific sleep hygiene changes.

When Sleep Problems Persist Despite Good Sleep Hygiene

For some people, sleep hygiene alone is insufficient. Chronic insomnia, sleep apnoea, restless leg syndrome, or other sleep disorders might require specialist assessment. If sleep remains severely disturbed after implementing good sleep hygiene for several weeks, discuss with your GP. Sleep medicine specialists can conduct sleep studies and provide targeted treatment. Cognitive behavioural therapy for insomnia (CBT-I) is highly effective treatment, more effective than sleep medication long-term. CBT-I might be available through NHS psychological therapy services or privately.

Sleep medication should be short-term solution, not long-term management strategy. Sleeping tablets are appropriate for brief periods during crisis but create dependence if used regularly. They also do not produce natural sleep architecture. If currently using sleep medication, discuss with prescriber about gradually reducing and stopping. CBT-I and sleep hygiene provide sustainable, effective alternatives without medication side effects or dependence risk.

Appendix F: Guided Relaxation and Meditation Scripts

These scripts provide structured guidance for relaxation and meditation practices. You can record these scripts in your own voice to play back, have someone read them to you, or read them yourself and then practise from memory. Pause appropriately between instructions, speaking slowly and calmly.

Progressive Muscle Relaxation Script (15-20 minutes)

Find a comfortable position, either lying down or seated with your back supported. Close your eyes if comfortable doing so. Take three deep breaths, breathing in through your nose and out through your mouth, allowing yourself to settle into this time of relaxation. Notice your body in contact with the surface beneath you, allowing yourself to feel supported and safe.

We will progressively tense and release each muscle group in your body, moving from your feet to your head. As you tense each muscle group, hold the tension for about five seconds, then release completely, noticing the sensation of relaxation that follows. Allow yourself twice as long to experience the relaxation as you spent creating the tension. If any muscle group feels uncomfortable to tense, skip it and move to the next.

Begin by bringing your attention to your feet. Curl your toes downward, creating tension throughout both feet. Hold this tension... notice what it feels like... and now release. Let all the tension flow out of your feet. Notice the difference between tension and relaxation. Allow your feet to feel heavy and completely relaxed. Pause for ten seconds. Now flex your feet, pulling your toes up towards your shins. Feel the tension in your feet and lower legs. Hold... and release. Notice your feet and lower legs becoming soft and loose. Pause for ten seconds.

Move your attention to your lower legs. Press your heels down and tense your calf muscles. Feel the tightness through your calves. Hold this tension... and now release completely. Feel the relaxation spreading through your lower legs. Pause for ten seconds. Now tense your thigh muscles by straightening your legs and tightening your thighs. Hold this tension... noticing it... and now let go. Feel your legs becoming heavy, relaxed, sinking down. All the tension flows away. Pause for ten seconds.

Bring awareness to your hips and buttocks. Squeeze your buttocks together, creating tension. Hold... and release. Feel the muscles softening. Pause for ten seconds. Now tense your abdomen, pulling your belly button towards your spine. Create tightness through your stomach. Hold... and now release, allowing your belly to be soft and loose. Notice your breathing returning to its natural rhythm. Pause for ten seconds.

Move to your hands. Make tight fists with both hands, tensing all the small muscles. Hold this tension... and release. Let your fingers gently uncurl. Notice the feeling of relaxation in your hands. Pause for ten seconds. Extend your fingers and tense your forearms. Hold... and release. Feel your forearms becoming loose and heavy. Pause for ten seconds.

Tense your upper arms by bending your arms and tensing your biceps. Hold... and release. Let your arms fall softly to your sides. Notice them becoming heavy and relaxed. Pause for ten seconds. Shrug your shoulders up towards your ears, creating tension across your shoulders and upper back. Hold... and now let your shoulders drop. Feel them settling into a comfortable, low position. Notice the release of tension. Pause for ten seconds.

Bring attention to your neck. Gently press your head back, creating tension in your neck. Be careful not to strain. Hold... and release. Let your neck be soft. Pause for ten seconds. Now press your chin towards your chest, feeling different neck muscles engage. Hold... and release. Allow your neck to settle into neutral, comfortable position. Pause for ten seconds.

Move to your face. Scrunch your whole face, squeezing your eyes shut, wrinkling your nose, pursing your lips. Hold this tension... and now release. Feel your entire face softening. Let your jaw be loose, teeth not touching, lips soft. Pause for ten seconds. Raise your eyebrows up towards your hairline, tensing your forehead. Hold... and release. Feel your forehead becoming smooth and soft. Pause for ten seconds.

Now take a few moments to scan through your entire body. Starting from your feet, mentally check each area, ensuring it is fully relaxed. If you notice any remaining tension anywhere, breathe into that area and imagine the tension dissolving on each exhale. Allow your body to sink deeper into relaxation with each breath. Pause for twenty seconds.

You are now deeply relaxed throughout your entire body. Enjoy this feeling of complete relaxation. You can return to this state any time you need to. When you are ready to finish this practise, begin to gently wiggle your fingers and toes. Take a deep breath, and slowly open your eyes, returning your awareness to the room around you. Take your time sitting up, allowing yourself to transition gradually back to your day.

Body Scan Meditation Script (20 minutes)

Settle into a comfortable position, lying down if possible. Allow your eyes to close gently. Begin by taking three full breaths, breathing in deeply and exhaling completely. With each breath, allow yourself to arrive more fully in this present moment, letting go of the concerns of your day. Notice the points of contact between your body and the surface beneath you, feeling yourself supported.

Bring your attention now to your left foot. Notice whatever sensations are present in your left foot. You might feel tingling, warmth, coolness, pressure, or perhaps no particular sensation. Whatever you notice is fine. There is no right or wrong way to feel. Simply observe your left foot with gentle, curious attention. Pause for ten seconds. Now expand your awareness to include your entire left leg, from your toes up through your ankle, your calf, your knee, your thigh, all the way to your hip. Notice all the sensations present in your left leg. Pause for ten seconds.

Shift your attention now to your right foot. Again, notice whatever sensations are present without trying to change anything. Pause for ten seconds. Expand awareness to include your entire right leg, from toes to hip, observing all sensations present. Pause for ten seconds. Notice both legs now, and the sense of your lower body resting heavily, supported by the surface beneath you.

Bring attention to your lower torso – your hips, buttocks, lower back, and abdomen. Notice sensations of contact with the surface beneath you. Notice your breathing, the gentle rise and fall of your belly with each breath. You do not need to control your breathing, just notice it. Pause for ten seconds. Move attention to your upper torso – your chest, upper back, and shoulders. Notice your breathing here, the expansion and contraction of your chest with each breath. Notice your heartbeat if you can sense it. Notice any tension in your shoulders. Pause for ten seconds.

Bring attention to your left hand. Notice the sensations in your palm, the back of your hand, each finger. Pause for five seconds. Expand awareness to include your entire left arm – your wrist, forearm, elbow, upper arm, and shoulder. Notice all sensations present. Pause for ten seconds. Now shift attention to your right hand, noticing all the sensations there. Pause for five seconds. Expand awareness to include your entire right arm. Pause for ten seconds. Notice both arms now, and how they are resting.

Bring attention to your neck and throat, noticing any sensations present, any areas of tension or ease. Pause for five seconds. Move attention to your face. Notice your jaw – are your teeth clenched or is your jaw soft? Notice your lips, your cheeks, your nose. Notice your eyes, the eyelids resting gently closed. Notice your forehead, whether it feels tense or smooth. Notice your scalp. Pause for ten seconds.

Now expand your awareness to include your entire body. As if from a distance, sense your whole body lying here. Notice your body breathing. Notice all the various sensations throughout your body. You might notice your mind wandering during this practise – this is entirely normal. When you notice your mind has wandered, gently, kindly, bring your attention back to your body. Pause for twenty seconds.

Take a few more moments to rest in awareness of your breathing, feeling your body breathing itself, without any effort from you. Pause for twenty seconds. When you are ready to end this practise, begin to deepen your breathing slightly. Gently wiggle your fingers and toes. Slowly stretch if you wish. Open your eyes when ready, taking your time to transition back to your day.

Loving-Kindness Meditation Script (15 minutes)

Find a comfortable seated position with your back supported. Rest your hands gently in your lap or on your knees. Close your eyes or maintain a soft downward gaze. Take a few deep breaths, arriving in this moment. Allow your breath to return to its natural rhythm.

Begin by bringing to mind someone who loves you unconditionally. This might be a grandparent, a dear friend, a pet, or anyone whose love for you is simple and pure. Bring this being clearly to mind. Feel their warmth and affection for you. Allow yourself to receive their love. Pause for ten seconds. Now, repeat the following phrases silently, directing them toward yourself, perhaps imagining that person speaking these words to you: May I be happy. May I be healthy. May I be safe. May I live with ease. Pause for five seconds.

Repeat these phrases several times, allowing the intention behind the words to resonate. May I be happy. May I be healthy. May I be safe. May I live with ease. If you notice resistance or self-judgment arising, that is okay. Simply notice it, and gently return to the phrases. Pause for twenty seconds.

Now bring to mind someone you care about – a friend, family member, or someone you feel fondness for. Visualise them clearly. Bring to mind their good qualities, what you appreciate about them. Pause for five seconds. Now direct the phrases of loving-kindness toward them: May you be happy. May you be healthy. May you be safe. May you live with ease. Repeat several times, genuinely wishing these qualities for them. Pause for twenty seconds.

Now bring to mind a neutral person – someone you see regularly but do not know well. Perhaps a shop assistant, a person you see on your commute, or a neighbour you have not spoken with. Recognise that this person, like you, seeks happiness and wishes to avoid suffering. Direct the loving-kindness phrases toward them: May you be happy. May you be healthy. May you be safe. May you live with ease. Pause for twenty seconds.

Now, if you feel ready, bring to mind someone you have difficulty with. Start with someone mildly difficult rather than the most challenging person in your life. Recognise that this person, like all beings, seeks happiness and wishes to avoid suffering, even if their actions are unskillful. Acknowledging the humanity in this difficult person, offer them loving-kindness: May you be happy. May you be healthy. May you be safe. May you live with ease. Notice any resistance that arises. You do not need to condone harmful behaviour to wish someone well. Pause for twenty seconds.

Finally, expand your awareness to encompass all beings everywhere. All people, animals, and living things. All beings, near and far, known and unknown, all beings in all directions. Offer loving-kindness to all beings: May all beings be happy. May all beings be healthy. May all beings be safe. May all beings live with ease. Feel the expansiveness of this intention extending outward without limit. Pause for twenty seconds.

Gently allow this practise to come to a close. Take a deep breath. Notice how you feel. Slowly open your eyes if they were closed. Take a moment before moving back into activity, carrying with you the warmth and openness cultivated in this practise.

Appendix G: Mood and Symptom Monitoring Forms

Regular monitoring of your mood, symptoms, and functioning helps you recognise patterns, track progress, identify early warning signs of decline, and communicate effectively with healthcare professionals. This appendix provides templates for various monitoring forms.

Daily Mood Diary

The daily mood diary provides simple tracking of overall mood each day. Create a chart with dates down the left side and a rating scale from zero (worst possible mood) to ten (best possible mood) across the top. Each evening, rate your overall mood for that day and mark it on the chart. Over time, this creates visual representation of mood patterns. You might notice mood is worse on certain days of week, that mood gradually improves with treatment, or that mood fluctuates in response to events.

Enhanced daily mood diary adds more detail. In addition to overall mood rating, record: highest and lowest mood points during the day, significant events or stressors, sleep quality previous night (rated zero to ten), exercise (yes/no and duration), social contact (yes/no and who), medications taken as prescribed (yes/no), and therapy homework completed (yes/no). This richer data helps identify what influences your mood positively and negatively.

Weekly Symptom Checklist

The weekly symptom checklist provides structured tracking of specific depression symptoms. List common depression symptoms down the left side: low mood, loss of interest or pleasure, fatigue or low energy, sleep disturbance, appetite changes, difficulty concentrating, feelings of worthlessness or guilt, thoughts of death or suicide, agitation or slowing, and any other symptoms you experience. Each week, rate severity of each symptom from zero (not present) to ten (extremely severe). Track this weekly throughout treatment to see which symptoms improve, which persist, and whether new symptoms emerge.

Comparing weekly symptom checklists over time demonstrates progress that might not be apparent day-to-day. You might notice that sleep has improved from seven to three even though mood remains problematic, or that suicidal thoughts have reduced from eight to zero, indicating important progress even if overall mood has not fully lifted. This specific symptom tracking provides more nuanced picture than overall mood rating alone.

Functioning Assessment

Depression affects functioning across life domains. Weekly functioning assessment tracks practical impacts of depression and monitors functional recovery. Rate from zero (unable to perform) to ten (performing normally) across key domains: self-care (showering, dressing, eating regular meals), household tasks (cleaning, laundry, shopping, cooking), work or educational functioning (if applicable), social engagement (spending time with others, responding to contacts), leisure activities (engaging in hobbies, interests, or enjoyable activities), and overall quality of life.

Functional impairment often persists after mood symptoms improve. You might feel somewhat better but still struggle with work or social activities. Tracking functioning separately from mood identifies areas needing specific attention. Some interventions such as behavioural activation or occupational therapy specifically target functional recovery.

Early Warning Signs Monitoring

For people with recurrent depression, monitoring personal early warning signs enables rapid intervention preventing full relapse. Create personalised list of your early warning signs based on previous episodes. Common early warning signs include sleep disturbance (particularly early morning waking), increased irritability, social withdrawal, loss of interest in usual activities, reduced self-care, increased negative thinking, reduced concentration, return of specific thoughts characteristic of your depression, changes in appetite, and increased fatigue. Check your warning signs list weekly, noting presence or absence of each sign.

If you notice two or more warning signs emerging, this signals need for action. Your relapse prevention plan (see Appendix C) specifies what actions to take. This might include increasing social contact, reinstating helpful activities, contacting your therapist or GP, reviewing coping strategies, or in some cases temporarily increasing medication if previously reduced. Early intervention when warning signs first appear often prevents full relapse.

Medication and Treatment Log

If taking medication or receiving other treatments, maintaining detailed log helps you track treatments tried, effectiveness, side effects, and optimal regimes. Record medication name, dose, start date, end date if discontinued, reason for stopping if applicable, effectiveness rating (zero to ten), side effects experienced, and any other relevant notes. This log ensures you do not retry medications that previously did not work or caused unacceptable side effects. It provides your GP or psychiatrist with clear history if you need to change clinician.

Similarly, record psychological therapy attended: therapist name, type of therapy (CBT, counselling, etc.), number of sessions, dates of treatment, effectiveness rating, what was helpful, what was unhelpful, and whether you completed therapy or ended early with reason. This therapy log helps you and future therapists understand what approaches have been tried and how helpful they were.

Appendix H: Communication Aids for Talking About Depression

Communicating about depression with family, friends, employers, or healthcare professionals can feel difficult. These templates and guidelines provide structure for difficult conversations.

Telling Someone You Have Depression: A Script Guide

Choose the right time and place for this conversation. Select a time when you will not be rushed and when the other person is not distracted or stressed. Choose a private, comfortable setting. Begin the conversation by indicating you need to share something important: 'I need to talk with you about something important to me. Do you have time now?' Ensure they can give you their full attention before continuing.

Explain what you are experiencing in clear, specific terms: 'I have been diagnosed with depression' or 'I have been experiencing symptoms of depression including [name specific symptoms such as low mood, loss of interest, sleep problems].' Avoid minimising or apologising for having depression. You would not apologise for having diabetes; depression is an illness not a personal failure.

Describe how depression has affected you: 'This has been affecting my [work, relationships, daily activities, etc.]. I have found it difficult to [specific examples].' Concrete examples help people understand depression's impact, particularly if they have not experienced depression themselves.

Explain what treatment you are receiving or planning to pursue: 'I am working with a therapist', 'I have started medication', 'I am on waiting list for therapy', or 'I am planning to see my GP.' This reassures the person that you are taking active steps and provides context for why they might notice changes in you.

Specify what support would be helpful from them: 'What would help me most is [specific request such as checking in weekly, helping with specific practical tasks, being patient when I am not sociable, understanding when I need to cancel plans].' Specific requests are more helpful than general 'please support me.' Different people can provide different types of support; match requests to the person and relationship.

Reassure them and address their concerns: People often worry they said or did something to cause your depression, or feel helpless about how to help. You might say: 'This is not caused by anything you did. Having people I trust who I can talk to honestly makes a difference. You do not need to fix this; just being understanding helps.'

Be prepared for various reactions. Some people will respond with understanding and support. Others might minimise your experience, offer unhelpful advice like 'just think positive', react with their own anxiety or distress, or distance themselves. These reactions reflect their own limitations or discomfort with mental health topics, not your worth or the validity of your experience. If someone responds unhelpfully, recognise this reflects on them, not you.

Workplace Disclosure Communication Guide

Deciding whether and how to disclose depression at work requires careful consideration of your specific workplace culture, relationship with your manager, legal protections, and personal comfort. If you decide disclosure is appropriate, this guide provides structure.

Request formal meeting with your manager: 'I would like to arrange a meeting to discuss a health matter affecting my work. Could we meet privately?' This frames the conversation professionally and ensures privacy. Some people prefer having HR present; this depends on workplace culture and your relationship with your manager.

Prepare written summary before the meeting including: condition ('I have been diagnosed with depression'), how it affects your work ('I am finding concentration and meeting deadlines challenging'), treatment you are receiving ('I am attending therapy and my GP has prescribed medication'), prognosis ('My doctor expects improvement over coming months with treatment'), and specific adjustments you are requesting ('Could I have flexible hours for therapy appointments, reduced workload temporarily, or regular brief check-ins to discuss progress').

During the meeting, refer to your written summary to ensure you cover everything important. Remain factual and professional. You are not asking for special treatment; you are managing a health condition that temporarily affects your capability, similar to someone managing diabetes or a physical injury. Frame requests as temporary accommodations supporting your return to full functioning.

Follow up the meeting in writing, thanking manager for their time, summarising what was discussed, confirming any agreed adjustments, noting any actions either of you committed to, and specifying review date. This creates written record protecting you if problems arise later.

Letter to GP Requesting Referral Template

If you struggle to communicate clearly during GP appointments due to anxiety or depression symptoms, preparing a written summary helps ensure your GP understands your needs. This template provides structure:

Dear Dr [Name], I am writing to request a referral for depression treatment. I have been experiencing the following symptoms for [duration]: [list specific symptoms, including mood, sleep, appetite, energy, concentration, social functioning, thoughts of self-harm]. These symptoms are affecting my [work, relationships, daily functioning – be specific]. My mood is [describe – consistently low, variable, worse in mornings, etc.]. I have tried [list any self-help strategies attempted]. I have previously experienced depression before / this is my first episode. I am requesting [referral to therapy, review of medication, referral to psychiatrist, or whatever you are seeking]. Thank you for your help. Yours sincerely, [Your name].

Bring this letter to your appointment or send it in advance. This ensures you communicate key information even if you become anxious or emotional during the appointment.

Appendix I: Glossary of Terms

This glossary defines key terms used throughout this book and in mental health services. Understanding terminology helps you communicate with healthcare professionals and understand written information about your condition.

Key Mental Health Terms

Anhedonia: Loss of interest or pleasure in activities previously enjoyed. A core symptom of depression.

Antidepressant: Medication prescribed to treat depression. Main types include SSRIs, SNRIs, and tricyclics. Works by affecting brain neurotransmitters.

Cognitive Behavioural Therapy (CBT): Structured psychological therapy focusing on relationships between thoughts, feelings, and behaviours. Strong evidence base for depression treatment.

Cognitive distortions: Systematic errors in thinking that maintain negative mood. Examples include catastrophising, all-or-nothing thinking, and mind-reading.

Comorbidity: Presence of two or more conditions simultaneously. Depression commonly occurs with anxiety disorders, substance use disorders, or physical health conditions.

Dysthymia: Older term for persistent depressive disorder. Chronic low-grade depression lasting two years or more.

Episode: Period of illness. A depressive episode has defined beginning and end. Some people experience single episode; others experience recurrent episodes.

Major depressive disorder: Clinical diagnosis requiring presence of at least five depression symptoms for at least two weeks, including either low mood or anhedonia, causing significant functional impairment.

Psychomotor changes: Visible changes in movement and activity. Psychomotor retardation involves slowing of movement and speech. Psychomotor agitation involves restlessness and inability to sit still.

Recurrence: New episode of depression after period of recovery from previous episode. Differs from relapse, which is return of symptoms before full recovery achieved.

Remission: Period without significant symptoms following treatment. Full remission means virtual absence of symptoms; partial remission means notable improvement but some symptoms remain.

Rumination: Repetitive, passive focus on symptoms of distress and their possible causes and consequences. Maintains and worsens depression.

Suicidal ideation: Thoughts about suicide. These range from passive thoughts about death to active plans to end one's life. Always requires assessment and appropriate intervention.

Treatment-resistant depression: Depression that has not responded adequately to at least two different antidepressant trials of adequate dose and duration. Requires specialist input and may respond to combination treatments or novel approaches.

Treatment Terms

Behavioural activation: Therapeutic approach focusing on increasing engagement in valued activities to improve mood. Often component of CBT but can be delivered as standalone treatment.

Collaborative care: Model integrating mental health treatment into primary care with care coordinator linking services.

Community Mental Health Team (CMHT): Specialist NHS multidisciplinary team providing assessment and treatment for people with severe or complex mental health problems.

Crisis Resolution and Home Treatment Team: Specialist NHS team providing intensive home-based support during mental health crisis, aiming to avoid hospital admission.

Electroconvulsive therapy (ECT): Medical treatment involving brief electrical stimulation of brain under anaesthesia. Very effective for severe depression but reserved for cases where other treatments have failed or when urgent treatment is needed.

Maintenance treatment: Continuing treatment after recovery to prevent relapse. Might involve continued antidepressant medication or periodic therapy sessions.

Mindfulness-Based Cognitive Therapy (MBCT): Group therapy programme combining mindfulness meditation with CBT elements. Specifically developed to prevent depression relapse.

Stepped care: Model where treatment intensity increases if less intensive treatment is ineffective. Starts with least restrictive effective intervention and steps up if needed.

Talking Therapies: NHS service providing psychological therapies for depression and anxiety. Allows self-referral in most areas.

References

American Psychiatric Association. (2013). Diagnostic and statistical manual of mental disorders (5th ed.). American Psychiatric Publishing.

Beck, A. T. (1967). Depression: Clinical, experimental, and theoretical aspects. Harper & Row.

Burns, D. D. (1980). Feeling good: The new mood therapy. William Morrow.

Cipriani, A., Furukawa, T. A., Salanti, G., Chaimani, A., Atkinson, L. Z., Ogawa, Y., ... & Geddes, J. R. (2018). Comparative efficacy and acceptability of 21 antidepressant drugs for the acute treatment of adults with major depressive disorder: A systematic review and network meta-analysis. The Lancet, 391(10128), 1357-1366.

Cooney, G. M., Dwan, K., Greig, C. A., Lawlor, D. A., Rimer, J., Waugh, F. R., ... & Mead, G. E. (2013). Exercise for depression. Cochrane Database of Systematic Reviews, (9), CD004366.

Cryan, J. F., & Dinan, T. G. (2012). Mind-altering microorganisms: The impact of the gut microbiota on brain and behaviour. Nature Reviews Neuroscience, 13(10), 701-712.

Cuijpers, P., Berking, M., Andersson, G., Quigley, L., Kleiboer, A., & Dobson, K. S. (2013). A meta-analysis of cognitive-behavioural therapy for adult depression, alone and in comparison with other treatments. The Canadian Journal of Psychiatry, 58(7), 376-385.

Dunlop, B. W., & Nemeroff, C. B. (2007). The role of dopamine in the pathophysiology of depression. Archives of General Psychiatry, 64(3), 327-337.

Edinger, J. D., & Means, M. K. (2005). Cognitive-behavioral therapy for primary insomnia. Clinical Psychology Review, 25(5), 539-558.

Erickson, K. I., Voss, M. W., Prakash, R. S., Basak, C., Szabo, A., Chaddock, L., ... & Kramer, A. F. (2011). Exercise training increases size of hippocampus and improves memory. Proceedings of the National Academy of Sciences, 108(7), 3017-3022.

Gariepy, G., Honkaniemi, H., & Quesnel-Vallée, A. (2016). Social support and protection from depression: Systematic review of current findings in Western countries. British Journal of Psychiatry, 209(4), 284-293.

Grosso, G., Pajak, A., Marventano, S., Castellano, S., Galvano, F., Bucolo, C., ... & Caraci, F. (2014). Role of omega-3 fatty acids in the treatment of depressive disorders: A comprehensive meta-analysis of randomized clinical trials. PLoS One, 9(5), e96905.

Hardeveld, F., Spijker, J., De Graaf, R., Nolen, W. A., & Beekman, A. T. (2010). Prevalence and predictors of recurrence of major depressive disorder in the adult population. Acta Psychiatrica Scandinavica, 122(3), 184-191.

Hofmann, S. G., Asnaani, A., Vonk, I. J., Sawyer, A. T., & Fang, A. (2012). The efficacy of cognitive behavioral therapy: A review of meta-analyses. Cognitive Therapy and Research, 36(5), 427-440.

James, S. L., Abate, D., Abate, K. H., Abay, S. M., Abbafati, C., Abbasi, N., ... & Abdollahpour, I. (2018). Global, regional, and national incidence, prevalence, and years lived with disability for 354 diseases and injuries for 195 countries and territories, 1990–2017: A systematic analysis for the Global Burden of Disease Study 2017. The Lancet, 392(10159), 1789-1858.

Kuehner, C. (2017). Why is depression more common among women than among men? The Lancet Psychiatry, 4(2), 146-158.

Kuyken, W., Warren, F. C., Taylor, R. S., Whalley, B., Crane, C., Bondolfi, G., ... & Dalgleish, T. (2016). Efficacy of mindfulness-based cognitive therapy in prevention of depressive relapse: An individual patient data meta-analysis from randomized trials. JAMA Psychiatry, 73(6), 565-574.

Martell, C. R., Addis, M. E., & Jacobson, N. S. (2001). Depression in context: Strategies for guided action. W. W. Norton & Company.

Martin, L. A., Neighbors, H. W., & Griffith, D. M. (2013). The experience of symptoms of depression in men vs women: Analysis of the National Comorbidity Survey Replication. JAMA Psychiatry, 70(10), 1100-1106.

Nolen-Hoeksema, S., Wisco, B. E., & Lyubomirsky, S. (2008). Rethinking rumination. Perspectives on Psychological Science, 3(5), 400-424.

Rock, P. L., Roiser, J. P., Riedel, W. J., & Blackwell, A. D. (2014). Cognitive impairment in depression: A systematic review and meta-analysis. Psychological Medicine, 44(10), 2029-2040.

Schuch, F. B., Vancampfort, D., Richards, J., Rosenbaum, S., Ward, P. B., & Stubbs, B. (2016). Exercise as a treatment for depression: A meta-analysis adjusting for publication bias. Journal of Psychiatric Research, 77, 42-51.

Segal, Z. V., Williams, J. M. G., & Teasdale, J. D. (2002). Mindfulness-based cognitive therapy for depression: A new approach to preventing relapse. Guilford Press.

Steiger, A., & Kimura, M. (2010). Wake and sleep EEG provide biomarkers in depression. Journal of Psychiatric Research, 44(4), 242-252.

Stetler, C., & Miller, G. E. (2011). Depression and hypothalamic-pituitary-adrenal activation: A quantitative summary of four decades of research. Psychosomatic Medicine, 73(2), 114-126.

Sullivan, P. F., Neale, M. C., & Kendler, K. S. (2000). Genetic epidemiology of major depression: Review and meta-analysis. American Journal of Psychiatry, 157(10), 1552-1562.

Trauer, J. M., Qian, M. Y., Doyle, J. S., Rajaratnam, S. M., & Cunnington, D. (2015). Cognitive behavioral therapy for chronic insomnia: A systematic review and meta-analysis. Annals of Internal Medicine, 163(3), 191-204.

World Health Organization. (2019). International statistical classification of diseases and related health problems (11th ed.). WHO.

World Health Organization. (2020). Depression and other common mental disorders: Global health estimates. WHO.

www.ingramcontent.com/pod-product-compliance
Lightning Source LLC
LaVergne TN
LVHW052246200926
848481LV00002B/293
* 9 7 9 8 2 3 2 2 7 0 8 4 1 *